Excel

Get the Results You Want!

SmartStudy 7

English

Ally Chumley

PASCAL PRESS

Reprinted 2019, 2020, 2022, 2024, 2025

ISBN 978 1 74125 602 4

Pascal Press
PO Box 250 Glebe NSW 2037
www.pascalpress.com.au

Publisher: Vivienne Joannou
Project editors: Mark Dixon and Rosemary Peers
Edited by Michael Wyatt
Proofread by Barbara Bessant
Answers checked by Cassandra Freeman
Cover and typesetting by Kim Webber
Printed by Vivar Printing/Green Giant Press

Students
All care has been taken in compiling this book, but please check with your teacher about the exact requirements of the course as these can change from year to year.

TABLE OF CONTENTS

TABLE OF CONTENTS

Unit 7: Narrative Text—Descriptive narrative

Unit 8: Narrative Text—Poetry

Unit 9: Persuasive Text—Marketing text

Unit 10: Persuasive Text—Opinion piece

Unit 11: Persuasive Text—Film review

Unit 12: Persuasive Text—Online discussion forum

STUDY STEPS TO SUCCESS!

Step 1 Reading Work

- In each chapter, read the main text.
- Read the annotations on the text. These notes identify key features of the text and will be useful as you complete the questions and activities in each section.
- The main texts have been categorised as either informative, narrative or persuasive. However, some texts have features of more than one category and so the categorisation in this book depends upon the specific elements of style they contain. These, in turn, depend on each particular writer's purpose for creating that text. For example, someone writing a biographical text may have been more interested in telling a good story than merely providing factual information about the subject's life. They may have given the text all the hallmarks of a narrative.

Step 2 Comprehension Work

- Read and answer the questions, using the hints to help you.
- Check each multiple-choice answer to ensure that it is the best response to the question.
- Re-read your longer answers to ensure that they make sense.

Step 3 Spelling Work

- Read all of the information, rules and hints provided about spelling.
- For most questions, use the List Words provided to complete your answers.
- For open or creative questions, avoid writing basic or obvious responses.

Step 4 Vocabulary Work

- Read all of the information and hints provided about improving your vocabulary.
- Check that you have the skills and knowledge you need to successfully complete the topic.
- Complete the questions and activities to test your knowledge and skills.

Step 5 Grammar Work

- Read all of the information, rules and hints provided about grammar.
- Check that you have the skills and knowledge you need to successfully complete the topic.
- Complete the questions and activities to test your knowledge and skills.

Step 6 Punctuation Work

- Read all of the information, rules and hints provided about punctuation.
- Check that you have the skills and knowledge you need to successfully complete the topic.
- Complete the questions and activities to test your knowledge and skills.

Step 7 Writing Work

- Read the information about language forms and structures.
- Refer back to the main text to understand these forms and structures in context.
- Answer the questions to test your knowledge and understanding.

Step 8 Writing Sample

- Study the writing sample carefully, reading all of the explanatory notes.
- Compare this text with the main text studied throughout the chapter so far, to reinforce your learning.

Step 9 Writing Your Own Sample

- Check that you understand the terms and techniques relevant to this task.
- Using the sample text and the explanatory notes as a guide, compose a similar text inside the scaffold. You may wish to do this on separate paper or electronically, in order to give yourself more room.

Step 10 Check Your Answers

- Check all of your answers at the back of the book.
- Whether or not you got the answers right, read through the whole answer section. Sample answers are provided along with explanations of why multiple-choice options are right or wrong.
- If you cannot understand a particular answer, revise the chapter notes and text annotations or ask your teacher for help.
- You should always attempt a question, even if you aren't confident in your answer, because in English you may still get some marks for a good attempt. Reading sample answers will help you write better answers next time.

Step 11 Tips for the Sample Tests

- These useful tips appear on page 122. Read them before you attempt one of the Sample Tests.

Step 12 Sample Tests

- Two Sample Tests are provided at the end of the book.
- Before attempting the Sample Tests, make sure that you have completed all of the work in the book and have worked through the answers to all questions that you answered incorrectly.
- Set aside the time allowed for the paper and complete it under test conditions—no sneaking a look at your notes!
- Work through the answers (at the end of the book) to any questions that you were unsure about. Write down your total marks for each section in the Your Score boxes at the end of each part of the paper, then add them up to get a total percentage for the test.

HOW TO USE THIS BOOK TO STUDY FOR A CLASS TEST, HALF-YEARLY OR END-OF-YEAR EXAM

Depending on your teacher or school, you will be given a variety of tests and exams each year. There may be a single-topic test, a test that covers a number of topics, a semester test or exam, or even a half-yearly or yearly exam.

Step 1

Find out which topics will be covered in the class test.

- To do this, look at your class workbook/textbook, laptop/tablet or online study program, and ask your teacher.
- For example, your class test may be on grammar.

Step 2

Match the topics that your test is on to the topics in this book.

- For example, each unit has questions on grammar.

Step 3

Use this book to study the topics being tested.

- Pages 6, 16, 26, 36, 46, 56, 66, 76, 86, 96, 106 and 116 all cover grammar. You can do the questions on these pages to study for your class test on grammar.

Note:

- When you are using this book to study for a **half-yearly** test, follow the same steps as above—the only difference being that you will have more topics to revise, of course.
- When you are using this book to study for an **end-of-year** test, you will more than likely need to study the whole book.

READING
Types of Questions

Literal questions—the answer is right in front of you

This is the simplest type of reading task question that asks you to find a 'literal' answer.

To answer these questions you just have to locate specific facts and details to find the meaning.

For some literal questions you might have to:

- find facts, details and other forms of information from the text
- consider certain features of the text, including spelling, punctuation or common language techniques
- recount (or retell) details, sometimes in your own words
- consider the order in which facts are presented in a text
- recognise synonyms that are used for particular details and search for slightly different words from those in the question
- use your vocabulary
- use your comprehension
- identify who, what, where, when and how.

Interpretive questions—the answer requires a synthesis of textual details

This type of question asks you to interpret the meaning of words, phrases and sentences.

To answer these questions you will have to combine facts and details to synthesise the meaning.

For some interpretive questions you might have to:

- synthesise meaning by putting various facts together to reach a conclusion—we synthesise meaning from texts all the time without even realising it
- consider multiple aspects of the text at once
- use logic to find additional meaning beyond the words
- interpret the meaning of facts and details as the meaning of some parts of the text may not be obvious from just a straightforward reading
- do simple calculations to find an answer
- look at language-related matters, such as meanings conveyed by certain words, phrases or symbols
- think about the connotations of words—meanings that extend beyond the words on the page
- describe, recount, explain, compare, summarise or give reasons
- make small but important distinctions between ideas. The words *bad*, *evil*, *naughty* and *diabolical* all mean a similar thing—but they have quite distinct shades of meaning. We might call a disobedient puppy naughty but not evil. Likewise, we wouldn't call a murderer naughty.

READING
Types of Questions

Applied questions—the answer is conceptual and is not present in the text

These questions require you to understand a text's implications—the logical extension of facts and connotations. A composer can imply meaning, rather than simply state it. This allows us to extract meanings that go beyond the literal denotation (straightforward meaning) of the words a writer uses.

To answer these questions you have to apply multiple skills to infer the meaning.

Students sometimes confuse the terms 'imply' and 'infer'. Put simply, the composer implies meaning in a text and the responder infers meaning from the text.

For some applied questions you might have to:

- explain, prove, judge, evaluate, predict, solve, discuss or critique aspects of the text
- make an informed judgement or evaluation based on evidence from the text
- apply 'assumed knowledge'—information or understanding that the writer assumes you possess already
- interpret facts using additional knowledge from outside the text, such as allusions
- consider facts or details in specific combinations to arrive at a logical conclusion
- consider what you already know about textual features and their effects on meaning
- consider the usual rules of genre, form or type of text
- 'read between the lines' to infer meaning from the text
- 'read beyond the lines' to understand implications
- engage your senses
- apply thinking skills to develop insights and personal opinions
- consider what information may be missing from the text.

INFORMATIVE TEXT

Informative book extract

READING WORK

Aptronyms

This passage is an extract from an informative book about the strange quirks of language that the author admires.

An aptronym is a name aptly suited to its owner because of the job it does. The theory is that people who have unusual names are sometimes attracted to the profession they suggest. That must be why Rem Koolhaus decided to become an architect, or why Justin Case sells insurance. Meteorologists Storm Field, Sara Blizzard and Dallas Raines all report the weather on television. One banking firm in Oregon, USA takes the unfortunate names of its two directors, Cheatham & Steele.

School teachers seem to fall under the aptronym spell. We know of a metalwork teacher called Mr Steel, a woodwork teacher called Mr Timbers, a biological anatomy teacher Mrs Boddey, English teacher Ms Read, music teacher Mrs Triplett and physical education teacher Ms Cartilage. Other school staff with job-appropriate names are Mr Wheeler, leader of the cycling club and Pastor Toogood, the school chaplain.

Aptronyms also lurk in medical waiting rooms, causing patients to smile … or flee. For skin complaints, you'll need a dermatologist. Try one of these specialists—Dr Rash, Dr Skinner, Dr Spott or Dr Whitehead. Gastro problems should be referred to Dr Gutman, of course. For tooth issues how about making an appointment with one of these dentists? Dr Aichen, Dr Ken Hurt, Dr Puller, Dr Yankum, Dr Randall Toothaker, Dr Fillmore, Dr EZ Filler, Dr Nasti, Dr Les Plack and Dr De Kay?

For more serious health problems, you may need an operation. Let's hope you don't find yourself under the care of one of these surgeons: Dr Risk, Dr Fear, Dr Payne, Dr Yell, Dr Gore, Dr Graves, Dr Hackman, Dr Savage, Dr Killam, Dr Slaughter, Dr Mallett, Dr Mes, Dr Kutteroff, Dr Feinmesser and, more positively, Dr Truluck!

Your faith in the law might be called into question if you were represented by Argue & Phibbs or injury compensation specialists Payne & Fears. If your opponent's lawyer is Sue Yoo, you could be in for some trouble. But if your own defence attorney's name is Scott Free, you might expect to get off with a caution.

The world of elite sports is replete with aptronyms. Who hasn't heard of Usain Bolt, the Olympic sprint champion, or Tiger Woods, the golfer? What about Margaret Court, Australia's own tennis champ in the 1960s and 70s? Baseball has its fair share of appropriately named players—pitchers Early Wynn and Jack Armstrong spring to mind. Here are some other sporting aptronyms you may have missed: tennis player Anna Smashnova, Olympic hurdlers Maria Stepanova and Vania Stambolova, runners Greggmar Swift and Dee Dee Trotter, fencer Jeff Spear, Russian volleyballer Yekaterina Gamova, French soccer goalkeeper Dominique Dropsy and Olympic pole vaulter Kim Yoo Suk. Hey, just for the record, I don't think you suck, Kim. I'm confident you can rise above your name!

- **The meaning of the title and the topic** is clearly defined at the beginning to provide a context for the reader's comprehension.
- A **connective statement** is used to create a transition into the main discussion.
- This **summary statement** functions as a neat linking sentence that maintains the flow of the text.
- **Personification** is used to make aptronyms seem to have motives. This adds variety and interest to the text. The word *also* provides a means of linking this paragraph with the former one.
- A **contrast** is used to finish off the list.
- The **second person mode** is used to create a sense of personal involvement. The reader is addressed directly as 'you'.
- The author uses specific examples to make **jokes** where they are appropriate as a way of commenting upon the irony of aptronyms.
- **Rhetorical questions** are used to provoke thought and reinforce the universality of the aptronym phenomenon.
- The phrase 'Here are some other…' signals that a **list** is to follow.
- The writer ends with a **witticism** that plays on one of the most amusing aptronyms. This provides the impact that the ending of such an article needs to make a lasting impression.

INFORMATIVE TEXT

Informative book extract

COMPREHENSION WORK

Literal questions

Hint: Read the text carefully to locate specific facts and details.

1 What three appropriate names are given for meteorologists?

____

2 What job does Dr Yankum do? ______________________________

3 What specific roles did Early Wynn and Jack Armstrong have as baseballers?

____

Interpretive questions

Hint: These questions require you to combine facts and details to synthesise the meaning.

4 What is the purpose of this rhetorical question from the extract?

'Who hasn't heard of Usain Bolt, the Olympic sprint champion, or Tiger Woods, the golfer?'

____

5 Why is the name 'Cartilage' apt for a physical education teacher?

____

6 How many schoolteachers are mentioned in the extract? ______________________

Hint: Only one answer option is correct. Use the process of elimination to work through the options.

7 Which of these medical practitioners' names would sound the most frightening for someone about to have surgery?

a Dr Slaughter **b** Dr Gutman **c** Dr Fillmore

8 Which alternative spelling of Russian volleyballer Yekaterina Gamova's surname shows what it implies?

a game over **b** gamover **c** gammova

9 Why is Dr Les Plack's name appropriate for a dentist?

a because a 'plack' is a tool dentists use

b because dentists encourage people to brush regularly to minimise plaque

c because 'Doctor' is not a term used to refer to dentists

10 Which sentence is used to move from law-related aptronyms to sports-related ones?

a The world of elite sports is replete with aptronyms.

b Here are some other sporting aptronyms you may have missed.

c If your opponent's lawyer is Sue Yoo, you could be in for some trouble.

Applied questions

Hint: This question requires you to understand a text's implications to infer meaning from the text.

11 What do the last two lines about Kim Yoo Suk imply?

a that Kim is bad at pole vaulting **b** that the writer doesn't believe Kim is bad at pole vaulting

c that the writer believes that Kim is bad at pole vaulting

12 How do we know that Rem Koolhaus's name must be pronounced 'Cool House'?

a because the letters *au* are always pronounced as 'ou', as in *our*.

b because the syllable 'Kool' refers to his job as a dermatologist

c because to be considered an aptronym, his name has to refer to his job as an architect

INFORMATIVE TEXT

Informative book extract

SPELLING WORK

List Words

All of the words in the box below appear in the text 'Aptronyms'.

unusual	profession	architect	unfortunate	complaints
specialists	appointment	operation	surgeons	represented
anatomy	defence	elite	champion	confident

1 Rewrite these misspelt list words.

List word	Correct spelling	List word	Correct spelling
a speshalists	______	**b** confadent	______
c proffesion	______	**d** apointment	______
e arcitect	______	**f** eleet	______
g surgens	______	**h** represanted	______

2 There is one word from the list in each of these sentences but it is spelt incorrectly. Find the word and write it correctly on the line provided.

a Doctors sometimes have to treat people who've had unusuel accidents. ______

b My biology lesson was on the anatemy of the human body. ______

c The case for the defents was presented by lawyer, Scott Free. ______

d I wouldn't want a surgeon named Dr Killam performing an operashon on me! ______

e It is unfortunit that our dentist is called Dr Nasti, because he's actually a really nice man! ______

f Jeff Spear is a world champien in the sport of fencing. ______

g Anna Smashnova made two complaince about the umpire of the tennis match. ______

3 Unscramble the letters to form words from the list.

a pessionfro ______

b splaintmoc ______

c tonymaa ______

d surgeson ______

e chartitec ______

f monaphic ______

4 Use slashes (/) to separate the list words in these letter chains. Spare letters have been added to both ends of each chain to trick you. Cross these out. There are three list words hidden inside each chain.

a ABELITEUNUSUALREPRESENTEDES

b DECOMPLAINTSSURGEONSUNFORTUNATERY

c NOPROFESSIONARCHITECTCHAMPIONAR

d OSANATOMYCONFIDENTDEFENCEIS

5 Fill in the missing vowels to complete words from the list.

a sp_c_ _l_sts

b _pp_ _ntm_nt

c _nf_rt_n_t_

d _p_r_t_ _n

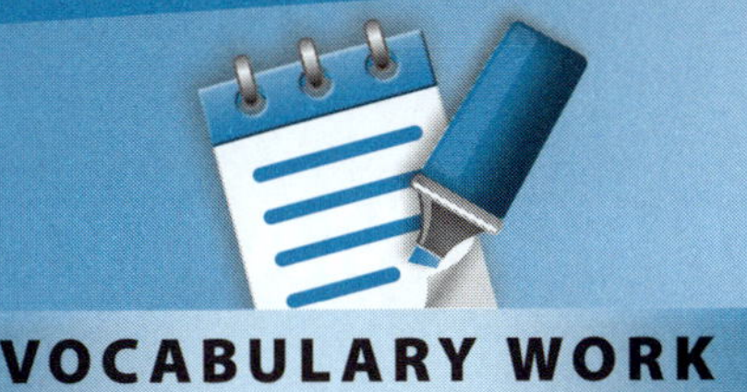

INFORMATIVE TEXT

Informative book extract

VOCABULARY WORK

In our writing we should always seek to use the most **precise** word, not just the simplest.

1 Circle the correct definition for each of these words.

a aptly	definitely	or	appropriately
b insurance	confidence	or	protection against loss
c meteorologists	weather researchers	or	comet scientists
d directors (of a company)	leaders	or	accountants
e patients	a tolerant attitude	or	people under medical care
f dermatologist	skin specialist	or	teeth specialist

2 Are these word meanings correct? Write *true* or *false* next to each meaning provided. *Hint: Look back at how the words are used in the text 'Aptronyms' for clues.*

Word	Meaning	True or False?
a positively	optimistically	______________
b compensation	changes	______________
c attorney	lawyer	______________
d caution	tension	______________

3 Find synonyms for these words. *Hint: Look back at how the words are used in the text 'Aptronyms' for clues.*

a problems	is______________
b decided	ch______________
c firm	com______________
d operation	sur______________
e faith	tr______________

Antonyms are words that mean the opposite of a given word.

4 Circle the correct form of the antonym of each of these words from the text 'Aptronyms'.

a specialists	amateurs	experts
b unfortunate	fortunate	fortunately
c unusual	usual	usually

An **idiom** is an expression used by speakers from a particular place, group or time period.

5 Here are some idioms from the extract. Match the idiom with its meaning by writing in the correct letter references.

Idiom	Meaning
a just in case	_____ you've lost
b to get off scot-free	_____ to escape a brush with the law without any penalty
c to do the bolt	_____ clumsiness in a person's ball skills
d game over	_____ in preparation for a negative event that may happen
e dropsy	_____ you are really bad at doing that task
f you suck	_____ to run away quickly

INFORMATIVE TEXT

GRAMMAR WORK

Verbs are words that identify actions. They show nouns doing, having or being various things. For example, in *The surgeon is operating*, the verb (*is operating*) shows that the noun (*surgeon*) is performing an action.

1 Which word in each of these sets is a verb? *Hint: Try putting the word into a sentence to see how it functions. Does it name an action or state of being?*

a think, you, we ________ **b** game, hurdling, runner ________

c golfer, woods, playing ________ **d** expect, law, attorney ________

e injury, court, called ________ **f** patient, healthy, need ________

g yell, graves, pain ________ **h** dental, visit, toothache ________

i specialist, rash, scratch ________ **j** teaching, school, English ________

k bicycle, leader, cycling ________ **l** anatomy, biology, study ________

m weather, reporting, television ________ **n** become, architect, house ________

o have, profession, name ________ **p** job, owner, attracted ________

2 Which is the verb in this sentence?

Baseball has its fair share of appropriately named players. ________

3 Which three words are used as verbs?

Aptronyms also lurk in medical waiting rooms, causing patients to smile.

________ ________ ________

4 Which words in this passage are verbs? Circle each of them.

Meteorologists Storm Field, Sara Blizzard and Dallas Raines all report the weather on television. One banking firm in Oregon, USA takes the unfortunate names of its two directors, Cheatham & Steele.

5 Which words in this passage are verbs or verb phrases (including auxiliary or 'helper verbs')? Circle them.

Your faith in the law might be called into question if you were represented by Argue & Phibbs or injury compensation specialists Payne & Fears.

6 **a** Write a sentence showing how the word *question* can be used as a noun.

____

b Now write another sentence showing how the word *question* can be used as a verb.

____

7 In each pair, which word can be used both as a noun and a verb? Circle one from each pair.

a	report	weather	**b**	law	post
c	record	restore	**d**	issues	tissues
e	fear	pain	**f**	play	perform

8 **a** Choose one word you circled in Question 7 and write a sentence showing how it can be used as a noun.

____

b Now write another sentence showing how the same word can be used as a verb.

____

INFORMATIVE TEXT

Informative book extract

PUNCTUATION WORK

Capital letters appear as the first letter of a sentence. They are also used for proper nouns (such as the names of people, places and events) and the pronoun *I*.

1 Look at each sentence below and write the words that should begin with a capital letter. *Hint: Refer back to the text to help you.*

a meteorologists storm field, sara blizzard and dallas raines all report the weather on television.

____

b one banking firm in oregon, usa takes the unfortunate names of its two directors, cheatham & steele.

____

c but if your own defence attorney's name is scott free, you might expect to get off with a caution.

____

d who hasn't heard of usain bolt, the olympic sprint champion, or tiger woods, the golfer?

____

e what about margaret court, australia's own tennis champ in the 1960s and 70s?

____

We use **question marks** to indicate when someone is asking a question. Even rhetorical questions require question marks, even though these types of questions are not intended to be answered. **Exclamation marks** are used to express surprise, astonishment or any other such strong emotion.

2 Add question marks or exclamation marks to complete each sentence.

a I think some of these aptronyms are hilarious

b Dr Skinner is a very appropriate name for a skin specialist, isn't it

c Is Usain Bolt a sprinter or a long-distance runner

d How confident are you that your dental operation will be painless

e Are you serious—a dentist called Dr EZ Filler worked on your teeth yesterday

f Get a load of this—my gastroenterologist is called Dr Gutman

g Can you imagine the embarrassment if Dr Hackman or Dr Kutteroff had to perform an amputation

h Who'd have thought there'd be a bank called Cheatham and Steele

3 There are ten punctuation mistakes in this passage drawn from the text. Circle the mistakes. *Hint: The abbreviations Mr, Mrs and Ms do not take full stops after them.*

school teachers seem to fall under the aptronym spell. We know of a metalwork teacher called mr steel, a woodwork teacher called Mr timbers, a biological anatomy Teacher Mrs Boddey, English teacher ms read, music teacher Mrs Triplett and physical education teacher Ms Cartilage. Other school Staff with job-appropriate names are Mr Wheeler, leader of the cycling club, and pastor toogood, the school chaplain.

INFORMATIVE TEXT

Informative book extract

WRITING WORK 1

Informative book extracts

An **informative book** is a text that provides true information about a topic drawn from real life. Informative books vary widely and are written for multiple purposes. They are classified as non-fiction because they deal with true information. The one from which our extract comes was written to inform the reader of an amusing trend that the writer has noticed in language. The text provides an entertaining summary of the phenomenon of aptronyms. The information provided is organised by topic, leading the reader to see a rare but definite trend emerging that suggests some people may indeed be subconsciously attracted to jobs and professions that match their name.

In this type of text factual details are important but the writer's main purpose is to entertain, not simply to inform. Writers of this type of information often make an effort to present their material in a way that engages and maintains their readers' interest in the topic.

The extract is written in second person mode, using the present tense. This gives the text a sense of immediacy, involving the reader personally. The author gives us the impression that there are many instances of aptronyms to report on. This is achieved through the provision of multiple examples and specific details.

In the extract featured in this chapter, the writer's tone is very important. The tone of a text can be summarised as the writer's attitude toward the topic, as revealed by the language they use.

Structural features of the text 'Aptronyms' include:

- a structure made of chapters (with this extract being the first section of one chapter)
- an introductory statement at the beginning of each chapter
- paragraphs in the chapter arranged in logical order
- paragraphs that each detail one specific topic or aspect of the topic
- humorous personal observations to end each section within a chapter.

Language features used in an informative book extract include:

- authorial comments giving us clues about what the author actually thinks about the topic
- connective phrases used as links between groups of sentences
- rhetorical questions
- use of the pronoun 'you'
- lots of interesting details
- examples that illustrate the author's key points.

1 Which of the following best describes this passage?

a an informative fiction book

b a non-fiction news article

c an informative book extract

d a fictitious story

2 Select three other chapter titles that you might expect to encounter in the book from which the extract is drawn. *Hint: Think about the description of the book given on the reading page.*

a Crazy place names

b Casserole recipes

c World's weirdest first names

d Palindromes—words spelt the same forwards and backwards

e Shocking crimes

f Circus performers through the centuries

g Amazing ants

h Meerkats make you laugh out loud

3 What is the main purpose of the text 'Aptronyms'?

____

____

4 **Each of** these thoughts is summarised in a few words in the text 'Aptronyms'. Write these summaries into the table to show the order in which they are presented in the text.

- Medical specialists sometimes have apt names that make patients smile.
- Aptronyms have also been discovered among school teachers.
- The definition of an aptronym is provided.
- Some medical specialists' names fill the patient with fear.
- Three weather reporters have appropriate names, considering their professions.
- There is a theory that some people may be attracted to a profession because it reflects their name.

Order	Thought
First	**a**
Second	**b**
Third	**c**
Fourth	**d**
Fifth	**e**
Sixth	**f**

5 Write one sentence in which the author uses an exclamation mark to convey a humorous observation.

____

6 How many sentences are used to properly introduce the topic of this extract? ______________

7 Write a word or phrase to describe the subtopic of each of the six paragraphs in the extract. The first one has been done for you, as it is the only paragraph with multiple topics

a Paragraph 1 introduction with examples from multiple job types

b Paragraph 2 ____

c Paragraph 3 ____

d Paragraph 4 ____

e Paragraph 5 ____

f Paragraph 6 ____

8 If you had to edit the text 'Aptronyms' to be no more than 200 words in length, which lines would you delete? Refer to specific line numbers in your answer and explain your reasoning. *Hint: On average, a line of text contains about 12 words.*

____

____

9 Which specific job type mentioned in the extract offers the best aptronyms, in your opinion? Give reasons for your choice.

____

INFORMATIVE TEXT

Informative book extract

WRITING SAMPLE

Here is a sample text showing you how to structure and write a text that forms part of a chapter of an informative book.

Sample text	Notes
The Great Houdini 	**Use a chapter heading that summarises the content.** This heading is the name of the illusionist, a logical and clear way in which to structure the book.
The world-famous escape artist and mystic, Harry Houdini, has gone down in history as one of the most well-known illusionists of all time. Born Erik Weisz, the Hungarian superstar began his career as a humble and not-very-successful magician.	**Write an introductory statement to begin each section or chapter.** Here the third person storytelling mode is used in the past tense, describing a person from history. A contrast between his early and later career is presented to foreshadow the content to come.
The 'Great Houdini' was most noted for his death-defying escapes from ropes, handcuffs or heavy chains, wooden chests, steel cages and other elaborate traps that seemed impossible to open. Before enthralled audiences he would free himself and exit his prison.	**Begin with a sentence that reveals the content most relevant to the overall topic of the book.** In this case, the topic is illusionists. Although factual statements are important, the descriptive and emotive language used tells us that the writer's main purpose is to entertain.
By 1827, Houdini had attracted a great deal of public attention. He'd staged a daring handcuff escape at a Grand Rapids police station. Reporters gathered and gazed up into the air as the shackled Houdini hung from a rope attached to a crane. In two minutes, the great Houdini had released himself to rapturous applause.	**Present the details of one story or piece of content that you'd like to focus on as a feature.** This story starts with a sentence giving the details of the setting for one of Houdini's escapes.
The years 1898–1926 saw Houdini accomplish many feats, causing his fans to reach, gasping, into their wallets. It seems America just couldn't get enough of the Great Houdini. He staged all sorts of terrifying acts, including having himself restrained in a straitjacket and buried alive.	**Arrange the content in paragraphs and present them in logical order.** Each features only one specific subtopic or aspect of the content, organised by year. The author gives us the impression that there are many escapes and other feats to report on. We're given multiple examples and specific details.
The Great Houdini could hold his breath for three minutes or more, which came in handy for his favourite crowd-pleasing trick. Hanging upside-down in a water-filled glass tank, Houdini would amaze audiences by calmly working his way out of locks and chains while completely submerged underwater.	**Present supporting details using a variety of language features.** The structural details of the trap, hyphenated adjectives and the use of emotive language make the material more interesting.
In a book he penned, Houdini revealed that the application of pressure on certain parts of locks could bring them undone easily. Other tools he used included hidden picks, keys and strings. But it wasn't all fakery.	**Add interesting details.** The most obvious piece of information that would interest readers is how Houdini accomplished his escapes.
Apart from just hanging around, Houdini also spent a good deal of time exposing the fraudulent activities of competitors.	**Maintain an engaging tone that suits the level of formality.** The phrase 'just hanging around' is a pun on the suspension tricks Houdini performed. It adds a sense of conversation or informality to the tone.
Tragically, Harry Houdini couldn't make one final escape—from death. In 1926, he was admitted to a Detroit hospital where he died of a burst appendix. Faithful to the end in upholding his mystical public image, his death occurred on the spookiest night of the year—Halloween.	**Provide a punchy ending to conclude.** This one uses the idea of escapes to convey the details of how Houdini died. These final comments give us clues about what the author actually thinks about the topic.

INFORMATIVE TEXT

Informative book extract

WRITING YOUR OWN SAMPLE

Write your own sample on the lines provided.

- **Use a chapter heading that summarises the content.** Use a heading name that offers a logical and clear way in which to structure the book.
- **Write an introductory statement at the beginning of each section or chapter.** Decide which storytelling mode and tense is the most appropriate choice for this content.
- **Begin with a sentence that reveals the content most relevant to the overall topic of the book.** Remember that factual details are important but the tools you use to convey them, such as descriptive or emotive language, are also vital if your reader is to remain interested.
- **Present the details of one story or piece of content that you'd like to focus on as a feature.** Begin with a key point, in a topic sentence. Then add specific details, facts, data, statistics, names and/or quotations.
- **Arrange the content in paragraphs and present them in logical order.** Each paragraph should feature only one specific subtopic or aspect of the content. Organise information chronologically (in order of timing), or use another method that works for your topic. Provide multiple examples and specific details.
- **Present supporting details, using a variety of language features.** Provide the information in sufficient detail to ensure an adequate coverage of the topic. The use of special features (such as emotive language) makes the material more interesting.
- **Add interesting details.** In informative books, material should be interesting to the reader with lots of interesting details. Try to identify the most obvious piece of information that would interest your readers.
- **Maintain an engaging tone that suits the level of formality.** The writer's tone is very important in influencing the reader's views of the topic.
- **Provide a punchy ending to conclude.** Use your final comments to give the reader clues about what you think or feel about the topic.

INFORMATIVE TEXT

Informative article

READING WORK

Strange things dogs eat

Vets get to see some pretty unusual things in their line of work. Dogs have been known to eat some very strange things—from clothing to Christmas lights. Colby, a golden retriever, not only managed to eat a lightbulb, swallowing it down in one piece. He then managed to pass it out the other end, entirely intact.

In one case, a Jack Russell terrier ate a whole turtle, getting pieces of shell stuck in her throat and nasal cavity. After surgery, the dog was fine but the turtle was not. Another weird meal involved a Rottweiler eating a pair of reading glasses, apparently with no ill effects. More than one pet lover has awoken to find their false teeth missing from their night table.

Various people have reported that their dogs have devoured candles, a Rolex watch, a dress, cash, three mobile phones, six plastic tubs of Playdoh, a coffee mug, and the lights and tinsel from a Christmas tree. Especially bizarre is the boxer who reportedly tried to eat her own tail, breaking it in several places. The same dog also swallowed a box of macaroni and cheese (including the cardboard and foil dry noodle pack), a plastic shopping bag, numerous shoes and her new leather collar.

Some dogs have more expensive tastes than others. One such mutt ate 170 dollars that he found in his owner's jeans pocket. An even more costly meal was eaten by a beagle. He ate his owner's diamond engagement ring. After following the dog around for a few days, the owner managed to retrieve it.

A Labrador named Lucy once gulped down a 9cm-long pocketknife. She didn't even require surgery. She just vomited it back up a few days later. Less fortunate was the Chihuahua that ate nine sewing needles. They migrated through the dog's body, lodging in various organs. He required some careful surgery, but amazingly made a full recovery.

Spooky the poodle ate a large chocolate Easter bunny, foil and all. Another disgraceful doggie gobbled up a whole frozen turkey that he took out of the freezer on his own. But at least these pooches were eating foods, unlike a cattle dog named Woof, who developed a penchant for rubber duck bath toys. When he was finally taken to the vet and given an X-ray, the owner discovered five little duckies inside.

One pet, a husky, loved to eat boxer shorts and knitted socks. This particularly fussy dog would somehow remove the elastic from the waistbands of the shorts and leave them uneaten. But it's a three-year-old great Dane that takes the biscuit for gobbling up a record quantity of foreign matter. After he began vomiting, his owners took him for a scan and found no fewer than 43 socks in his belly.

- The **title** clearly reveals the topic of the article.
- The writer begins by mentioning a **key source of information**—veterinarians. This adds a sense of authenticity and reliability to the facts that will be presented in the article.
- The writer is careful to use a **euphemism** for the passage of the lightbulb through the dog's digestive tract. This is because the writer has a general audience in mind who might otherwise be offended.
- Here we see a **contrast** between the dog and the turtle's states of health. The fact that the turtle wasn't 'fine' is stating the obvious but the writer does it here simply for an amusing understated effect.
- **Specific product names** are given to enhance the reader's ability to comprehend the strangeness of these dogs' actions. By alluding to commonly known products we can more easily picture the details.
- **Non-essential information is presented in parentheses** in order that the reader isn't too distracted from the main ideas.
- A **colloquialism** for 'dog' is used to preserve the informal, friendly and engaging tone that makes the text appear very accessible to a range of readers.
- Specific **attention to detail** adds authenticity and believability.
- An **idiomatic expression** is used to emphasise this unusual behaviour.
- **Alliteration** is used to create a humorous effect.
- A **connective phrase** is used to create a smooth transition between this sentence and the next, which introduces another anecdote.
- The text **ends with a startling fact** about a very extreme example of odd dog behaviour, providing perhaps the best (most extreme) illustration of the topic.

INFORMATIVE TEXT
Informative article

COMPREHENSION WORK

Literal questions
Hint: read the text carefully to locate specific facts and details.

1 What was the name of the dog that ate an Easter bunny? ______________________

2 What did the husky eat?

____

3 What sharp objects were eaten by a Labrador and a Chihuahua?

____

Interpretive questions
Hint: These questions require you to combine facts and details to synthesise the meaning.

4 'Another disgraceful doggie gobbled up a whole frozen turkey that he took out of the freezer on his own.'

Of which literary technique is the term 'disgraceful doggie' an example? ______________________

5 The text indicates that Woof was X-rayed by whom? ______________________

6 How many different dog breeds are mentioned in the extract?

____

Hint: Only one answer option is correct. Use the process of elimination to work through the options.

7 Which of these was not something eaten by a dog in this text?

a money **b** car keys **c** clothing

8 Why did the great Dane's owners take him for a scan?

a he began vomiting **b** they'd discovered all their socks in his tummy

c he was refusing to eat his food

9 Which of the following statements is true?

a The writer of this text seems to dislike dogs.

b The writer of this text seems to be critical of dogs.

c The writer of this text seems to be amused by dogs.

10 The phrase 'ill effects' in line 12 is used to make which point?

a The dog who ate the reading glasses became ill.

b Sickness is caused by dogs eating objects that aren't food items.

c The dog was unharmed after eating something it shouldn't have eaten.

Applied questions
Hint: This question requires you to understand a text's implications to infer meaning from the text.

11 What conclusion can we draw from the text?

a dogs never get hurt from eating strange objects

b some of the dogs were lucky to have escaped harm

c eating Christmas lights is harmless and normal dog behaviour

12 What is the main message of this text?

a Huskies eat weird things. **b** Dogs sometimes eat strange things. **c** Dogs like all kinds of foods.

INFORMATIVE TEXT

SPELLING WORK

List Words

All of the words in the box below appear in the text 'Strange things dogs eat'.

swallowing	weird	cavity	apparently	devoured
bizarre	several	numerous	engagement	diamond
lodging	amazingly	disgraceful	elastic	biscuit

1 Rewrite each misspelt word in these sentences on the line provided. *Hint: All the misspelt words are list words.*

- **a** Dogs eat some truly bizzare things. ______
- **b** There's a danger of a sharp object lodgeing in the throat of the dog. ______
- **c** My dog has a wierd interest in eating dead lizards. ______
- **d** We've caught our dog licking the bathroom floor sevarel times. ______
- **e** The dog that ate a turtle had bits of shell stuck in its nasal cavaty. ______
- **f** The disgracfull behaviour of dogs turns some people off owning them. ______
- **g** My dog has aparrently lost his appetite. ______
- **h** Before eating boxer shorts, one dog removed the elastick from the waistband. ______
- **i** The two dogs raided their owner's chocolate stash and devored the lot. ______
- **j** My dog likes to sneak a buscuit or two off the plate when my back is turned. ______

2 Which two list words end with the suffix *ly*?

______ ______

3 Which two list words end with the suffix *ing*?

______ ______

4 Add the suffix *er* to one list word. ______

5 Add the suffix *ly* to two list words. ______ ______

6 Choose the correctly spelt word from these sets. Circle your selections.

a	swallowing	swalowing	swollowing
b	numerus	numeros	numerous
c	dimond	daimond	diamond
d	amazeingly	amazzingly	amazingly
e	engagement	engagment	enghagment

7 Write in a word beginning or ending to form list words from each of the following.

a ______ ver ______ **b** ______ gag ______ **c** ______ ren ______

d ______ our ______ **e** ______ zin ______ **f** ______ mer ______

8 How many syllables are in each of these words? *Hint: Syllables relate to the individual 'sounds' that combinations of letters make.*

a weird ___ **b** cavity ___ **c** biscuit ___ **d** bizarre ___

INFORMATIVE TEXT

Informative article

VOCABULARY WORK

1 Write a sentence that uses each list word to show that you understand their meanings.

apparently	engagement	amazingly	disgraceful

a ______________________________

b ______________________________

c ______________________________

d ______________________________

2 What is the meaning of the word 'lodging' in the context of the text 'Strange things dogs eat'?

____

3 Write the antonyms (opposites) of these words from the text. *Hint: Read around the word in its location in the text to help you grasp the meaning from its context.*

a strange (line 4) ______________ **b** fine (line 10) ______________

c new (line 20) ______________ **d** expensive (line 21) ______________

e found (line 22) ______________ **f** costly (line 22) ______________

g following (line 24) ______________ **h** down (line 26) ______________

i careful (line 30) ______________ **j** full (line 30) ______________

k large (line 31) ______________ **l** frozen (line 32) ______________

m unlike (line 34) ______________ **n** loved (line 37) ______________

o uneaten (line 39) ______________ **p** after (line 41) ______________

4 Complete these statements by changing the form of the list word to fit into the sentence.

a Lucy the Labrador decided to g______________ down a pocket knife.

b When one dog owner became e______________, her diamond ring was swallowed by her beagle.

c A Chihuahua had a lucky escape after vets found sewing needles l______________ in some of its organs.

d When Woof the cattle dog was X______________, five rubber ducks were found inside his belly.

There are many dog-related **idioms** in common use. Test your knowledge by completing these activities.

5 Which of these words is a colloquial term for a dog? Circle the correct one.

a pooch **b** poop **c** poosh

6 Can you think of two other colloquial words beginning with *m* that mean 'dog'—one with an affectionate tone and one with a critical tone? Unscramble the letters to identify the two words.

a tumt ______________ **b** gromlen ______________

7 Other idioms about dogs are listed below. Match them with their meanings by writing in the letters.

a Those kids are on a tight leash. _____ A dog is faithful and useful to its owner.

b Blue! _____ Those children are under the strict control of others.

c That stew would kill a brown dog. _____ She makes verbal threats but isn't likely to carry them out.

d Her bark's worse than her bite. _____ We all get our chance to achieve something positive in life.

e A man's best friend is his dog. _____ A name for a dog with red or ginger-coloured fur.

f Every dog has his day. _____ This food looks and tastes bad.

Modal verbs change the strength of a statement. Low modality verbs include *could*, *may* or *might*, in comparison to high modality verbs like *should*, *must* or *will*.

1 Choose the correct modal verb from each pair to complete the sentences. Circle your choices.

a Your dog ____________ (may / must) one day try to eat something that isn't food.

b This dog is so ill that unfortunately he ____________ (won't / will) live through the night.

c We ____________ (must / may) even be lucky enough to get that diamond ring back in a few days.

d The weird things that some dogs eat ____________ (can / didn't) perhaps hurt them.

2 Write the opposites of these modal verbs.

a can ____________ **b** could ____________

c shouldn't ____________ **d** will not ____________

e must ____________ **f** won't ____________

Adverbs are words we *add* to *verbs* in order to make them more descriptive and precise. For example, we could add the words *greedily* or *delicately* to describe how a dog ate its meal.

3 Create adverbs from the words in parentheses in these sentences and write them on the lines provided.

a There were five dogs ____________ (eager) looking for food treats.

b My dog bounded up ____________ (boisterous) and put his muddy paws all over me.

c The fox terrier crept up ____________ (silence) behind the cat, ready to attack.

d The Irish setter howled ____________ (mournful) at the moon.

e There were no more dog biscuits in the bowl and Jacko looked up at me ____________ (judgemental).

f Three big dogs stood in my path, growling ____________ (menace) at me.

g When Susie's Doberman bares his teeth, everyone ____________ (quick) backs away from him.

4 Unscramble these adverbs that describe how often some dogs eat strange objects.

a arelyr ____________ **b** fento ____________

c gularlyre ____________ **d** caocsioallyn ____________

5 Change each of these words from the text into their adverbial form.

a whole ____________ **b** new ____________

c expensive ____________ **d** full ____________

e day ____________ **f** later ____________

g body ____________ **h** fussy ____________

INFORMATIVE TEXT

Informative article

PUNCTUATION WORK

Apostrophes

Students often find punctuating the contraction *it's* and the pronoun *its* confusing. The contraction *it's* is short for *it is*. This is different from the possessive pronoun *its*. If you aren't sure which one is correct, try reading the sentence and replacing the word *its* with *it is*. If it makes sense, then add the **apostrophe**.

1 Circle the correct word in the brackets to complete these sentences. *Hint: Possessive pronouns (*his, hers, yours, its*) do not need apostrophes.*

- **a** The boxer is a great breed of dog because of (its / it's) intelligence and physical hardiness.
- **b** The poodle owes (its / it's) popularity to (its / it's) distinctive, curly coat.
- **c** (It's / Its) amazing that more dogs aren't harmed from eating strange objects.
- **d** The thing to consider when buying a pet is that (its / it's) going to require a long-term commitment.
- **e** Statistics tell us that pets get overfed because (its / it's) easy to spoil them with treats.
- **f** Our blue heeler is able to catch a frisbee in (its / it's) mouth.

Words that are **plural do not need apostrophes** unless they are showing ownership. *Hint: When showing possession with an apostrophe, check to see how many things are involved.*

2 Decide whether the bold words need apostrophes or not. Circle your choice for each one. *Hint: use the context to help you.*

a	Three **dogs** were walking in the park.	Apostrophe	No apostrophe
b	The dog ate my car **keys**.	Apostrophe	No apostrophe
c	Our garden is a great location for our two **dogs** favourite game.	Apostrophe	No apostrophe
d	The small **childs** fear of the big dog was obvious.	Apostrophe	No apostrophe
e	Tiger and Banjo are two **cats** I've had as pets.	Apostrophe	No apostrophe
f	The three **kittens** fur was standing up as the dog approached them.	Apostrophe	No apostrophe
g	The **childrens** mother had told them to take the dog for a walk.	Apostrophe	No apostrophe
h	The **dollars** my dog ate were going to be put in my bank account.	Apostrophe	No apostrophe
i	Two **ladies** handbags were chewed by my dog, Fred.	Apostrophe	No apostrophe

3 Rewrite these sentences, correcting the punctuation. *Hint: Look for incorrectly used apostrophes, capital letters, commas and full stops.*

- **a** in my neighbourhood the dogs bark at each other all day long

  ____

- **b** my dogs bark is worse than her bite

  ____

- **c** the husky is a breed of dog that can survive quite well in siberia

  ____

- **d** my brother received sixteen stitches in his leg after two dogs sank their teeth into it

  ____

- **e** veterinarians are sometimes compelled to report abusive owners for their neglect of dogs needs

  ____

INFORMATIVE TEXT

Informative article

WRITING WORK 1

Informative articles

Informative articles are texts that are designed to present non-fiction material. They may contain true accounts of events of interest to a wide range of people in the community. The content for informative articles is usually summarised in the first paragraph of the text, allowing the reader to access the basic details. The main body of the story is presented, with details given that flesh out the material in the opening paragraph.

Factual articles often have these features:

- a headline
- an introductory paragraph that foreshadows the content to come
- a logical order of presentation of the facts and details
- background information that provides a proper context for the reader
- action words, such as strong verbs and adverbs
- highly descriptive language, including adjectives and adjectival phrases
- quotations or indirect speech from authorities, witnesses or other commentators
- developments, lessons or questions arising from the story.

1 What role does the first paragraph of an informative article play?

____

2 Name one structural feature of an informative article designed to provide context for the reader.

____

3 What do we call the lines that are presented in quotation marks in factual texts?

____

4 What type of background information might be needed in an informative article about a crime? Tick all that apply.

☐ the place the event occurred
☐ the criminal's favourite fragrance
☐ the person(s) who committed the crime
☐ the motive for the crime
☐ the TV shows the witnesses prefer watching
☐ the temperature that day
☐ the first pet ever owned by the victim
☐ whether or not the criminal has been caught
☐ any unusual details about the crime
☐ clues or evidence left by the criminal
☐ the victim or victims of the crime
☐ the criminal's hopes and dreams
☐ the date the event occurred
☐ the time the event occurred
☐ the extent of any damage or injuries caused
☐ lessons to be learned from the incident

5 Circle *true* or *false* in response to these statements about information in articles.

a Informative articles present truthful material about people and events. True False
b An informative article may contain direct speech presented in exclamation marks. True False
c Informative articles always contain information that no-one is interested in reading. True False
d Facts and details are presented in random order. True False
e The appeal of informative articles can be enhanced with suitable images. True False

INFORMATIVE TEXT

Informative article

WRITING WORK 2

Informative articles may be separated into sections using **subheadings**. Article subheadings need to be interesting and capture the essence of what's in that section. Informative articles may also feature illustrations such as photos, diagrams, maps or other graphic elements.

6 Write two different subheadings that could be used for each of these topics. *Hint: Keep your titles fairly short to ensure that the message is clear.*

a A group of small children become lost in the dense bushland of the Blue Mountains, west of Sydney.

Subheading 1 ______________________________

Subheading 2 ______________________________

b Dolphins become stranded in shallow water outside a seaside restaurant after an unusually low tide.

Subheading 1 ______________________________

Subheading 2 ______________________________

c A Melbourne high-school maths teacher is identified as a member of an outlaw motorcycle gang.

Subheading 1 ______________________________

Subheading 2 ______________________________

d Researchers discover a fluid compound that can be swallowed to enable humans to breathe under water.

Subheading 1 ______________________________

Subheading 2 ______________________________

7 Describe the content of four photographs that would be suitable for presentation alongside each of these factual articles.

- ______________________________
- ______________________________
- ______________________________
- ______________________________

The text 'Strange things dogs eat' contains **adjectival phrases** that we commonly see in informative texts. These phrases give us clues about what the writer thinks and feels about the content.

8 Can you identify the adjectival phrases in these extracts? Underline them.

a Vets get to see some pretty unusual things in their line of work.

b Another weird meal involved a Rottweiler eating a pair of reading glasses …

c Especially bizarre is the boxer who reportedly tried to eat her own tail …

d Less fortunate was the Chihuahua that ate nine sewing needles.

e He required some careful surgery but amazingly, made a full recovery.

f Another disgraceful doggie gobbled up a whole frozen turkey …

g This particularly fussy dog would somehow remove the elastic from the waistbands …

INFORMATIVE TEXT

Informative article

WRITING SAMPLE

Here is a sample text showing you how to structure and write an informative article.

Ninjas to the rescue

✱ **Use a main heading that captures attention.**

A trio of muggers were foiled by a troupe of ninjas in Sydney in January 2017.

✱ **Write a clear summary of the story.** The content of the lead paragraph has been enhanced with a visual image.

Three nasty thugs got more than they bargained for when they staged a mugging near Burwood railway station in Sydney. The youths, aged between 16 and 20, had been harassing a German medical student while he was travelling on an inner city train.

✱ **Add contextual information to ensure the reader understands the place (or setting).** We encounter details about the number and ages of the muggers, the place of the attack and the identity of the victim.

When the man refused to hand over his wallet, they followed him from the railway station into a dark alleyway and began beating and kicking him in a cowardly attack. The student, on an eight-week exchange visit to Australia, cried out for help.

✱ **Give detailed information to show how the event unfolded.** We find vivid details about the demands for the man's wallet, the stalking and the physical attack that ensued.

And help came in a manner that sometimes happens in the movies, but rarely in real life.

✱ **Use a technique such as contrast to add drama.** Here it's the contrast between what happens in the movies versus real life.

By coincidence, the attack had occurred right outside the Ninja Senshi Ryu training school, where the *ninjitsu** class was being let out for the night.

✱ **Provide a key detail that allows the reader to predict what will happen next.** By revealing the presence of the ninjas at just the right time, the reader feels part of the action. This makes the reading experience more exciting.

Imagine the scene—these three delinquents are brutally assaulting an innocent tourist, when out of the shadows emerge five black-clad ninjas, in full traditional gear, running toward them at speed.

✱ **Try using a direct authorial statement to address the reader.** The reader is invited to 'imagine the scene' when the thugs first see the ninjas. This creates a dramatic pause in the action, prolonging the suspense.

The thugs showed by their actions that they did have some measure of common sense—they ran. And they ran fast. Led by *sensei** Kaylan Soto, the ninjas gave chase, giving the attackers the fright of their lives.

✱ **Use strong verbs and adverbs to add pace and excitement to the story.** Repetition is used to emphasise the action. Verbs like 'ran' and 'chase' add pace and make the text interesting to a greater variety of readers.

The victim came away with minor injuries and had his iPod and phone stolen, but these belongings were recovered shortly afterwards when police arrested two of the three suspects. The third perpetrator is still at large but most likely will be steering clear of dark alleys for some time to come.

✱ **Include a quote or report from an authority figure to add weight and credibility to the story.** Here we see police being referenced indirectly to clarify the outcome of the crime. The writer also makes a prediction about the likely future behaviour of the perpetrators.

****ninjitsu***—a Japanese martial art that emphasises stealth, tactical skill, and specialised knowledge of immobilising enemies through pressure points and lethal weaponry

****sensei***—a highly skilled ninjitsu instructor

✱ **Asterisk symbols in the text refer readers to definitions of specialised words to help them understand the text more clearly.** In this text they are Japanese terms related to the art of ninjitsu

Plan your sample on the lines provided.

- **Use a main heading that captures attention.**
- **Write a clear summary of the story.** You could enhance the content of the lead paragraph with visual images that illustrate the text.
- **Add contextual information to ensure the reader understands the place (or setting).** Your setting details could also include the specific time the event occurred.
- **Give detailed information to show how the event unfolded.** Use a logical order. Include vivid details to add to the reader's understanding of what happened. This adds credibility to the story and raises the reader's sense of interest in what happens next.
- **Use a technique such as contrast to add drama.** For example, you might want to describe your fears about what might have happened in contrast to the actual outcome that occurred.
- **Provide a key detail that allows the reader to predict what will happen next.** By revealing a certain vital detail at the right time, you're helping the reader feel part of the action.
- **Try using a direct authorial statement to address the reader.** You could invite the reader to 'imagine the scene'. Use descriptive language (with adjectives and adjectival phrases) to inspire the reader to find out how the story ends.
- **Use strong verbs and adverbs to add pace and excitement to the story.** Use repetition to emphasise the action. Punchy verbs make the text more interesting. Quality descriptions can make informative texts appeal to a greater variety of readers than would usually be in that target audience.
- **Include a quote or report from an authority figure to add weight and credibility to the story.** You may wish to report someone's exact words using direct speech, for example. You could also make a prediction.
- **Asterisk symbols in the text refer readers to definitions of specialised words to help them understand the text more clearly.** Decide which words, if any, need further clarification in your text.

UNIT 3

INFORMATIVE TEXT

Procedure

READING WORK

The perfect espresso brew

At C Ya Latté, we pride ourselves on the precision with which we make our coffee. We expect all C Ya Latté baristas to follow this procedure to ensure that we maintain the high quality of our products.

Extracting the coffee—machine method

When making the perfect espresso, it is the pressure that makes the difference. Hot water under pressure extracts the best flavour from the coffee. Correct espresso extraction should take around 25 seconds.

- First select the customer's preferred amount of ground coffee by pressing the appropriate button so the grounds are released into the group handle. The machine is set as follows:

  two pulls = one shot
  three pulls = double shot
  four pulls = extra-large double shot.
- Next press down firmly with the tamp to level and compact the coffee smoothly. The coffee is ground to a particular degree of coarseness to allow just the right amount of water to flow around the coffee grounds. If you pack the coffee into the group handle correctly, you can be sure of extracting the perfect shot, which should have a rich reddish brown crema.
- Then attach the group handle to the machine very firmly and press the appropriate button to allow hot water to flow through the coffee. The flowing coffee should have a thick nectar-like consistency.
- After the shot is extracted, turn the handle upside down over the collection container and tap out the cake of coffee. It should come out in one piece and be firm and fairly dry. Discard it immediately.

Immediately after pouring the shot, turn your attention to steaming the milk.

Steaming the milk—machine method

- Begin with half a jug of cold milk.
- Hold the jug at an angle so you can see inside.
- Insert the steam wand as deeply as possible and to one side of the milk jug.
- Open the steam valve fully.
- Keeping the steam wand to one side, quickly lower the jug so that the wand is just below the milk's surface. The milk should start to hiss and whirlpool at this point, which will break down any large bubbles. The hissing becomes less frequent as the milk heats up. Continue until the milk reaches 63–65 °C and the bigger bubbles have been broken down. By the time steaming is complete the total volume in the jug should have doubled.
- Bang the jug on the counter top to settle the milk.
- Pour the milk over the espresso as soon as possible after steaming.
- Finish with a swirl or create another pattern with the milk as you pour the last of the froth into the cup.

- The **title** is designed to clearly identify the topic.
- The **company name** is given to identify the café and to assert the owner's authoritative right to enforce this procedure upon staff.
- **Subheadings** are used to organise the information in a logical way.
- **Connective words and phrases** are used to ensure that the points are presented in proper sequence, and that the order is noted by the reader.
- The **layout** is adjusted to ensure that the information is as accessible and clear as possible. It also provides an effective means of summarising details rather than writing out long sentences.
- **Commanding language** is used to emphasise the fact that this is a procedure that staff are expected to follow without deviation.
- This **directive** provides the link between the two portions of the text.
- **Connectives** are used, again indicating the order in which the steps should be taken.
- **Jargon** specific to barista work is used and by this we can see that the author assumes a level of comprehension in the reader.
- **Specific figures** are used for the barista's reference. This implies that the text may be re-read while on the job.
- The word 'finish' provides a **transition** to the concluding step, signalling that this is the final step in the procedure.

INFORMATIVE TEXT

Procedure

COMPREHENSION WORK

Literal questions

Hint: Read the text carefully to locate specific facts and details.

1 What is the name of the café mentioned in this text?

a The Perfect Espresso Brew **b** Procedure **c** C Ya Latté

2 How many pulls make a double-shot espresso? ______________________

3 Why does the barista need to turn the group handle upside down and tap it?

____

Interpretive questions

Hint: These questions require you to combine facts and details to synthesise the meaning.

4 What are the two main pieces of equipment involved in steaming the milk?

a the jug and the steam wand **b** the steam wand and the group handle

c the jug and the spoon

5 From its use in the context, what phrase does the symbol '°C' represent?

a Celsius points **b** degrees Celsius **c** days Celsius

6 What is the meaning of the word 'grounds' in this text?

____

7 Considering the structure of the text, what are the two key stages in coffee making?

____

8 What should the steamed milk look like when it is ready for pouring into the coffee cup?

____

9 What is a final recommendation mentioned at the end of the process?

a pour the milk as soon as possible **b** make a pattern with the froth

c hold the milk jug at an angle

10 The main points about extracting the espresso are summarised in correct order by which of the following?

a select the amount, pack the group handle, allow hot water to flow through, empty the group handle

b give four pulls, pack the group handle, press the button on the machine, empty the group handle

c take the customer's order, pack the group handle, press down firmly, steam the milk

Applied questions

Hint: These questions require you to understand a text's implications to infer meaning from the text.

11 If the espresso doesn't have a rich, reddish crema, what are the two most likely causes?

____

12 Which of the following would be the most appropriate addition to clarify this procedure text?

a a diagram of the coffee machine and its parts **b** a photo of a customer

c a picture of coffee beans

INFORMATIVE TEXT

SPELLING WORK

List Words

All of the words in the box below appear in the text 'The perfect espresso brew'.

maintain	flavour	machine	consistency	whirlpool
pressure	preferred	coarseness	angle	surface
extraction	released	attach	valve	espresso

Spelling is much easier when we break down a word into its parts. Many are made up of a **base word** and a **prefix** (added to the beginning of the base word) or a suffix (added to the end).

1 Write the list words upon which each of these is based.

a angular ______ **b** flavoured ______

c machinery ______ **d** pressurised ______

e attachment ______ **f** maintenance ______

2 Write answers to these questions.

a Which list word could take the suffix *ment* to form a new word? Write it on the line provided.

______

b Choose three list words that could take the suffix *ing* to form a new word and write them on the line.

______ ______ ______

3 Write the plural forms of these words from the text.

a procedure ______ **b** handle ______

c water ______ **d** wand ______

4 Use these sets of consonants and vowels to form words from the list.

a sssncr eeoa ______ **b** ttncrx aeio ______

c rrrpdf eee ______ **d** ccssnnty eio ______

5 Which word is the only compound word in the list? ______

6 Which list words contain double consonants next to each other? ______

7 Which list word has a 'shen' sound at the end? ______

8 Which list word contains the letters *ch* that are pronounced 'sh'? ______

9 Find list words that contain the following vowel blends and circle the word with the matching sound.

Vowel blends	List word	Sounds like the vowel in …		
a ai	______	day	hair	park
b oo	______	float	took	cool
c ea	______	pie	peace	head
d oa	______	hour	goat	board
e ir	______	her	it	eye

INFORMATIVE TEXT

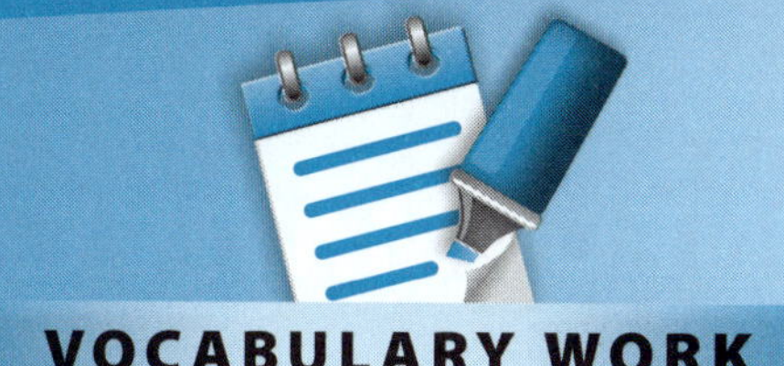

VOCABULARY WORK

1 Write a list word to match each definition.

List word	Definition
a	accuracy (line 2)
b	method (line 4)
c	programmed (line 12)
d	even (line 16)
e	red coloured (line 20)
f	froth on the top of fresh espresso (line 20)
g	amount (line 38)
h	curly pattern (line 41)

Synonyms are words that mean the same as a given word and **antonyms** mean the opposite.

2 Complete these synonym and antonym activities by reading each word in its context in the text 'The perfect espresso brew'. Write the words that appear in the text on the lines provided.

a Which word is a synonym for the word 'about' (line 9)? ____________

b Which word is a synonym for the word 'hard' (line 16)? ____________

c Which word is a synonym for the word 'specific' (line 17)? ____________

d Which word is a synonym for the word 'push' (line 21)? ____________

e Which word is an antonym for the word 'wet' (line 26)? ____________

f Which word is an antonym for the word 'outside' (line 30)? ____________

g Which word is an antonym for the word 'slowly' (line 33)? ____________

h Which word is an antonym for the word 'halved' (line 38)? ____________

i Which word is an antonym for the word 'start' (line 41)? ____________

j Which word is an antonym for the word 'first' (line 42)? ____________

3 What do we call a person who is trained to make coffee using a specialised machine? ____________

There are many **idioms** that relate to tea and coffee culture in the English language.

4 Write in the missing word from these idioms. Choose from the words below.

storm	sugar	piece	cup	milk	crème
icing	cookie	tea	cake	pie	biscuit

a I wouldn't sell it for all the ____________ in China.

b Scoring the final goal was the ____________ on the cake.

c That way you can have your ____________ and eat it too.

d The whole thing is just a ____________ in a teacup.

e A spoonful of ____________ makes the medicine go down.

f These artists are the crème de la ____________.

g Snow skiing is not my ____________ of tea.

h That really takes the ____________.

i That's the way the ____________ crumbles.

j It's really easy—a ____________ of cake.

k It's no use crying over spilt ____________.

l It's just a fantasy—____________ in the sky.

INFORMATIVE TEXT

Procedure

GRAMMAR WORK

Nouns

We call words that name things **nouns**. Nouns name people, places, events, things, ideas, thoughts and emotions. Two categories of nouns are common and abstract.

Common nouns name things that you can sense with your five physical senses. They have independent existence in reality. Common nouns include words like *bird, book, light, grass* and *storm.* Common nouns do not begin with capital letters unless they are positioned at the start of a sentence.

Abstract nouns name things that exist (such as ideas, thoughts and emotions) but do not have any form or substance that can be perceived with the physical senses. They refer to concepts rather than actual things. *Dreams, sadness, taste, luck* and *wisdom* are all abstract nouns.

1 Underline the common nouns in these clauses.

- **a** how to make coffee
- **b** the machine has been programmed
- **c** find out what the customer would like
- **d** try steaming the milk
- **e** all our staff do it like this
- **f** we want to offer the best quality product we can
- **g** there is a rich aroma
- **h** they're attracted to the café

2 Underline all of the common nouns in this passage from the text 'The perfect espresso brew'. *Hint: Take note of how they are used as some words have been used here as adjectives instead of nouns.*

After the shot is extracted, turn the handle upside down over the collection container and tap out the cake of coffee. It should come out in one piece and be firm and fairly dry.

3 Underline the abstract noun in this sentence.

Immediately after pouring the shot, turn your attention to steaming the milk.

4 Which type of nouns are these? Circle your choice. *Hint: Consider the context of each word in the text before you decide on the answer.*

a coffee	common or abstract	**b** water	common or abstract
c button	common or abstract	**d** machine	common or abstract
e precision	common or abstract	**f** quality	common or abstract
g attention	common or abstract	**h** customer	common or abstract
i milk	common or abstract	**j** bubbles	common or abstract
k volume	common or abstract	**l** jug	common or abstract
m espresso	common or abstract	**n** froth	common or abstract
o cup	common or abstract	**p** pattern	common or abstract

Transitional words and phrases link one part of a text to another. They often make statements about timing and the order of events. For example, *finally* and *afterwards* are both transitional words. Transitions may be made using single words or multi-word phrases.

5 In which lines of the text are these transitional expressions used? Write in the line numbers.

a first	line _____	**b** next	line _____	**c** then	line _____
d after	line _____	**e** immediately after	line _____	**f** begin with	line _____
g start to	line _____	**h** continue until	line _____	**i** by the time	line _____
j as soon as possible	line _____	**k** finish	line _____	**l** the last of	line _____

INFORMATIVE TEXT

Procedure

PUNCTUATION WORK

A **clause** is a string of words related to a single idea. A clause is a phrase that contains a **subject**—a person or thing—and a **verb**. The subject and verb may be composed of more than one word. **Commas** help make meaning clearer by separating one clause from another in a sentence.

1 Decide whether each of the following is a phrase or a clause. Circle *phrase* or *clause* for each one. *Hint: Phrases are just strings of words that lack a subject and/or verb, disqualifying them from being considered clauses.*

a	when making the perfect espresso	Phrase	Clause
b	hot water under pressure	Phrase	Clause
c	after the shot is extracted	Phrase	Clause
d	keeping the steam wand to one side	Phrase	Clause
e	any large bubbles	Phrase	Clause
f	the total volume in the jug should have doubled	Phrase	Clause

2 Place a comma after the first clause in each of these sentences to make the meaning clearer.

a When the bus pulled up ten school students ordered six lattes and four cappuccinos between them.

b Although it's not our most popular drink we've been selling a lot more chai teas lately.

c Despite the hot weather this week we've been just as busy as ever.

d Since we took on two new baristas last April we've more than doubled our profits at the café.

3 Place two commas in each of these sentences to make the meaning clearer. *Hint: It's the meaning of a sentence, not its length, that determines how many commas are needed.*

a Two of our regular customers Theo and Olga nominated us for a community service award.

b At closing time one of our baristas tripped and sprained her ankle giving everyone a nasty shock.

c The barista shook chocolate powder over the frothy drinks then taking a thin wooden stick in his fingers he delicately made a swirling pattern on top of each one.

Commas can be used to **separate** items in a **list**.

4 Rewrite these sentences containing lists on the lines provided, using commas to separate the items. *Hint: In a list there is no comma between the second last and the last noun. The word* and *is used as the separator in place of the comma.*

a To make instant coffee at home you'll need instant coffee powder hot water milk sugar

____

b The barista made three coffees two teas a hot chocolate

____

c We ordered raisin toast carrot cake lemon slice two almond biscuits a blueberry muffin

____

5 What symbol, usually associated with mathematics, is used to present the information about the machine's settings in the text? ________

INFORMATIVE TEXT
Procedure

WRITING WORK 1

Procedures

Procedures are informative texts that provide clear, easy-to-follow steps that result in a particular outcome or product. Some common procedure texts are instruction manuals, recipes, game rules and written directions. Procedures are written to explain to the reader how to make or do almost anything. They may appear in point form rather than as prose paragraphs, a feature which makes them different from other informative texts.

The basic features of any procedure text are:
- a literal, informative title
- a clear structure, including subheadings, numbered steps or dot points
- a progression of actions or a method leading to the outcome or product named in the title
- the present tense
- explanatory pictures, photos and diagrams
- assumed knowledge of measurements, abbreviations, key procedural words, standard equipment relevant to the type of procedure and key verbs commonly used in procedures.

To ensure that a procedure is effective, we must:
- use language economically, providing only the most essential details
- use clear expression
- use accurate punctuation
- use the present tense
- use action verbs
- give factual descriptions
- use simple, literal language.

1 How is a procedure text different from other informative texts?

____

____

2 Write two topics that procedure texts could be written to explain.

____________________ ____________________

3 Why are bullet points useful in procedural texts?

____

4 Which of the following is not a feature of a procedure text? Circle one.

a adjectival phrases **b** action verbs

c present tense **d** factual descriptions

5 List three aspects of the structure of procedure texts that make them easy to understand.

______________ ______________ ______________

6 What visual features can add clarity to procedure texts? List three.

______________ ______________ ______________

7 Complete this table of language features by writing in the missing examples. *Hint: Use the letter and line number clues to help you.*

Feature	Example from the text	Effect in the text
action verbs	from line 10 of the text **a** p _ _ s _ _ _ g	Specific action verbs help the reader understand precisely what to do in the procedure.
present tense	from line 29 of the text **b** B _ _ _ n with h _ _ f a j _ g of _ o l_ m _ l k.	This gives the procedure immediacy and gives the impression that the reader is being personally instructed.
standard equipment	from line 11 of the text **c** _ r _ u _ h _ _ _ l _	Readers of a procedure text are likely to be familiar with the specific equipment mentioned.
measurements	from line 36 of the text **d** _ _ – _ _ °C	Measurements and other numerical data help make the text specific to its purpose. Measurements are literal, factual elements of procedure texts.
subheadings	from line 6 of the text **e** _ x _ _ _ _ _ _ _ _ _ _ _ _ _ _ _ _ _ —machine method	Subheadings provide the text with a strong organisational structure that allows the reader to quickly access relevant information in the proper sequence.

8 Is 'The perfect espresso brew' a suitable title for the sample text? Explain your answer.

____

____

9 Who do you think most likely wrote the text 'The perfect espresso brew'? Explain your reasoning. *Hint: This is not the name of a person but their position. Think about why the text has been written.*

____

____

10 Which of the following best describes the text 'The perfect espresso brew'? Tick one.

- ☐ a recipe
- ☐ instructions
- ☐ a narrative
- ☐ an opinion

11 Read the text 'The perfect espresso brew' and write a point-form summary of the method of extracting the espresso.

- ______________________________
- ______________________________
- ______________________________
- ______________________________
- ______________________________

INFORMATIVE TEXT

Procedure

WRITING SAMPLE

Here is a sample text showing you how to structure and write a procedure.

Human versus shark: how to survive a shark attack

✱ **Use a literal title with no figurative language techniques.** The phrase 'how to' shows that this is a practical guide for the reader.

What to do when you encounter a shark while swimming

Step 1. Try not to panic.
Step 2. Alert others quickly so they can help (or at least escape the situation themselves).
Step 3. Keep your eyes on the shark at all times.
Step 4. If you can get away, do so—as fast as you can! But if you're trapped with no hope of escape, remain still.

✱ **Make sure each subheading clearly outlines the topic of its section.** It should be literal. A numbered list of steps gives the text its structure. Action verbs emphasise the importance of the actions.

What to do when you're trapped in deep, open water

Step 5. Try to slowly back away.
Step 6. Try to back yourself up against something, like a boat or even another swimmer, to reduce the shark's approach angles.
Step 7. If the shark begins circling you, it is about to attack. You must try to physically fight it off.

✱ **Use bold headings throughout the procedure to break it into clear steps.** Here the numbers continue from the last section to emphasise that these follow the first four steps. The last step leads into the topic of the next section.

Three methods for fighting off a shark

Method 1: Eye poking? Worth a try, but difficult.
During an attack, the shark rolls its eyes back and a membrane closes over them. You could just make it angrier.

Method 2: Nose punching? Worth a try, but dangerous.
It isn't easy when you're in the water to muster enough energy to deliver a crippling blow. The snout is dangerously near their teeth. You could quickly end up with your fist in their jaws.

Method 3: Gill gouging? Your best bet by far.
Sharks hate anything touching their gills. Jamming your fingers or an object into the gills on the sides of its head is the best method for fending off an attack.

✱ **Organise headings logically.** This heading follows on logically from the previous section. It is intended to guide the reader who has considered all the earlier steps. It provides summary information—three methods are presented for fighting off a shark: the first two are assessed as difficult and dangerous, leading the reader to see that the third method is the most likely to succeed. Subheadings address the reader in a conversational manner, as this makes the text seem more friendly. Phrasing them as questions helps reinforce this tone.

If the worst comes to the worst

If you are injured in a shark attack:
Your first priority is to get away from the shark. **Your second priority** is to stop the bleeding. **Your third priority** is to get help as soon as you can. Remember: many people have survived shark attacks, even after sustaining severe injuries. Keep fighting off the shark despite your injuries. Your life is certainly worth fighting for!

✱ **Include the most important information so that the reader's attention is focused upon it.** The subheading expresses a common idiom. Bold type is used to emphasise the order of the priorities. A final note offers a reminder to the reader that brings logic and rational thinking back to the text after they've been led to consider the worst possible outcome.

How to avoid sharks

- Never swim or surf alone at dawn, dusk or night-time.
- Never enter water where fish are swarming or feeding.
- Never swim in risky areas—caves, bridges, in murky water or around fishing haunts. Bait attracts sharks.
- Never swim in deep water with a dog. Their erratic movements and strong scent attract sharks.
- Never swim with an injury. Blood attracts sharks.

✱ **Conclude the text by giving practical information.** Preventive measures are included to show that this procedure is a last resort that shouldn't be necessary if swimmers act sensibly around the water. This section functions as a conclusion that encourages responsible thinking and planning to avoid the attack scenario discussed.

Plan your sample on the lines provided.

- **Use a literal title with no figurative language techniques.** Identify the topic and include the phrase 'how to' to show that this is a practical guide for the reader.

- **Make sure each subheading clearly outlines the topic of its section.** It should be written in literal language. Provide a numbered list of steps to give the text its structure. Use action verbs to emphasise the importance of the actions to be taken.

- **Use bold headings throughout the procedure to break it into clear steps.** Consider how you will use numbering to emphasise how each section follows on chronologically from the last. The last step should lead into the topic of the next section.

- **Organise headings logically.** The heading for this section should follow on logically from the previous section to guide the reader who has read and considered all the earlier steps. Provide summary information of major points. You may like to give the reader your own assessment of each one. Use the subheadings (or another method) to address the reader in a conversational manner. This makes the text seem more friendly. Phrasing the subheadings as questions helps reinforce this tone.

- **Include the most important information so that the reader's attention is focused upon it.** Emphasise priorities by using subheadings that draw the reader's attention to them. Bold type may be used to emphasise the order of the priorities.

- **Conclude the text by giving practical information.**

INFORMATIVE TEXT

Online article

READING WORK

Strange coincidences

Alexander Fleming

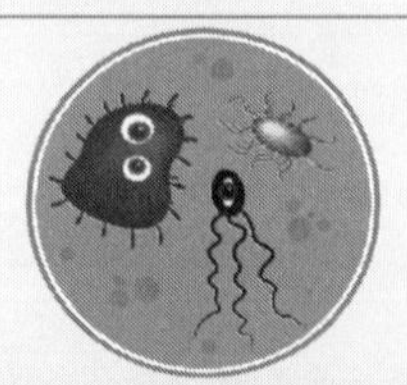

A life-saving, germ-killing medicine was discovered by a researcher who decided not to bother with the washing up one evening in 1928.

Alexander Fleming went home from his laboratory without cleaning out a petri dish that contained a culture of staphylococcus—a nasty bacterium. After a few days, a blueish fuzz had grown in it. That fuzz turned out to be a mould that killed the staphylococcus bacteria in the dish. He'd accidentally discovered the antibiotic properties of penicillin, a drug that has saved countless lives.

The Ebbin brothers

In 1974 a passenger in a taxi in the little town of Hamilton, Bermuda was unlucky enough to become involved in an accident. Neville Ebbin, a 17-year-old local, was killed when the taxi struck his moped. A year later, the same passenger was reminded of this unpleasant incident as he rode in a taxi along that same route with the very same cab driver, Willard Manders. As bad luck would have it, his thoughts were interrupted by a sudden thump. The taxi had collided fatally with a youth on a banged-up old moped. It was Erskine Ebbin, Neville's 17-year-old brother.

Anne Parrish

When American novelist Anne Parrish was browsing through some old books in a Paris bric-a-brac shop, she came across one title that had been a childhood favourite—*Jack Frost and Other Stories*. She'd been given a copy of that book more than fifty years earlier by her grandfather. She'd lost her original copy over the years, having moved house many times. She felt it was a stroke of luck to find a copy in France, of all places. So for sentimental reasons, she bought it. The well-used copy in her hands was old and tattered. As she looked through the pages, she recalled fond memories of reading those stories as a child. Showing it to her husband, they turned to the inside cover. There the name of the book's former owner was written—Anne Parrish, 209 North Weber Street, Colorado Springs.

Violet Jessop

In 1911 an ocean liner stewardess named Violet Jessop was aboard RMS *Olympic* when it collided with a British warship, HMS *Hawke*. Fortunately, there were no fatalities that day. Violet was assigned to work on the *Olympic*'s sister ship, RMS *Titanic*, the following year. On the vessel's first and only voyage, it struck an iceberg and quickly sank. The sinking of the *Titanic* has entered into folklore as the most devastating passenger liner accident on record. Jessop survived the disaster. Undaunted by her bad luck at sea, Jessop served with the British Red Cross on HMHS *Britannic* in World War 1. The *Britannic* was the third sister in this trio of ill-fated ships. In 1916 Jessop again survived disaster. This time a torpedo hit the ship, causing an explosion that killed thirty people and sank the ship. Violet Jessop went back to work for the White Star Line in 1920 and the remainder of her career at sea ended uneventfully.

- The article's **title** identifies the general topic.
- **Subheadings** take the form of people's names. Because the first name (Alexander Fleming) is familiar to us, we presume that the others named are also real people.
- A **specific date** is given which adds credibility to the story.
- An **important term is defined**, showing that the writer realises that the average reader may not have this knowledge.
- Details are given to enhance the **precision** of the text.
- This line is a **pun** on the common expression 'As luck would have it …'.
- The **title of the book is shown in italics**, consistent with the usual practice of referring to titles in written texts.
- **Contractions** are used to help the text flow while still preserving an appropriate register.
- **Small physical details** enable the reader to visualise the scene.
- The reader is left to make the **connection** between the address and the fact that Anne Parrish lived in America in her childhood.
- The **names of the ships must be presented in italics.**
- The author only **briefly mentions** the *Titanic* disaster as this is not the main point of the article. The reader is presumed to know about the sinking of the *Titanic* but not the disasters involving the other two ships.
- There is **no overall conclusion** given in this article, as each section of the text (under each subheading) has its own conclusion built in.

INFORMATIVE TEXT

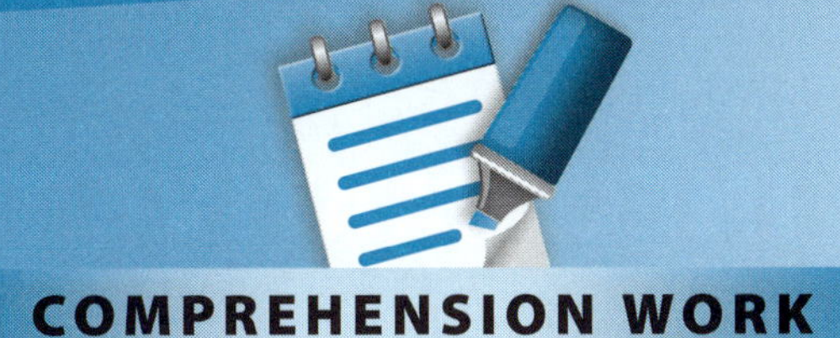

COMPREHENSION WORK

Literal questions

Hint: Read the text carefully to locate specific facts and details.

1 What life-saving antibiotic was discovered by Alexander Fleming?

a bacterium **b** staphylococcus **c** penicillin

2 Explain the causes of the three accidents of the ships Violet Jessop worked on.

____

____

3 How many times did Anne Parrish buy the book *Jack Frost and Other Stories*? ______________

4 List all the people who are mentioned in the text.

____

Interpretive questions

Hint: These questions require you to combine facts and details to synthesise the meaning.

5 In what year did the RMS *Titanic* sink? ______________

6 What item did Alexander Fleming fail to clean in his lab? ______________

7 To what is the term 'unpleasant incident' referring in line 15 of the text?

a a fight with a taxi driver **b** Erskine Ebbin's death **c** a collision with a moped

8 Which of the following is a logical conclusion to make about the hometown of the Ebbin brothers?

a It is a huge city with many roads and many taxis.

b It is in Hamilton, New Zealand.

c It is a fairly small town with only a few taxis.

9 What feature is it reasonable to assume was included in the book *Jack Frost and Other Stories*?

a a sound recording **b** pictures **c** a DVD

10 Why did Anne Parrish buy the book in Paris?

a because her name was written in the book

b because it revived fond memories of her childhood

c because she wrote the book

Applied questions

Hint: This question requires you to understand a text's implications to infer meaning from the text.

11 What is surprising about Anne Parrish's book being found in a bric-a-brac shop in France?

a It was the same book she'd owned fifty years earlier when she'd lived in America.

b It was a different copy of her favourite book.

c It was her book but it had someone else's name and address written inside.

12 Why is the coincidence involving the Ebbin brothers especially surprising?

____

____

List Words

All of the words in the box below appear in the text 'Strange coincidences'.

researcher	bacteria	incident	interrupted	original
laboratory	accidentally	route	novelist	bought
mould	passenger	collided	childhood	tattered

1 Write the plural forms of these words from the text 'Strange coincidences'.

a researcher __________ **b** incident __________

c laboratory __________ **d** novelist __________

2 What is the singular form of the word 'bacteria'? __________
Hint: Scan the text for the answer.

3 Which two words are the only single-syllable list words?

__________ __________

4 Which list words contain the vowel blend 'ou'? __________

5 Which list word can be shortened to 'lab'? __________

6 Which list word has two silent letters? __________

7 Write the list words to which each of the words below is most closely related.

a mouldy __________ **b** incidentally __________

c originated __________ **d** collision __________

e passage __________ **f** children __________

8 Find an antonym (opposite) in the list for each of the following.

a on purpose __________ **b** sold __________

c uninterrupted __________ **d** a copy __________

9 Write these list words and underline all the vowels in each.

a researcher __________ **b** route __________

c collided __________ **d** laboratory __________

10 Arrange all the list words in alphabetical order.

__________ __________ __________

__________ __________ __________

__________ __________ __________

__________ __________ __________

__________ __________ __________

INFORMATIVE TEXT

Online article

VOCABULARY WORK

1 What is the meaning of these list words? Write definitions in your own words.

- **a** mould ______________________________
- **b** collided ______________________________
- **c** route ______________________________
- **d** tattered ______________________________
- **e** incident ______________________________

2 Write one list word to fit each of the following definitions:

- **a** a person who works in a field of scientific enquiry ______________
- **b** according to random forces ______________
- **c** prevented from continuing as planned ______________
- **d** first of its kind ______________

3 Link each list word in the box on the left with one in the box on the right. Write a letter on the lines provided to form each match. *Hint: they are linked by their contexts.*

a researcher	________	travel
b laboratory	________	literature
c bacteria	________	shopping
d passenger	________	disease
e novelist	________	knowledge
f bought	________	chemistry

4 In the table below, use the affixes (prefixes and suffixes) to change list words into new forms. *Hint: you can use the base words of the list words to make new forms.*

Affixes	List word	New form
a the prefix *un*		
b the suffix *y*		
c the suffix *ed*		
d the suffix *ly*		

5 There are many idioms relating to luck, chance and coincidence. Complete these by writing in the missing words.

law pot management feet stars Fate

Idiom	Meaning
a She's landed on her ______________.	She has had good fortune in life after a poor start.
b Thank your lucky ______________.	Be grateful for your good luck.
c I'll take ____________ luck.	I'll accept whatever is available without knowing beforehand.
d More good luck than good ______________.	It happened by chance and wasn't anyone's achievement.
e As ____________ would have it …	As sometimes happens because of coincidence …
f It's Murphy's ____________.	If something can go wrong, it will go wrong.

INFORMATIVE TEXT

GRAMMAR WORK

Prepositions are words that show relationships between others, usually nouns or pronouns. They may start phrases and link words so that we can understand how they relate to each other. For example, *under, into, up, with* and *around* are all prepositions.

1 Underline the prepositions in these sentences.

- **a** If you look at that petri dish, you'll see mould growing in it.
- **b** Inside his laboratory, Fleming worked patiently on isolating bacteria.
- **c** Tomorrow's biologists will have knowledge that goes beyond what we know today.

2 Look at these pairs of words and circle the preposition from each pair.

a off / other	**b** tonight / against	**c** future / down	**d** cover / over	**e** beside / table
f into / accident	**g** taxi / to	**h** transport / from	**i** in / outer	**j** pass / by

3 Add the missing prepositions to complete these sentences.

- **a** The lady who'd bought the book was delighted __________ her purchase.
- **b** The patient was cured __________ two doses of penicillin.
- **c** There have been two major accidents __________ that intersection in recent years.
- **d** Many passengers were sucked ______________ the water with the ship when the *Titanic* went down.

4 Underline all the prepositions in this passage.

In 1974 a passenger in a taxi in the little town of Hamilton, Bermuda was unlucky enough to become involved in an accident. Neville Ebbin, a 17-year-old local, was killed when the taxi struck his moped. A year later the same passenger was reminded of this unpleasant incident as he rode in a taxi along that same route with the very same cab driver, Willard Manders. As bad luck would have it, his thoughts were interrupted by a sudden thump. The taxi had collided fatally with a youth on a banged-up old moped. It was Erskine Ebbin, Neville's 17-year-old brother.

When we need to express the idea that someone or something 'possesses' or owns something, we use an apostrophe of possession. For example, *Lee's shirt* or *Maya's hat* are both expressed with a **possessive apostrophe**. For singular nouns (and for plural nouns that don't end in 's'), we add an apostrophe followed by 's'; for example, *the book's former owner, children's stories*. For plural nouns ending in 's', we simply add an apostrophe at the end; for example, *readers' entertainment*.

5 Rewrite these expressions using an apostrophe of possession. The first one has been done for you as an example.

- **a** the owner of the book *the book's owner*
- **b** the wheels of the car ______________________
- **c** the luck of Anne Parrish ______________________
- **d** the discoveries of scientists ______________________
- **e** the deaths of the passengers ______________________

It's important to learn how to **punctuate** sentences correctly. A sentence begins with a capital letter and has one of three possible ending marks: a full stop, a question mark or an exclamation mark. Sentences may also include commas and other punctuation marks; this allows writers to make themselves understood more clearly.

INFORMATIVE TEXT
Online article

PUNCTUATION WORK

1 Correct the punctuation of these sentences by rewriting them. *Hint: Look for missing capital letters, sentence ending marks and commas.*

a as fleming repeatedly taught his students the staophylococcus bacterium is a dangerously infectious bug

___

b is the town of hamilton in bermuda

___

c anne parrish came home from paris with the very same book shed owned as a child

___

d imagine the odds of two brothers being killed at the same place by the same driver just a year apart

___

e how lucky is violet jessop to have survived three accidents at sea

___

Hyphens are used to join closely related words together.

2 Write the hyphenated terms that appear in the text 'Strange coincidences' on the lines provided. *Hint: They appear on line numbers 3, 13, 18, 22, 27 and 40.*

___-___ ___-___ ___-___

___-___ ___-___

3 Identify these punctuation marks.

a , ___ **b** ' ___ **c** ? ___

d ' ' ___ **e** - ___ **f** ! ___

g : ___ **h** ; ___ **i** . ___

Contractions are two words that have been joined together to make one word. In contractions, apostrophes show that one or more letters have been left out. For example, *hadn't* is the contraction of *had* and *not*. Using contractions makes our writing more like conversational language or everyday speech.

4 For each of the following, write out the words that have been contracted in their full forms.

a would've ___ **b** can't ___

c shouldn't ___ **d** they'll ___

e he'd ___ **f** we're ___

g haven't ___ **h** we'll ___

5 **Conjunctions** are words that join two words, phrases, clauses or sentences together. Which word in each pair is a conjunction? Shade the bubble to select your answer.

a ◯ and ◯ the **b** ◯ he ◯ but

c ◯ went ◯ because **d** ◯ although ◯ in

e ◯ or ◯ now **f** ◯ while ◯ under

g ◯ this ◯ whether **h** ◯ except ◯ a

INFORMATIVE TEXT

Online article

WRITING WORK 1

Online articles

Online articles are informative texts that are designed to attract and maintain the attention of a wide audience of readers. They are non-fiction texts presenting factual accounts of events that have happened in the past. The possibilities for topics and themes of online articles are limitless. In online articles, the details are presented in logical (usually chronological) order.

Online articles often contain these **textual features:**

- a heading that clearly describes the topic or theme so internet search engines can tag the keywords
- subheadings, which may also be hypertext links for ease of navigation by the reader
- the main body broken into short, readable chunks of text
- a logical order of presentation of the facts and details
- a conversational tone assisted by the use of contractions
- connective phrases that help unify the article
- language features that affect the pace, including short sentences
- specific details, facts, data, statistics, names or quotations
- an exciting, dramatic or humorous element at the end of the article
- engaging techniques such as rhetorical questions
- images that illustrate the topic
- visual features that affect the readability, including dot points or bold highlighting of keywords
- quotes
- jargon when a specialised topic is being presented
- keywords in the body text for ease of tagging and indexing by internet search engines.

Online articles may also include **interactive features** such as:

- photographs and other illustrative material
- links to related information so the reader can research the story
- a facility for leaving personal comments about the article
- a facility for engaging in a discussion forum.

1 Could the online article in this chapter be classified as a fiction or a non-fiction text? ______________________

2 Name two structural features of online articles that help make the content easy to navigate.

______________________ ______________________

3 Which is easier to locate on a specific topic: an online article or a magazine article? Explain your answer.

____

____

4 Which of the following best describes the writer's purpose for the text 'Strange coincidences'? Tick one.

☐ The writer is persuading readers to accept a particular opinion about the topic of coincidences.

☐ The writer intends to inform readers about some strange coincidences.

☐ The writer intends to narrate a story about a strange coincidence to readers of fiction.

INFORMATIVE TEXT
Online article

WRITING WORK 2

5 Demonstrate your understanding by inserting the missing words into these sentences.

access	worldwide	stories	related	appeal	target	indexed	large

a An online article presents facts in ways that ____________ to a particular ____________ audience.

b They are sometimes composed of multiple ____________ or snippets that are ____________ in some way.

c Online articles make up a ________ proportion of the content of the ____________ ____________ web.

d They contain keywords that can be tagged and ____________ by search engines for ease of ____________.

6 Complete this table of language features by finding examples of each in the text 'Strange coincidences'.

Feature	Example from the text	Effect in the text
a contraction	**a**	Contractions help create a conversational tone in the text.
an exciting, dramatic or humorous element	**b**	Such moments are often found at the end of the article, as a means of leaving a strong impact upon the reader.
a subheading	**c**	Subheadings help provide a strong organisational structure for the text and enable easier navigation by the reader.
a date	**d**	Specific details, such as dates, add authenticity and authority to the facts being presented in the text.
jargon naming a type of bacterium	**e**	
jargon naming a piece of laboratory equipment	**f**	
an address	**g**	

7 Mark these statements about the text 'Strange coincidences' as *facts* or *opinions* by ticking the appropriate column.

Statements about the text	Fact	Opinion
a Antibiotics like penicillin are the greatest ever discoveries of medicine.		
b All laboratory researchers should leave their petri dishes unwashed.		
c Penicillin kills staphylococcus bacteria.		
d The taxi driver was reckless and should have had his licence cancelled.		
e Hamilton is a town in Bermuda.		
f Erskine and Neville Ebbin were brothers.		
g Neville Ebbin was killed in a collision with a taxi.		
h Anne Parrish is an American novelist.		
i *Jack Frost and Other Stories* is a really great children's book.		
j If you've ever moved house since childhood you will definitely lose some of your favourite books.		

INFORMATIVE TEXT

Online article

WRITING SAMPLE

Here is a sample text showing you how to structure and write an online article.

Shipwreck survivor, Hugh Williams

In a strange quirk of history, the survivors of five separate shipwrecks had the name Hugh Williams.

Lucky Hugh!

A man named Hugh Williams survived two separate ferry disasters in the same year. So should this Hugh Williams consider himself lucky or unlucky?

These sinkings occurred in the Menai Strait of Wales and involved the vessels *Tal-y-Foel* and *Abermenai*. Another shipwreck in 1785 saw all aboard drown except another man named Hugh Williams. In 1860 a small ship sank in the same waters. The sole survivor was—unbelievably—a passenger named Hugh Williams. Our tally so far is three men called Hugh Williams who survived a total of four shipwrecks.

Bad Karluk

Historical research turns up yet another shipwreck survivor named Hugh Williams. This fellow was aboard the *Karluk*, an Arctic exploration vessel.

The *Karluk* became trapped in ice, forcing the crew to abandon ship. Most died but among the survivors was our old friend Hugh Williams, a seaman who is fondly remembered for his bravery. Hugh's frostbitten toe had to be removed by a companion to avoid infection. The surgical instrument was a pair of garden shears. And the anesthetic? Ice, of course!

Unlucky for Hugh

But for those parents thinking of naming their son Hugh Williams as a precaution, you may wish to note that not all people with this name survive shipwrecks. The luck of this Hugh Williams ran out.

Michigan's Captain Hugh Williams of Lightship 82 drowned near Buffalo when his vessel went down in the 1913 storm. The captain wrote a final farewell to his wife in indelible ink on a door panel, which was recovered and delivered to his family intact. The message was brief but poignant: 'Goodbye, Nellie. Ship is breaking up fast. WILLIAMS.'

Read discussion thread *Comment*

Sources:

Amazing coincidences

'Hugh Williams' a popular name among shipwreck survivors

- **Use a heading that clearly outlines the topic.** Online headlines must be factual and literal so that the keywords can be tagged and indexed by internet search engines.
- **Write a brief introduction to the topic.** In online texts readers don't want to stay on one page for long. They need well-organised text presented in short chunks.
- **Use a subheading to introduce the first element of the article.** This one includes a pun on the phrase 'Lucky you!'
- **Begin with an interesting aspect of the story.** This text uses a rhetorical question as an engaging technique to create interest
- **Present the details of the story in logical order.** Begin with a key point and add specific details, facts, data, statistics, names or quotations.
- **Use more subheadings to maintain the reader's interest in the story.** Use them as hypertext links to allow readers to navigate easily. This writer has used puns, this one being a pun on the phrase 'bad luck'.
- **Ensure the most interesting aspects come through strongly in the article.** This maximises reader interest in every statement. A connective phrase links the items.
- **Your language should be conversational.** Each element must relate to the topic or theme. Varied language features include short sentences, dot points or highlighting of keywords to add interest.
- **Continue the pattern of using subheadings.** This ensures that you don't overwhelm the reader with material.
- **Keep your purpose in mind.** In this case, the author is writing simply for the readers' entertainment.
- **Reserve some exciting, dramatic or humorous elements for the end of the article.** Here we see a final detail that makes this Hugh Williams the 'odd one out'—as he actually does go down with his ship.
- **Provide links to related information so the reader can research the story further.** The internet allows readers to interact with articles in numerous ways, leaving personal comments about the article and engaging in discussion forums

INFORMATIVE TEXT

Online article

WRITING YOUR OWN SAMPLE

Plan your sample on the lines provided.

- **Use a heading that clearly outlines the topic.** Make it factual and literal.
- **Write a brief introduction to the topic.** Organise and present your text in short chunks.
- **Use a subheading to introduce the first element of the article.**
- **Begin with an interesting aspect of the story.** Use an engaging technique to create interest
- **Present the details of the story in logical order.** Begin with a key point and add specific details, facts, data, statistics, names or quotations. Present information that is interesting to your readers. Keep the details in logical order so the reader can easily follow the story. This approach enables you to develop each point methodically, giving a logical flow and coherence to the whole piece.
- **Use more subheadings to maintain the reader's interest in the story.** Use them as hypertext links to allow readers to navigate easily.
- **Ensure the most interesting aspects come through strongly in the article.** This maximises reader interest in every statement. Use connective phrases as links.
- **Your language should be conversational.** It should feel that you're speaking directly to the reader. Each element must relate to the topic or theme. Use varied language features including short sentences, dot points or highlighting of keywords to add interest. Be selective about the details. Presenting quotes is another great way to make the article interesting.
- **Continue the pattern of using subheadings** to ensure that you don't overwhelm the reader with material.
- **Keep your purpose in mind.** In this case you're writing simply for your readers' entertainment. Remember that you're communicating with real people who have real-life experience. Use that to your advantage.
- **Reserve some exciting, dramatic or humorous elements for the end of the article.**
- **Provide links to related information so the reader can research the story further.** The internet allows readers to interact with articles in numerous ways, leaving personal comments about the article and engaging in discussion forums. Giving the reader options for further reading helps validate the reliability of your article.

NARRATIVE TEXT

Journal

Earthbound

Sunday, 5 August

This is my fourth and final mission.

I must admit I'm feeling just as nervous this time around. Last night I couldn't sleep for thinking about that 45-minute re-entry, 3000 degrees of searing heat threatening to incinerate the shuttle as we returned to the Cape.

Every day I thank God that Jacko was able to restore power to that pressure door before it was too late. I'm going to try to get some sleep.

Monday, 6 August

I never told Samuel that anything went wrong on my last mission but I think he senses that something was amiss. I hate keeping secrets but I don't want to terrify him and the kids any more than they already are. I can't believe that some NASA desk sucker decided to inform them of the one-in-76 odds of a fatal mission failure that we gamble against whenever we proceed with a launch. Anyway, I'll tell him everything when I get back from this final job.

This mission takes me to the International Space Station for a month-long assignment to upgrade the communications system. It isn't particularly dangerous—no tethered work outside this time. Despite the knowledge that this will be a routine job, I can't shake the fear that something will go wrong. It's probably just because I know it's my last mission. Nature has a strange sense of irony sometimes.

Wednesday, 8 August

It will be good to get my feet back on the ground. But there's a profound sadness mixed in with the relief of knowing that I'll have survived a career in space. No doubt I'll feel like all grounded astronauts when I finally get my wings clipped and become earthbound—and desk-bound.

No-one else can understand that feeling—that feeling way beyond adrenaline. Nothing will ever compare to that experience. I remember my first time—becoming totally lost in the panorama spread before me. It was surreal, like a dream: the great blue sphere rolling past, under clouds that seemed to be brushed onto the background of the sea like oil paint. And the golden wings of the satellite spread out and glittering in the black void, welcoming me to the universe.

- The **title has been added for literary effect**. Some journal writers like to add such effects, while others may treat their journal more like a diary—a record of events rather than a text involving reflective 'life writing' with literary flair. This title has multiple meanings which we'll explore later.
- The **date** is written at the beginning of each entry. The entries are presented in sequence.
- The demonstrative adjective 'this' clearly **identifies the topic** that is dominating the writer's thoughts throughout this section of the journal. The adjective 'final' signals that she is retiring from space travel.
- Specific details are given that contain **jargon** related to the work performed by astronauts.
- Verbs like 'searing' and 'incinerate' carry **emotive connotations** to enhance the drama of the text.
- The writer makes statements that are flagged as **confidential**, giving the reader a sense that they are being made privy to secrets.
- An invented **colloquialism** is used to reveal the writer's feelings about this person.
- A **conversational transition** is created using this informal word.
- The mention of this well-known asset helps **anchor the text in reality**. Perhaps the writer has a sense that the journal might one day be read by people other than herself and is adding these details for that reason.
- **Personal feelings and thoughts** are expressed in journal writing. Here we see the writer grappling with her mixed emotions about leaving the space program.
- **Repetition** is used to emphasise the significance of the 'feeling' of going into space.
- Strong **visual imagery** adds to the emotive effect.

NARRATIVE TEXT

Journal

COMPREHENSION WORK

Literal questions

Hint: read the text carefully to locate specific facts and details.

1 On what day and date was the last journal entry written?

____

2 Who is 'Samuel'?

____

3 What is 'the great blue sphere'?

____

Interpretive questions

Hint: These questions require you to combine facts and details to synthesise the meaning.

4 The words 'my last mission' refer to which of the following?

a the astronaut's second mission **b** the astronaut's third mission **c** the astronaut's fourth mission

5 The title of the text 'Earthbound' has two meanings. What is the negative meaning?

a travelling back to Earth **b** being unable to leave Earth again **c** being tangled up on Earth

6 Which phrase means that soon the astronaut won't be going on any more flights into space?

a whenever we proceed with a launch **b** Nothing will ever compare to that experience.

c when I finally get my wings clipped

7 Why is the astronaut upset at one of NASA's employees? *Hint: Only one answer option is correct. Use the process of elimination to work through the options.*

a The person failed to fix the pressure door of the craft, nearly causing a fatal mission failure.

b The person sucks his desk while at the office.

c The person scared the astronaut's family by revealing an alarming statistic.

8 How does the astronaut think she will feel after her last mission is over?

____

9 What is one thing the astronaut mentions that she really doesn't like about her job?

a the adrenaline surge she gets when she's on a mission

b not being able to sleep **c** keeping secrets

10 The description of clouds that seemed to be 'brushed onto the background of the sea like oil paint' is an example of which literary technique? ______________________________

Applied questions

Hint: This question requires you to understand a text's implications to infer meaning from the text.

11 When the author wrote this text, who was her intended audience? ______________________________

12 What does the last line of the third journal entry (line 37) imply?

a There's a 'Welcome' sign on the wings of the satellite.

b NASA employees are welcome to visit outer space.

c Unless you've been in space it's hard to appreciate the wonder of the universe.

SPELLING WORK

List Words

All of the words in the box below appear in the text 'Earthbound'.

fourth	failure	career	incinerate	astronauts
panorama	mission	adrenaline	sphere	terrify
fatal	launch	satellite	profound	glittering

1 Which list words have double consonants next to each other?

____

2 Which list word begins with three consonants? ______________________________

3 Organise these words according to their first vowel sound by writing them in the correct cells.

astronauts	incinerate	fourth	failure	satellite
glittering	fatal	launch	mission	panorama

First vowel sound is short 'a' as in the word *cat*	First vowel sound is short 'i' as in the word *hit*	First vowel sound is long 'a' as in the word *day*	First vowel sound is long 'aw' as in the word *paw*
a	**b**	**c**	**d**

4 Change these list words into plurals.

a mission ______________________ **b** failure ______________________

c launch ______________________ **d** career ______________________

e sphere ______________________ **f** satellite ______________________

5 Circle the misspelt word in each sentence.

a The Earth looks blue to astronuats in space.

b The rocket failed to properly launsh.

c A team was deployed to repair the sattelite.

d Without a heat shield, the speed of re-entry into the atmosphere would insinerate any capsule.

e The glittaring stars lit up the night sky.

f A surge of addrenaline shot through me as the countdown began.

g A carere with NASA can take many years of study to achieve.

6 Write affixes (prefixes and suffixes) to complete these words. *Hint: Use the phrases to help you.*

a incinera______	(past tense verb)	The plants around the launch site were ________________.
b terrify ______	(adjective)	Going into space for the first time is ________________.
c fatal______	(noun)	We managed to avoid even a single ________________.
d launch______	(present tense verb)	NASA ________________ their newest satellite today.
e fail______	(past tense verb)	A silicone seal ______________, causing the fuel leak.
f panorama______	(adjective)	The views from the space craft were ________________.
g spher______	(adjective)	We saw a ______________ object in the night sky.
h glitter______	(past tense verb)	The captain's eyes ________________ as he told the story.

NARRATIVE TEXT

VOCABULARY WORK

1 Write these words from the text next to the correct definitions.

shuttle	searing	amiss	proceed	final	admit	restore
void	surreal	pressure	survived	gamble	threatening	senses

a ______________ risk **b** ______________ scorching
c ______________ transport craft **d** ______________ wrong
e ______________ empty space **f** ______________ unreal
g ______________ last **h** ______________ concede
i ______________ dangerous **j** ______________ repair
k ______________ force **l** ______________ perceptions
m ______________ lived **n** ______________ go ahead

2 These prefixes and suffixes are drawn from Greek and Latin roots. What do they mean? *Hint: Use their context in the text to help you work out their meanings.*

a *astro* (as in 'astronaut') means ______________
b *pan* (as in 'panorama') means ______________
c *spher* (as in 'sphere') means ______________

An **acronym** is a term in which each letter stands for a word in a multi-word name and is pronounced as a word. For example, *NATO* stands for *North Atlantic Treaty Organisation.*

3 What do the letters in the acronym 'NASA' stand for?

a North American Space Adventurers
b National Aeronautics Space Administration
c New American Space Shuttle Agency

4 Think of a verb, an adjective and an adverb that could be used to build a sentence that includes the noun. Write each set in the labelled spaces.

Noun	Adjective	Verb	Adverb
a space			
b astronaut			
c flames			
d satellite			
e exploration			
f accident			

We frequently hear **idioms** based on real space exploration and science fiction.

5 Match each highlighted idiom to its meaning by writing the correct letters on the lines provided.

a My teacher is **on another planet** today. ____ aliens
b That medicine made me feel all **spaced out**. ____ Get ready to start.
c Don't tell me you've seen **little green men**? ____ not thinking clearly; distracted
d '**3, 2, 1, blast off!**' ____ strangely distracted from reality

NARRATIVE TEXT

GRAMMAR WORK

Pronouns take the place of nouns already mentioned in a text. Personal pronouns refer to specific people and things; for example, *I, we, he, she* and *they*. Pronouns change according to who is speaking. Possessive pronouns show ownership; for example, *mine, yours, his* and *hers*.

1 List the pronouns used in the text 'Earthbound' in relation to each of the following nouns. *Hint: Some of these are contracted pronouns (such as* she'll *for* she will*). There will be lots of repeats in your list.*

a the astronaut ____________________

b the astronaut's mission buddies ____________________

c Samuel ____________________

Adjectives describe nouns and pronouns. They can describe people, objects, ideas, feelings and places.

2 In the text 'Earthbound' which adjectives are used to describe each of the following? *Hint: Use the line numbers to help you.*

a heat ____________________ (line 7)

b mission failure ____________________ (line 16)

c job ____________________ (line 18)

d sadness ____________________ (line 27)

e astronauts ____________________ (line 28)

f time ____________________ (line 33)

g sphere ____________________ (line 34)

h wings ____________________ (line 36)

i void ____________________ (line 37)

3 Change these nouns into adjectives. For example, the noun *star* becomes *starry* as an adjective.

a nerves ____________________ **b** sleep ____________________

c heat ____________________ **d** power ____________________

e secret ____________________ **f** knowledge ____________________

g comparison ____________________ **h** memory ____________________

i cloud ____________________ **j** gold ____________________

4 Complete this activity in two stages. First complete this list of eighteen words from the text. All of the words are to do with thinking, feeling and speaking. Refer to the line numbers to help you.

a f __________ g (line 4) **b** t __________ g (line 5)

c t __________ k (line 9) **d** t __________ d (line 12)

e s __________ s (line 13) **f** h __________ e (line 13)

g t __________ y (line 14) **h** b __________ e (line 15)

i I __________ m (line 15) **j** t __________ l (line 17)

k s __________ s (line 27) **l** r __________ f (line 27)

m k __________ g (line 27) **n** f __________ l (line 28)

o u __________ d (line 31) **p** r __________ r (line 32)

q d __________ m (line 34) **r** w __________ g (line 37)

G	A	G	C	S	H	L	H	R	Z
N	I	J	T	M	E	L	E	E	F
I	L	N	R	E	O	N	Q	L	C
L	K	I	F	D	L	W	S	I	X
E	N	S	U	O	Y	L	T	E	U
E	O	P	X	V	R	U	M	F	S
F	W	E	L	C	O	M	I	N	G
S	I	Y	B	W	F	E	H	U	V
U	N	D	E	R	S	T	A	N	D
O	G	P	D	X	E	Y	T	S	S
Q	P	L	N	R	X	B	E	S	E
Z	O	Y	R	T	U	K	E	P	V
T	H	I	N	K	I	N	G	K	E
V	F	S	N	B	D	M	Z	O	I
Y	W	A	M	A	E	R	D	Q	L
D	H	R	S	U	Z	S	V	A	E
T	R	E	M	E	M	B	E	R	B

Now find the words in the puzzle.

NARRATIVE TEXT

Journal

PUNCTUATION WORK

A **sentence** is a group of words that expresses a complete idea, feeling or thought. Sentences begin with a capital letter and end with a full stop, question mark or exclamation mark. Sentences can be short, depending on what you want to express. It's best to avoid using too many commas in a sentence.

1 Add the correct punctuation marks to complete these sentences that have been adapted from the text 'Earthbound'.

- **a** im feeling just as nervous as i always do before a launch
- **b** i hate keeping secrets from samuel and the kids but I dont want to frighten them about the risks
- **c** ill tell my family all about my experiences when I get back from this final mission
- **d** i must admit im looking forward to getting my feet back on the ground
- **e** jacko was able to restore power to the pressure door before it was too late
- **f** i can't believe that someone disclosed the odds of a fatal mission failure to my loved ones
- **g** nothing will ever compare to my first experience of going into space
- **h** looking back i remember becoming totally lost in the panorama spread before me
- **i** the clouds seemed to be brushed onto the background of the sea like oil paint
- **j** the golden wings of the satellite were glittering in the black void of space

2 Which end punctuation mark correctly completes each sentence? Write its name and symbol. *Hint: One missing punctuation mark goes inside the quotation marks.*

Sentence	Name of punctuation mark	Symbol
a Is this the astronaut's final mission	______________	______
b Twenty five minutes before launch, I called home	______________	______
c The controller yelled, 'Abort, abort'	______________	______
d We're going to burn up	______________	______
e There would be no second chances not this time	______________	______
f Why would anyone want to be an astronaut	______________	______

3 Where should the comma be placed in each of these sentences? Add one or more commas to each. *Hint: Commas separate listed items except for the second-last and last items, where we use 'and' instead.*

- **a** Yuri Gagarin John Glenn Neil Armstrong and Buzz Aldrin are all famous astronauts.
- **b** Many nations use satellites including Australia Japan China Russia and the United States of America.
- **c** The five Space Shuttle orbiters were named *Columbia Challenger Discovery Endeavour* and *Atlantis.*
- **d** The planets in our solar system are Mercury Venus Earth Mars Jupiter Saturn Uranus and Neptune.

An **ellipsis** (the plural is ellipses) is a set of three equally spaced full stop marks (…) to show that something has been left out of a sentence. An ellipsis can also signal a pause or an unfinished thought or statement. For example, *'There was a loud explosion, then …' her voice trailed off as she began to cry.*

NARRATIVE TEXT
Journal

WRITING WORK 1

Journals

We keep **journals or diaries** to record our personal experiences and thoughts. Journals are usually private texts that are not designed to be shown to others, at least until after the writer's death. Here are some of the main features of journal writing.

Structural features of journals include:

* a series of chronological entries over a period of time
* entries written at regular or irregular intervals
* entries marked with a date, day and sometimes even a time of the day.
* salutations (for example, *Dear Diary*)
* sign-offs (usually the author's name).

Language features of journals include:

* informal descriptions of events from the point of view of the journal's writer (including anecdotes)
* expressions of thoughts about the past, including detailed personal revelations about the writer's private thoughts and feelings
* foreshadowing of plans for the future
* a consistent narrative voice that provides a sense of the author's unique identity
* diction (word choice) that reveals the author's historical context, personal background, attitudes and values
* idioms
* colloquial language
* allusions
* jokes and humour that is highly specific to just the author's immediate circle of family and/or friends
* a range of tenses used between and sometimes inside entries
* emotive language used to express the writer's feelings
* conjunctions and connectives to preserve a logical and consistent flow of linked ideas
* limited use of figurative language
* direct expression of personal opinions and judgements.

1 What is the main purpose of a journal? ______________________

2 Which two language features of journals help maintain a consistent flow from one idea to another?

____

3 What is another term for an informal description of an event from the writer's point of view?

____

4 In what order are we most likely to encounter the events in a journal?

____

5 Give two examples of emotive words or phrases found in the text. *Hint: Think beyond just the usual 'feeling words' to expressions that provide interesting, intense or exciting insights and descriptions.*

____

6 There are many types of journal. Unscramble these terms.

a resigtre ____________	**b** dairy ____________
c pointapment koob ____________	**d** parcskobo ____________
e iclechron ____________	**f** gol ____________

NARRATIVE TEXT

Journal

WRITING WORK 2

Writing about journals

People keep **journals** for all sorts of reasons. Some are just a record of private experiences and thoughts for the author's personal use as a record of their life. Others are official, legal documents such as a record of workers clocked on or off the job. Some journals contain scientific observations, botanical drawings, details about maps, routes and distances. Still others are used to document a process, such as an artist's diary or portfolio.

7 Match the journals with their likely owners by writing the correct names in the spaces.

Journal owners	Journal	Content
Scott Burrell (a car windscreen repairman who works at customers' residences)	**a**	Entries about people and places encountered during travels, flight and accommodation details, observations about sights seen, photos
Mohendas Gupta (a finance student currently on an exchange program from India to Australia)	**b**	Notes about university assessment tasks, web addresses for Australian immigration authorities and visa requirements, doodles
DI Woodbridge (a Detective Inspector with the NSW Police)	**c**	Personal observations about being forced to leave home to escape violence on the streets, feelings about lost loved ones, hopes for a better future
Ainsley Ryback (an aspiring novelist who has just moved to an apartment in Melbourne)	**d**	Short descriptions of gameplay experiences, lists of new games to explore, notes about cheats, website and email addresses
Ringo the Clown (a puppeteer and clowning actor who can be booked for children's parties)	**e**	Client bookings, addresses of clients, order list of parts, log of hours worked, notes on quotes provided to clients, note to pick up a forgotten tool
May Chang (a backpacker currently travelling in Nepal)	**f**	Detailed descriptions of thoughts and feelings about new experiences at boot-camp training, entries anticipating future events, descriptions of new friends
Matthew Flinders (an explorer who charted much of Australia's coastline)	**g**	Reflections on the success of a party, list of items to buy from joke shop, telephone number of local puppeteers, doodle of possible new business card
Private Miriam Rosas (a new Army recruit studying at the Australian Military College, Duntroon)	**h**	Descriptions of travels by ship, reflections about the dangers of the voyage, hand-sketched maps and sea routes, diagrams of plants and animals found
Marat Samut (a twelve-year-old boy living in Cyprus in disputed territory during a skirmish)	**i**	Hour-by-hour notes of appointments and movements to different places, telephone numbers of witnesses, reminders to write reports
Cody Jamieson (a thirty-year-old gaming enthusiast currently testing new Microsoft products)	**j**	Descriptions of moving house, list of items to buy for home, ideas for a new book, list of literary agents, entries about missing old friends

NARRATIVE TEXT

Journal

WRITING SAMPLE

Here is a sample text showing you how to structure and write a series of journal entries.

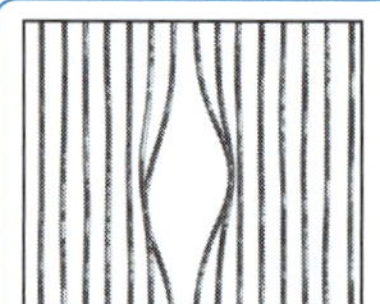

First day of freedom

✱ Use a literal title.

Friday, 30 September 2016

Today is my first day of freedom in nine years. Still can't believe it all happened. But there's no changing history. I'm so grateful that I was able to serve out my sentence in a fairly decent place. It would've been much worse for me if I didn't get moved out of Goulburn. Today, I had the best feed I've had in a loooong time. I couldn't decide between a meatlovers pizza and a cheeseburger and fries, so I had all three! Go son!

✱ **Choose a style for dating the entries.** This author uses a formal dating format. Truncation provides economy; we read 'Still can't believe it all happened.' Because it is informal, little attention is paid to grammatically correct syntax. For example, we read 'It would've been much worse for me if I didn't get moved out of Goulburn.' The writer should've used 'hadn't been moved' here. The word 'long' is spelt with too many 'o's, a form of exaggeration used for emphasis.

Tuesday, 4 October 2016

I'm narrowing down the likely possibilities for my future. First thoughts were landscape gardener or handyman. I've been offered a job behind the bar at my local but I'm reluctant to put myself anywhere near booze at present, because for me booze tends to lead to trouble. So for now I guess I'll stick to yard work until NASA calls me with a better offer.

I'm moving house on the long weekend. Mum and Dad have bought me some basic furniture and dug out some boxes of gear that I'd left in their garage for the past decade! The delivery guy I spoke to said it looks like raining all weekend but I just smiled hearing that. After all those years inside, I couldn't care less if it rained on me and my stuff because at the end of the day I'm free under this big sky and that's all that matters.

✱ **Break up the text into chunks based on topics.** When the topic changes, the writer adds a space to show the focus has shifted. Colloquial language and idioms reflect the writer's historical and sociocultural setting. We read that he was offered a job at his 'local' (local hotel bar) and hopes to avoid 'booze' (alcohol). Later we read more idioms, like 'local rag' (newspaper) and 'my ugly mug' (my face). Irony injects humour into the entry to lighten the writer's own mood or for sarcastic effect. Here we read about the 'NASA' offer. The writer makes statements about thoughts and feelings in the entries dealing with personal experiences. His response to the threat of rain on moving day is 'I couldn't care less'.

Thursday, 6 October 2016

I'm living free and easy in a little fishing town called Lynch's Inlet, near the family farm. I thought I'd try my luck getting work doing small repair jobs and yard work. It's worked out well because I've been able to spend time with my farming folks. It's great being free to earn my own living. I enjoy the freedom that working outside gives me. I work four days a week and spend my free Fridays each week fishing. Who'd have thought that I'd be fixing fences and running after cows instead of fixing bank jobs and running from the cops?

✱ **Use conversational language with simple verbs and straightforward diction.** Contractions such as 'I'm' add to the informal effect. Repetition is used, sometimes unconsciously and other times for emphasis. We read words based on the root word 'free' numerous times. Rhetorical questions reflect the writer's internal questioning and sense of disbelief at his improved circumstances. We read 'Who'd have thought that I'd be fixing fences and running after cows instead of fixing bank jobs and running from the cops?'

Monday, 28 November 2016

Well, I'm famous! Today the local rag ran a story on my parents' farming enterprise and I had my ugly mug and name on the front page. Fancy having my name appear in print for reasons other than criminal! Things are looking up!

✱ **Exaggerate the use of exclamation marks to emphasise a humorous or exciting feature.** We read 'Fancy having my name appear in print for reasons other than criminal!'

NARRATIVE TEXT

Journal

WRITING YOUR OWN SAMPLE

Plan your sample on the lines provided.

✷ **Use a literal title.** Make sure the title accurately captures the substance of these journal entries.

✷ **Choose a style for dating the entries.** This choice can be left up to you. You could use a formal or simple system, naming just the day, or the whole date including the month and year. Use truncation for economy. Shorten sentences to make them read as if they are spoken rather than written language. Because your journal entries are meant to sound informal, you can get away with slippages in grammatically correct syntax. You could experiment with the spelling of some words to add special emphasis.

✷ **Break up the text into chunks based on topics.** When the topic changes, add a space to show that you have shifted the focus of the writing. Use colloquial language and idioms to reflect your own unique historical and sociocultural setting. What colloquialisms and idioms are peculiar to your setting or background? Use irony to inject humour into your entry, which can lighten the mood or create a sarcastic effect. Ensure that statements about thoughts and feelings dominate the entries that deal with personal experiences.

✷ **Use conversational language with simple verbs and straightforward diction.** Use contractions to add to the informal effect. Use repetition for emphasis. Which words would be worth repeating in your journal entries? Create rhetorical questions to reflect your own internal questioning of things that have occurred.

✷ **Exaggerate the use of exclamation marks to emphasise a humorous or exciting feature.**

UNIT 6

NARRATIVE TEXT

Biographical article

READING WORK

Felix Baumgartner

In 2012 Austrian adventurer Felix Baumgartner set a new world record unlikely to be broken anytime soon. He travelled to the edge of space in a hot air balloon then … he jumped out. At the staggering height of 36 000 metres your helmet's faceplate heats up, stopping you from seeing much. You can't breathe since you're on the northern side of the Earth's atmosphere. And you hurtle back to the planet at a speed of well over a thousand km/h. As a startling bonus you break the speed of sound without the protection of an aircraft simply by submitting to the law of gravity. Felix shot a headcam video of the mighty freefall—but it's mostly just spinning.

Baumgartner is no stranger to crazy jumps. He's BASE-jumped from Malaysia's iconic Petronas Towers and Taiwan's Taipei 101 tower. But his edge-of-atmosphere stunt really pushed his limits. Felix tells us what went through his head when he was up there, poised to plunge into oblivion: 'When I was standing there on top of the world, you become so humble you do not think about breaking records anymore, you do not think about gaining scientific data. The only thing you want is to come back alive.'

Felix worked with a team of aerospace experts whose first challenge was working out how to safely get him to the edge of the stratosphere. Then they needed to figure out how to enable Felix to withstand supersonic speeds and the massive pull of gravity. A carefully engineered pressure suit and capsule was developed to do the job. Felix's team also had to design the world's most reliable parachute to gently return him to his home planet. Their efforts paid off. The trip back to Earth took just over nine minutes, with around half of that time in sheer freefall. The world watched, breathing a collective sigh of relief when Felix's feet touched the ground safely. Felix accomplished his record-breaking freefall without even messing up his hair. Well, he *was* wearing a helmet.

The purpose of the mission was to observe the ability of the human body to cope with extreme conditions of pressure and temperature at the edge of space. Felix reported that the feat was a lot harder than he thought it would be. He felt he was about to lose consciousness from the wild spinning that he endured during the freefall but he managed to regain control at the critical moments. After five years of intensive training and preparation, research and development, Felix and his team have declared the mission a great success.

- The **title** is straightforward, simply giving the full name of the subject of the biographical article.
- The important details of the **date, the subject's name and the achievement** are provided in straightforward language in the first two sentences.
- The reader is invited to ponder the scale of the achievement through the use of **emotive adjectives** like 'staggering'.
- The verb 'hurtle' continues to build the **emotionally charged tone** of the text.
- **Informal terms** are used, such as 'shot', in keeping with the tone. Modern biographical writing tends to be less formal in tone than once was the case.
- These locations are mentioned because they represent some of Asia's tallest buildings, **emphasising** the lunacy of Felix's BASE-jumping stunts.
- An **alliterative description** of an action is given for added impact.
- Here the writer aims to present the facts in Felix's **own words**. This is an interesting way to contrast Felix's normality as a person with his superhuman feats of endurance and skill.
- This passage is **structured logically**, presenting the problem then the solution. This cause and effect structure is created with the use of connective statements such as 'whose first challenge was' and 'then they needed to figure out'.
- A **simple statement** reports the success of the mission.
- Audiences around the globe are treated as a single human breathing a sigh of relief in this **metaphorical description**.
- The lessons learned from the feat are **summarised by an indirect quote** from Felix himself.

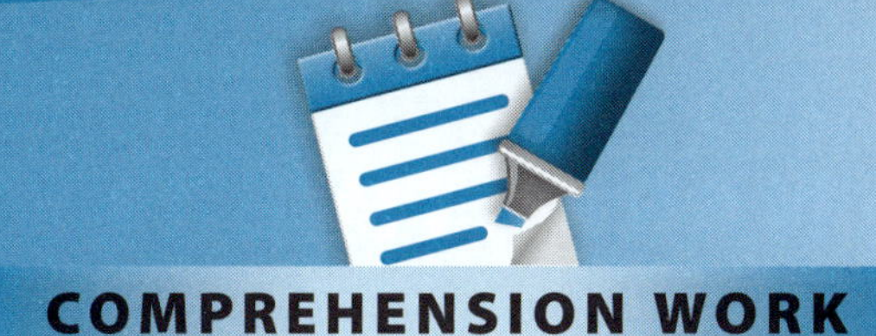

NARRATIVE TEXT

Biographical article

COMPREHENSION WORK

Literal questions

Hint: Read the text carefully to locate specific facts and details.

1 What did Felix Baumgartner use to transport himself to the edge of space?

____

2 In which country is the Taipei 101 tower? ______________________

3 How fast was Felix's freefall?

a over 36 000 metres per second
b over 1000 kilometres per hour
c over 1000 kilometres per second

Interpretive questions

Hint: These questions require you to combine facts and details to synthesise the meaning.

4 What force creates a massive pull on the body of a person travelling at high speeds? ______________

5 What does the term 'supersonic' mean?

a high above the Earth's atmosphere
b at light speed
c faster than the speed of sound

6 Which piece of equipment prevents jumpers from seeing very much?

____

7 What does the author say about the video footage Felix shot during his jump?

____

8 The author notes the need for reliability of which piece of gear?

a the headcam
b the tower
c the parachute

9 Which of the following items was designed to withstand supersonic speeds?

a pressure suit
b time capsule
c hot air balloon

10 Which statement best describes the stunt?

a The record was achieved through the combined efforts of Felix and his team.
b Felix's accomplishment was achieved solely through his own efforts.
c A team of aerospace experts forced Felix to jump out of a balloon on the edge of the Earth's atmosphere.

Applied questions

Hint: These questions require you to understand a text's implications to infer meaning from the text.

11 What quality of the human character does Felix say is most evident when you're about to make such a jump?

____

12 Which detail tells us that Felix was afraid before he jumped?

a the first sentence of the text
b the direct quote from Felix
c the phrase 'You can't breathe'

SPELLING WORK

List Words

All of the words in the box below appear in the text 'Felix Baumgartner'.

adventurer	thousand	stunt	consciousness	accomplished
metres	breathe	plunge	engineered	parachute
atmosphere	submitting	scientific	supersonic	hurtle

Do you remember the spelling rule for adding the suffix *ing* to words ending in *e*? Test yourself.

1 Add the suffix *ing* to these list words, changing their form where necessary.

a breathe ______________________ **b** parachute ______________________

c plunge ______________________ **d** hurtle ______________________

2 Change these words by adding the suffix *ed*. *Hint: For words ending in* e, *you just add the* d *of the suffix.*

a breathe ______________________ **b** parachute ______________________

c plunge ______________________ **d** hurtle ______________________

3 Unscramble these list words and write them on the lines provided.

a moatsphere ______________________ **b** sconsenscious ______________________

c gulpen ______________________ **d** treems ______________________

e thebear ______________________ **f** southand ______________________

4 Make list words out of these fragments by pairing them up. Write the finished words on the lines provided.

tific	engine	phere	chute	conscious	atmos
urer	para	super	scien	ered	ness
sonic	sand	accom	thou	plished	advent

______________________ ______________________ ______________________

______________________ ______________________ ______________________

______________________ ______________________ ______________________

5 Circle the correctly spelt word from these pairs. *Hint: You'll find them all in the text 'Felix Baumgartner'.*

a Austrialan	Australian	**b** baloon	balloon	**c** height	hieght
d plannet	planet	**e** Malasya	Malaysia	**f** oblivion	ablivion
g data	datar	**h** pressure	preshure	**i** unlikely	unlikly
j stagering	staggering	**k** hellmet	helmet	**l** aercraft	aircraft
m iconic	ikonic	**n** stratesphere	stratosphere	**o** with-stand	withstand
p efforts	efferts				

6 Cross out the extra letter in these list words.

a atmossphere **b** enginneered **c** subbmitting

d supersonnic **e** scientiffic **f** accommplished

NARRATIVE TEXT
Biographical article

VOCABULARY WORK

1 Insert the missing words to complete these sentences. *Hint: Re-read the text 'Felix Baumgartner' to help you.*

a Felix Baumgartner set a new world ______________________.

b The edge of space is about 36 000 ______________________ away.

c The faceplate of Felix's ______________________ heated up.

d Because there's very little oxygen up there, you can't ______________________.

e You break the speed of ______________________ as you hurtle back to Earth.

f Felix performed the stunt without the protection of an ______________________.

g Felix spent most of the freefall ______________________ out of control.

2 Write these words from the text next to their definitions to complete the table.

humble	freefall	gravity	engineered	oblivion
capsule	stratosphere	crazy	limits	iconic

Word	Definition
a	force of attraction between two objects that pulls things downward to the Earth
b	nothingness
c	designed to perform a specific task
d	enclosed unit
e	flight downwards with no resistance
f	the upper atmosphere
g	symbolic, well-recognised
h	meek and lowly
i	mad, insane
j	boundaries

3 Circle all the compound words in this list. *Hint: Compound words are made of two separate base words joined together.*

seeing	space	anytime	faceplate	stranger
freefall	withstand	helmet	engineered	supersonic
developed	challenge	anymore	standing	capsule

Pronouns take the place of nouns to help give sentences clarity and to avoid unnecessary repetition. For example, rather than writing *Felix successfully completed Felix's mission, with Felix's team supporting Felix,* we could use the pronouns *his* and *him. Felix successfully completed his mission, with his team supporting him.*

1 Look at the passage below and circle all the pronouns you find. *Hint: There are six in total.*

At the staggering height of 36 000 metres your helmet's faceplate heats up, stopping you from seeing much. You can't breathe since you're on the northern side of the Earth's atmosphere. And you hurtle back to the planet at a speed of well over a thousand km/h. As a startling bonus you break the speed of sound without the protection of an aircraft simply by submitting to the law of gravity.

2 To whom or what are these pronouns from the text referring? *Hint: Use your skim-reading skills.*

a He's (line 14) ______________ **b** they (line 23) ______________

c his (line 26) ______________ **d** their (line 27) ______________

3 Complete the table by writing in the variants of the phrases to match the tense correctly. Add auxiliary verbs as required.

Past tense	Present tense	Future tense
a	Felix is jumping from space.	**b**
c	**d**	Felix will be spinning.
The experts agreed on a plan.	**e**	**f**
g	The record is being broken.	**h**

Jargon is specialised language peculiar to a particular group of people. It is often related to a field of expertise, such as aerospace science.

4 Identify the jargon in each line by writing the relevant portion on the lines provided. *Hint: The answers will include words and phrases. Use the line numbers to help you.*

a a term meaning 'visor' (line 7) ______________

b a term meaning 'information collected' (line 20) ______________

c a term meaning 'space-flight related' (line 21) ______________

d a term meaning 'upper atmosphere' (line 22) ______________

e a term meaning 'faster than sound' (line 23) ______________

f a term meaning 'protective outfit' (lines 24–25) ______________

5 Place these terms from the text in the correct categories by listing them in the right places.

gravity, metres, edge, km/h, supersonic, limits

a units of measure ______________

b boundaries ______________

c aerospace science ______________

6 List all the proper nouns in the text 'Felix Baumgartner' in alphabetical order. Leave out any numerals in names and include each name in your list only once. *Hint: There are seven.*

______________ ______________ ______________ ______________

______________ ______________ ______________

NARRATIVE TEXT

Biographical article

PUNCTUATION WORK

1 List all the punctuation marks found in these lines from the text 'Felix Baumgartner'. List them in the order that they appear in the text.

a He travelled to the edge of space in a hot air balloon then … he jumped out. (lines 4–6)

____

b And you hurtle back to the planet at a speed of well over a thousand km/h. As a startling bonus you break the speed of sound without the protection of an aircraft simply by submitting to the law of gravity. (lines 9–12)

____

c Felix tells us what went through his head when he was up there, poised to plunge into oblivion: 'When I was standing there on top of the world, you become so humble you do not think about breaking records anymore, you do not think about gaining scientific data. The only thing you want is to come back alive.' (lines 16–20)

____

d Felix's team also had to design the world's most reliable parachute to gently return him to his home planet. Their efforts paid off. (lines 25–27)

____

e Felix accomplished his record-breaking freefall without even messing up his hair. Well, he *was* wearing a helmet. (lines 30–31)

____

f After five years of intensive training and preparation, research and development, Felix and his team have declared the mission a great success. (lines 37–39)

____

2 Which of the following phrases are correctly punctuated? Tick your choice.

a	Felix's helmet	☐	Earths' atmosphere	☐
b	the team's expertise	☐	the suits capabilities	☐
c	Austrias famous adventurer	☐	the balloon's ascent	☐
d	Malaysia's tallest tower's	☐	Taiwan's famous landmark	☐
e	the challenge's of flight	☐	the two scientists' expertise	☐
f	feeling's of humility	☐	conquering his fears	☐

3 List all the phrases that are hyphenated in the text 'Felix Baumgartner'.

____

4 Rewrite the following sentences as questions. *Hint: You may need to alter the order of some words.*

a Well, he *was* wearing a helmet. ______________________________

b Felix reported that the feat was a lot harder than he thought it would be. ______________________________

____

NARRATIVE TEXT

Biographical article

WRITING WORK 1

Biographical articles

Biographical articles inform readers about the life experiences and achievements of a particular person. Biography and autobiography is sometimes called 'life writing'. Biographical texts are written by one person about another, whereas autobiographical texts are written by the person themselves.

Biographical articles have these **structural features**:

- a topic concerning an achievement or life experience of one person from the point of view of another
- an opening statement that introduces the specific incident or aspect of the person's life being presented
- a sequence of events, usually presented in chronological order or in a 'cause-and-effect' structure
- detailed information about selected events
- visual content, such as photographs, maps and illustrations, to support the textual content.

There are a number of specific **language features** common to biographical articles. They include:

- first or third person storytelling mode
- the past tense (and the present tense for current information about the subject if they are alive at the time of publication)
- highly descriptive language
- the active voice
- conjunctions that link sentences together
- connectives that link paragraphs together in a chronological sequence
- foreshadowing of future events
- emotive language
- direct quotes presenting people's exact words
- indirect speech paraphrasing things people have said
- highly detailed factual information including dates and the names of people, places and events
- reference to significant events drawn from the social and historical context of the subject
- a summarising statement to conclude.

1 What are two forms of life writing?

____

2 Which tense is the most appropriate to use in a biographical article about a person still living today?

____

3 List three types of visual content often included in biographical articles.

__________ __________ __________

4 In which storytelling mode are biographical articles usually written? __________

5 What type of speech in biographical articles involves paraphrasing? __________

6 What are two types of highly detailed factual information found in biographical articles?

__________ __________

7 Which technique relates to the presentation of information about future events? __________

NARRATIVE TEXT

Biographical article

WRITING WORK 2

8 Convert this quote from the text 'Felix Baumgartner' into the third person, as if the author of the biography is reporting Felix's words as indirect speech. Write the new version on the lines provided.

'When I was standing there on top of the world, you become so humble you do not think about breaking records anymore, you do not think about gaining scientific data. The only thing you want is to come back alive.'

____

____

____

____

9 Identify and write out two connective phrases that appear in the text.

____

____

10 Change the tense of the following portion of the text into the present tense. Notice how it takes on a different tone and effect when the tense is changed.

The feat was a lot harder than he thought it would be. He felt he was about to lose consciousness from the wild spinning that he endured during the freefall but he managed to regain control at the critical moments.

____

____

____

____

11 Which of these quotes from the text contain exciting, strong descriptions that emphasise the drama of the actions being described? Circle *strong* or *neutral* for each one.

a	fearless exploits	Strong	Neutral
b	At the staggering height of 36 000 metres	Strong	Neutral
c	As a startling bonus	Strong	Neutral
d	And you hurtle back to the planet	Strong	Neutral
e	Felix shot a headcam video	Strong	Neutral
f	Felix tells us what went through his head	Strong	Neutral
g	poised to plunge into oblivion	Strong	Neutral
h	A carefully engineered pressure suit	Strong	Neutral
i	The trip back to Earth took just over nine minutes	Strong	Neutral
j	After five years of intensive training	Strong	Neutral
k	crazy jumps	Strong	Neutral
l	Felix worked with a team of aerospace experts	Strong	Neutral

NARRATIVE TEXT

Biographical article

WRITING SAMPLE

Here is a sample text showing you how to structure and write a biographical article.

Before *Twilight*

✱ **Use an interesting heading to attract the reader to the text.** This one has a double meaning—before the evening and before the publication of *Twilight*.

Stephenie Meyer says she's still in a spin over the runaway success of her first novel, *Twilight*. To date, the franchise—including the books, films and merchandise—have netted Meyer a staggering $6 145 100 000. Yes, that's billion not million!

✱ **Begin with the orientation to provide some context for the achievement to be described.** Here we read of the massive profits the books and films have made.

The idea for the series came to the writer in a dream that vividly presented a young couple in love. Meyer soon began to fall in love with her characters and was inspired to bring them to life by writing the story of the charming and mysterious Edward and his haunted true love, Bella.

✱ **Create a sense of context for what is to come.** The narrative is in the past tense in first person mode, adding a personal touch. We are told of a dream Meyer had that led her to write the book. The use of first person mode makes the author appear to know Stephenie Meyer personally, adding authority and authenticity.

When *Twilight* was launched teenagers across the globe instantly fell in love with the stories and multimillion dollar movie deals were made, searing the romance into the public consciousness for good. Savvy casting of the suave but tortured-looking Robert Pattinson and the naive emo chick Kristen Stewart has helped these characters stay popular.

✱ **Add supporting details to expand the context.** Extra description about the actors engaged to play the main characters amplifies the contextual details.

More books soon followed the original *Twilight*, including *New Moon*, *Eclipse* and *Breaking Dawn* Parts 1 and 2. Each went on to find similar success to the first instalment.

✱ **Organise the narrative chronologically.** Here the subsequent sequels to the original book are listed in their order of publication.

Stephenie Meyer is the mother of three young children and lives with her husband in Phoenix. She penned her famous debut novel in three months, during the height of Arizona's intense summer heat.

✱ **Present detailed information to build the idea that the subject is a real person.** We are introduced to the idea that Stephenie Meyer is a real person whose life was ordinary until the successful release of the book. There is a shift to the present tense, as the author is now describing Meyer's current situation in real time.

In the real world Meyer spent that summer waiting by the pool in hot, sticky humidity while her kids took swimming lessons. But in her mind she would retreat into the misty, wintry world of Forks, Washington State, where vampires try to blend in among the town's inhabitants.

✱ **Use contrast.** We are presented with information about Meyer's real-life situation that differs markedly from the romantic setting and plot of her novel. The humid heat of Phoenix, Arizona versus the cold rain in the novel's setting of Forks creates a strong contrast.

After thinking about her characters and dreaming up plans all day, she'd write mainly at night-time, completing anything from a page or two to an entire chapter in each session. This went on for three months.

✱ **Use connectives to form links between sentences.** Here a link is created with the phrase 'After thinking about her characters …', signaling consequences to come.

Meyer's preference for the novel's title was *Forks*, after the town in which the story is set. After searching for the rainiest town she could find, Meyer settled on this little village in Washington state.

✱ **Add interesting details such as secrets or little-known facts.** Extra details given here include the inspiration for the characters (a dream) and the reason for Meyer's choice of setting (one of the rainiest towns in America).

Meyer received eight rejections from publishers before having the manuscript accepted by Little, Brown and Company. Today *Twilight* has become a global phenomenon with sequels, movie deals and an enthusiastic resurgence of interest in all things vampire.

✱ **Conclude with an ending that makes a summary comment.** Here we have the contrast between the humble beginnings of Meyer's writing career and her global success today. This adds to the sense of the subject's achievement, making the article worth reading. Here we see the wild financial success that *Twilight* yielded for Meyer.

NARRATIVE TEXT

Biographical article

WRITING YOUR OWN SAMPLE

Plan your sample on the lines provided.

* **Use an interesting heading to attract the reader to the text.**

* **Begin with the orientation to provide some context for the achievement to be described.** The text should be concise since it functions primarily as an introduction.

* **Create a sense of context for what is to come.** The use of first person mode gives the text a sense of authority and authenticity.

* **Add supporting details** to expand the context. Give extra description to amplify the contextual details.

* **Organise the narrative chronologically.** In this way the reader is easily able to progress through related topics in a natural, chronological sequence that makes sense.

* **Present detailed information to build the idea that the subject is a real person.** Give details about aspects of their life that are relevant to the topic. You may find that the tense needs to shift to the present if your subject is to be described as they are today, in real time.

* **Use contrast.** This tool creates emphasis. Present markedly opposite or differing segments of information in close proximity to create a strong contrast.

* **Use connectives** to form links between sentences. You could use the first or the last part of a sentence to create links.

* **Add interesting details** that let the reader in on a few secrets or little-known facts. Think about what extra details you could offer to readers.

* **Conclude with an ending that makes a summary comment.** Contrast the past with the present, failure with success or some other features of the person's life. Try to convey a sense of the person's achievement that makes the article worth reading.

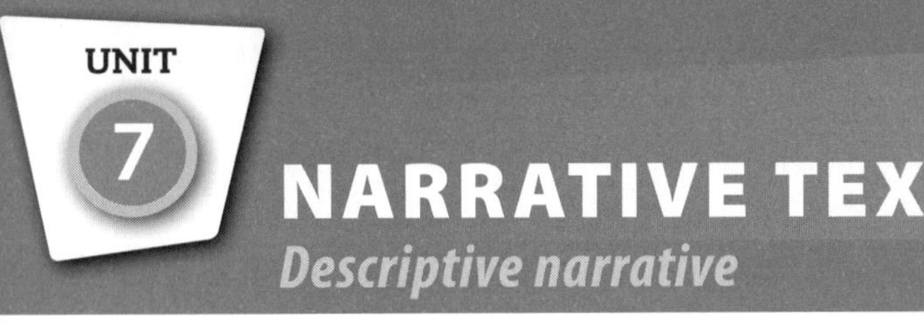

NARRATIVE TEXT

Descriptive narrative

Sitting in the rain

When Peter reached the park he glanced up and noticed dark, grey clouds forming overhead. He was hot and sticky. Weeks of humid summer weather had dragged on, baking the town and everyone in it. The grass under his feet was scorched and shrivelling into tinder-dry clumps. A heat haze shimmered in the distance.

Before long it started to rain. After overheating on his long walk he found the rain a welcome relief, so the boy didn't move straight away. He noticed that a man seated on a bench in the park hadn't bothered to move either. Shaking drips from his head Peter looked around until he spotted a good, sturdy tree to climb. He grasped hold of a lower branch, swung himself up and sat down, well-hidden from sight and sheltered from the rain by the broad, waxy leaves.

The grey sky threatened to open up to produce more than a drizzle. Peter could hear the rain becoming heavier. He decided he'd just have to wait it out. So he leaned a little closer against the trunk and settled himself. He looked over towards the man on the bench, and was surprised to find that he was still sitting there. The gentleman was smartly dressed in a perfectly tailored suit, charcoal grey. His curly hair gave an impression of nobility and was cut close, almost as if it were sculpted. The hair disappeared into a grey shirt collar, the colour identical to the suit, permitting no glimpse of his neck. The man's head was turned at such an angle that made it impossible to see his face, and from his vantage point Peter could see his steel-grey hair.

The steadily increasing rain still seemed to be having no impact on the man at all. He hadn't moved an inch. Perhaps the man was asleep, although his head was still upright. There was something about the man's bearing that intrigued Peter—distinguished and refined, yet content to sit in the drizzling rain with not a care for the damage to his lovely suit.

Peter climbed down from his branch and was just about to head for the seat to get a closer look when the heavens opened in a torrential downpour. People everywhere scurried for cover, running to their cars and toward the shelter of the trees. Water flowed freely onto Peter's head and shoulders, and coursed down his back, drenching him through. He shook it off vigorously as he leapt back under the tree to take shelter. He peered through the leaves and the rain, shaking his wet head in disbelief. The man was still sitting there! He still hadn't moved at all. He must have been soaked to the skin! As Peter stayed under the tree, trapped by the grey sheet of rain, it suddenly dawned on him that the man he was looking at was an iron statue.

- The **title** is literal but doesn't really give us an idea of the theme, which is that things aren't always what they seem to be.
- The text begins with a **connective statement** indicating that events have already occurred before the scene being described.
- The **connectives** 'before long' and 'after' create a sequence of events into which the narrator now thrusts the reader. We get the impression that we have now caught up and are observing the character in real time, as things happen to him.
- A **visual image** helps us picture the scene.
- The word 'grey' and its synonyms appear repeatedly throughout the text, emphasising the weather and **foreshadowing** the surprise ending.
- The character's thoughts are explained to us, making this an **omniscient narrative style**.
- **Clues** about the reason why the man wasn't moving are given in the details about his appearance. The word 'sculpted' is an example of carefully crafted diction (word choice).
- **Synonyms** are used for the same concept so that repetition is avoided. We encounter the words 'spotted', 'sight', 'looked' and 'angle' to indicate the line of sight or viewpoint Peter has. Then the phrase 'vantage point' is used for variety.
- **Adverbs** are used to provide details about the rain and give momentum to the story as it moves toward the conclusion.
- An **exclamation** cues the reader to feel the same sense of surprise that Peter does. The narrator positions the reader to interpret Peter's thoughts as our own.
- The **twist** is delivered in the last line of the text for added impact, leaving the reader with this sudden revelation that was not expected in an otherwise ordinary scene.

NARRATIVE TEXT

COMPREHENSION WORK

Literal questions

Hint: Read the text carefully to locate specific facts and details.

1 At the beginning why didn't Peter mind that it was raining?

a He was hot from his long walk. **b** He wasn't getting wet. **c** He enjoyed getting soaked.

2 In the sentence 'He decided he'd just have to wait it out', what is 'it' referring to?

____

3 What was the first thing that Peter noticed about the man on the bench?

a He had a grey suit on. **b** He was frowning at the rain. **c** He hadn't moved.

Interpretive questions

Hint: These questions require you to combine facts and details to synthesise the meaning.

4 Which phrase means that Peter adjusted his sitting position?

a settled himself **b** sheltered from the rain **c** sitting there

5 How do we know that Peter had no difficulty climbing the tree?

a because the use of the phrase 'swung himself up' implies that he did

b because he was a gymnast

c because the text says he took a long time to climb the tree

6 What two qualities of the tree's leaves gave some shelter from the rain?

____

7 When it first began how was the strength of the rain described? ______________

8 How did Peter first know the rain was becoming heavier?

a The man in the suit got up.

b He could hear it.

c He could see people running for cover.

9 List two adjectives in the text that describe the positive attributes of the man.

______________ ______________

10 Which statement best describes this text?

a The text is a narrative delivered in the third person.

b The text is an informative text delivered in the second person.

c The text is a persuasive text delivered in the first person.

Applied questions

Hint: These questions require you to understand a text's implications to infer meaning from the text.

11 Why did Peter shake his head in line 39?

____

12 Which detail incorporating a unit of measurement foreshadows the twist that the 'man' is a statue?

____

NARRATIVE TEXT

Descriptive narrative

SPELLING WORK

List Words

sheltered	nobility	angle	torrential	vigorously
gentleman	sculpted	upright	scurried	leapt
impression	disappeared	intrigued	drenching	statue

We make regular **plurals** by adding *s*. For example, *birds, horses, donkeys*. Some words must be altered in their form to make them plural. For example, *child* becomes *children* when made plural.

1 Use these spelling rules to turn these list words into plurals.

a impression ______________________ **b** statue ______________________

c angle ______________________ **d** gentleman ______________________

2 For words that end in *s*, *ss*, *sh*, *ch*, *z* or *x*, we add *es*. For example, *bonuses, messes, wishes, beaches, fizzes, boxes*. Convert these words to plurals.

a bench ______________________ **b** face ______________________

c bush ______________________ **d** buzz ______________________

e inch ______________________ **f** branch ______________________

g box ______________________ **h** hiss ______________________

3 Unscramble these mixed-up letter groups to make four list words.

gentleing nobshelt eredman drenchility

______________ ______________ ______________ ______________

4 Identify list words that have these affixes. Then tick *prefix* or *suffix* for each one to identify its type.
Hint: Prefixes are added to the beginning and suffixes are added to the end of base words.

a man ______________ ☐ Prefix ☐ Suffix **b** ion ______________ ☐ Prefix ☐ Suffix

c ly ______________ ☐ Prefix ☐ Suffix **d** ity ______________ ☐ Prefix ☐ Suffix

e in ______________ ☐ Prefix ☐ Suffix **f** up ______________ ☐ Prefix ☐ Suffix

g sculpt ______________ ☐ Prefix ☐ Suffix **h** ial ______________ ☐ Prefix ☐ Suffix

i ed ______________ ☐ Prefix ☐ Suffix **j** dis ______________ ☐ Prefix ☐ Suffix

5 Change these past tense words into three varieties of present tense words. The first one has been done for you as an example.

	Base word	***s* or *es***	***ing***
a realised	realise	realises	realising
b reached			
c formed			
d rained			
e noticed			
f decided			
g leaned			

NARRATIVE TEXT

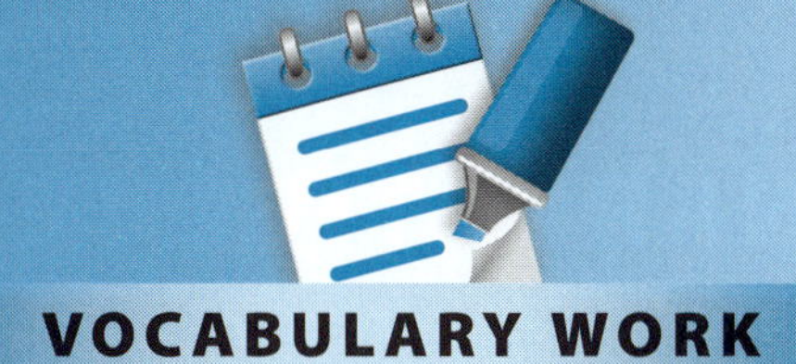

VOCABULARY WORK

1 Write antonyms for these words from the text 'Sitting in the rain'.

a before ____________ **b** hadn't ____________ **c** good ____________
d lower ____________ **e** perfectly ____________ **f** disappeared ____________
g identical ____________ **h** impossible ____________ **i** hidden ____________
j open ____________ **k** heavier ____________ **l** closer ____________
m could ____________ **n** asleep ____________ **o** down ____________
p disbelief ____________

2 Which of these phrases are in the past tense? Tick your choices.

- ☐ we are sheltering
- ☐ I sculpted a statue
- ☐ she suddenly disappears
- ☐ my heart is racing
- ☐ we scurried away
- ☐ he leapt under the shelter

3 Circle the odd word out in each set.

a rain, drizzle, shower, weather, downpour
b collar, shirt, tie, suit, hair
c statue, man, iron, sculpture
d caught, people, shoppers, pedestrians
e position, eyes, perspective, angle
f leapt, scurried, seat, ran, climbed
g leaves, foliage, branches, nature, tree, trunk
h boy, human, Peter, he

4 List all the grey things mentioned in the text.

a c____________ **b** h____________ **c** r____________ **d** s____________
e sh____________ c____________ **f** i____________ s____________ **g** ____________y

5 Write the base word of each of these list words.

a torrential ____________ **b** vigorously ____________
c sheltered ____________ **d** impression ____________
e intrigued ____________ **f** nobility ____________
g sculpted ____________ **h** disappeared ____________
i scurried ____________ **j** drenching ____________

Idioms about the weather are very common in the English language.

6 Can you finish these weather idioms by selecting the correct words to fill each gap?

day	cats	lightning	week	pours	sprung
cloud	bolt	storm	dawn	showers	sun
dry	fair	bone	night	silver	drowned

a It's raining ____________ and dogs.
b I'm saving for a rainy ____________.
c I'm chilled to the ____________.
d He's slower than a wet ____________.
e She's a ____________-weather friend.
f Every cloud has a ____________ lining.
g ____________ never strikes in the same place twice.
h It never rains but it ____________.
i Red sky at ____________, shepherd's delight.
j Spring has ____________.
k You look like a ____________ rat.
l Make hay while the ____________ shines.
m April ____________ bring forth May flowers.
n It's always darkest before the ____________.
o Like a ____________ from the blue.
p Any port in a ____________.

NARRATIVE TEXT

Descriptive narrative

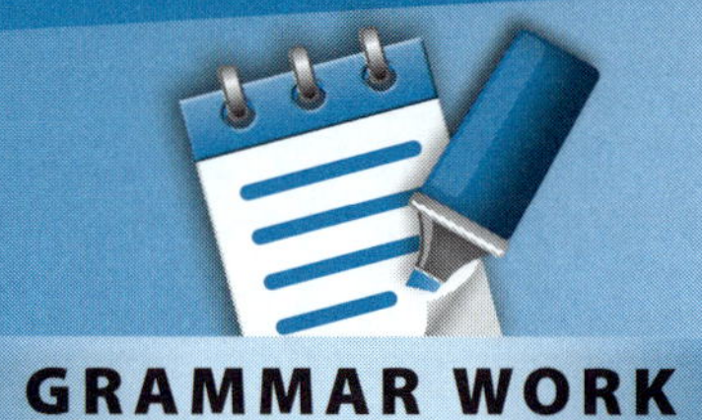

GRAMMAR WORK

Adjectives are words that describe nouns. We use them to make our descriptions richer and more detailed. We can describe nouns using single words (for example, *the large bird*) or adjectival phrases (for example, *the large, black, flightless jungle bird*).

1 List the adjectives in the first paragraph of the text 'Sitting in the rain' that describe the following:

a a walk ______________________ **b** a relief ______________________

c a tree ______________________ **d** a branch ______________________

e leaves ______________________

Adverbs are words that describe verbs. We use them to make our descriptions of actions more precise. Adverbs are single words, whereas adverbial phrases are made up of more than one adverb.

2 List the adverbs in the text 'Sitting in the rain' that describe the following.

a how someone is dressed ______________________ **b** how water is flowing ______________________

3 Find two examples of an adverb/adjective combination to describe the following.

a the rain ______________________ **b** a suit ______________________

4 Think of interesting adjectives to describe the nouns in this table. Write your answers in the spaces.

Noun	Feature 1	Adjective 1	Feature 2	Adjective 2
a boy	age		hair	
a girl	clothes		voice	
a dog	size		breed	
a tree	shape		height	
leaves	colour		texture	
a park	location		atmosphere	
a crowd	size		movement	
a storm	pace		action	
a house	appearance		colour	
a noise	pitch		sound	

5 Think of interesting adverbial phrases that could be used to describe the following actions. Write the whole sentence out. For example, *The zombie attacked* ***suddenly, violently*** *grabbing his victim around the legs.*

Action to describe	Adverbial phrase
water flowing	
an explosion	
a military invasion	
a man cooking	
a gamer playing	
a bulldozer working	
a lion stalking a deer	
water flowing	

6 Use the adjectives and adverbs in this list to enhance the following descriptions. Write them on the appropriate lines. quickly grey sudden unexpectedly iron

a The man in the ______________ suit was actually an ______________ statue.

b Peter ______________ took shelter before the ______________ rain drenched him.

c In summer, rainstorms can hit ______________, catching people off guard.

The rules for making words **possessive** tell us to add an apostrophe and the letter *s*. This works for most singular words.

1 Place the apostrophe and the *s* in the correct position to complete these possessive plurals.

a the trees branches (one tree)
b the peoples movements (a group of people)
c the bushs leaves (one bush)
d the bosss car (one boss)

2 Make these expressions singular or plural by adding punctuation.

a the boys mistake (two boys)
b the parks trees (one park)
c the trees trunks (three trees)
d the seasons changes (four seasons)

3 List the phrases with possessive apostrophes in the text 'Sitting in the rain'. *Hint: There are only two.*

______________________ ______________________

As well as using apostrophes to indicate possession, we also see them when we join words together to form **contractions**. The **apostrophe** shows where one or more letters is missing, having shortened a word to create the contraction.

4 Form contractions from these words and place the apostrophes in the correct places.

a did not ______________________
b had not ______________________
c could have ______________________
d does not ______________________
e he will ______________________
f they did ______________________

5 What exclamations are present in the text? Write out the expressions.

____

____

6 Are there any questions in the text 'Sitting in the rain'? Circle *yes* or *no*. Yes No

7 In which line of the text is a dash used? Write the line number on the line. *Hint: A dash (—) is not the same as a hyphen (-). Hyphens join words together, whereas dashes are part of the structure of sentences.* ________

8 Convert each of these sentences into two separate sentences by altering the wording and punctuation. Write the separate sentences on the lines provided. *Hint: Some words may need to be changed or deleted.*

a After his long walk the rain was a welcome relief, so the boy didn't move straight away.

____

b Shaking drips from his head Peter looked around until he spotted a good, sturdy tree to climb.

____

c The hair disappeared into a grey shirt collar, the colour identical to the suit, permitting no glimpse of his neck.

____

____

9 Fix the punctuation in this sentence from the text 'Sitting in the rain'. *Hint: Capital letters, commas and a full stop are missing.*

as peter stayed under the tree trapped by the grey sheet of rain it suddenly dawned on him that the man he was looking at was an iron statue

NARRATIVE TEXT

Descriptive narrative

WRITING WORK 1

Descriptive narratives

Descriptive narratives help readers form a vivid impression of the object or subject being described. They may be part of an overall narrative or may exist as a single, standalone text. People write descriptive narratives that are fiction and non-fiction texts.

The author usually begins by describing the overall scene, giving a general picture of what is happening or has happened. In a descriptive narrative, the writer builds a particular mood by providing details that create sensory and emotive images. Highly descriptive language with adjectives conveys precise details about the setting (the time and place). A complex sentence structure is employed to achieve richly descriptive sentences with multiple clauses. There may be a mixture of sensory imagery, including visual (sight), auditory (hearing), tactile (touch), olfactory (smell) and gustatory (taste) images. These help the reader imagine the scene.

Narrative voice is an important feature of descriptive narrative texts. This is the style of expression used by the storyteller in the text. Authors use a combination of real experiences and imagination to develop their narrative 'voice'. Sometimes narrators of descriptions will intrude into the text, appearing to address the reader directly.

When descriptive narratives form part of a larger work, such as a novel, authors may use special plot devices. One is a technique called **foreshadowing**, which provides clues about possible solutions to conflicts. They drop small hints that seem unimportant at the time but these may play a significant role later on. Another common plot technique is the **red herring**—a false lead or clue that is designed to distract the reader from the true resolution, preventing them from solving a mystery or predicting the ending. In the text 'Sitting in the rain', both of these devices are evident.

In summary, the **structural features** of a descriptive narrative are:
- a description of the overall scene at the very beginning
- a complex sentence structure
- richly descriptive sentences with multiple clauses
- connectives that link sentences together into cohesive paragraphs
- interesting plot devices such as foreshadowing and red herrings (in extended narratives that are part of a novel or short story).

The **language features** of a descriptive narrative include:
- the development of a particular mood
- highly descriptive language with adjectives that convey precise details about the setting
- sensory imagery created using similes and metaphors
- emotive language
- adverbs that strengthen the verbs describing the action
- authorial intrusion
- contrast.

1 How is a narrative description different from a novel?

____

2 What do connectives do to improve paragraphs? ________________________

3 Name two techniques used to create sensory imagery.

____

4 Describe the 'voice' of the narrator in the text 'Sitting in the rain'.

____

5 Find one example of each of these techniques in the text. Write them on the lines provided.

a a visual (sight) image ______________________________

b an auditory (sound) image ______________________________

c a tactile (touch) image ______________________________

6 Similes enhance the author's power to create strong descriptions. Create one simile to describe Peter.

____

7 What place is presented as the main setting in the text? ______________________________

8 **a** In what time period is the story set? ______________________________

b What clues are given to indicate the time period?

____

9 What parts of speech can be used to strengthen the impact of verbs? ______________________________

10 The text 'Sitting in the rain' contains some richly descriptive sentences. Can you identify the adjectives in these extracts? Write the adjectives on the lines provided. *Hint: Sometimes there are two adjectives, not just one.*

Extract from the text	Adjectives
dark, grey clouds forming overhead	**a** ______
	b ______
weeks of humid summer weather	**c** ______
	d ______
shrivelling into tinder-dry clumps	**e** ______
After overheating on his long walk	**f** ______
he spotted a good, sturdy tree to climb	**g** ______
	h ______
He grasped hold of a lower branch	**i** ______
by the broad, waxy leaves	**j** ______
	k ______
The grey sky threatened to open up	**l** ______
His curly hair gave an impression of nobility	**m** ______
Peter could see his steel-grey hair	**n** ______
content to sit in the drizzling rain	**o** ______
the damage to his lovely suit	**p** ______
the heavens opened in a torrential downpour	**q** ______
shaking his wet head in disbelief	**r** ______
was an iron statue	**s** ______

NARRATIVE TEXT

Descriptive narrative

WRITING SAMPLE

Here is a sample text showing you how to structure and write a descriptive narrative text.

An extraordinary undertaking 	**Create an interesting title.** This one contains a pun on the word 'undertaking'.
In a certain garden, still and dark, a strange sight presented itself under the silent witness of the moon. A cluster of seven lithe figures were intently digging at a patch of turf, uprooting it in little clumps.	**Describe the overall scene, giving a general picture of what is happening or has happened.** In this text the writer is describing a group of 'seven lithe figures' which we don't yet know are cats. The writer builds an intense, eerie and slightly mysterious mood as details of a night-time scene are presented. In a short description, it may also be appropriate to develop suspense. Here suspense is created by the use of the adjectives 'certain', 'still', 'dark', 'strange' and 'silent'.
Their grim purpose was revealed by the strengthening moonlight, which illuminated a sleek, lifeless body stretched out by the widening hole.	**Use highly descriptive language.** The language here conveys precise details about the appearance of the body, achieved using a complex sentence structure with multiple clauses.
A cold breeze shivered through the low brush that formed one border of the garden and the faint scent of wild freesias flavoured the air.	**Use sensory descriptions.** The breeze and the smell of freesias (delicately perfumed flowers) are described. By creating tactile (touch) and olfactory (smell) images, the writer is helping the reader imagine the scene.
Presently one of the seven signalled for the digging to cease. For a time the mourners stared at the forlorn figure on the grass, their breath creating small puffs of fog that mingled with the night mist.	**Use connectives to link sentences and paragraphs together smoothly.** The connective word 'presently' links the two paragraphs. The foreshadowing phrase 'for a time' links the first and second sentences, and signals that something else is expected to happen, thereby building mild suspense.
There was a slight swishing of tails and an audible shaking of forepaws free from the clinging dirt before the little group formed a respectful circle around the gravesite. The scents of earth and grass lingered.	**Use a combination of sensory images to engage as many senses as possible.** In this paragraph the senses of sight, hearing and touch are involved. Include emotional perceptions as you create descriptions.
Gathering around the body they tenderly conveyed it to the newly dug cavity. Then, with one accord, they soberly turned their backs on the grave, and in a sudden flurry worked their hind legs to fling the freshly displaced earth over their friend.	**Use verbs to describe the action and adverbs to enhance the descriptions.** Here we see the words 'tenderly' and 'soberly' used to express the ways in which actions are performed.
Anyone watching this scene may have been struck by the strange sophistication of the ritual. With no human to marshal them and no undertaker to instruct them, the seven animals gave their friend a hero's burial with only the solemn moon presiding. Then one by one they slid away into the deepening night.	**Use authorial intrusion to add variety.** Here, the narrator appears to be addressing the reader directly, echoing their unspoken thoughts about the scene. Contrast is drawn between the world of humans and the world of cats. Personification creates interesting imagery; here the moon is described as 'presiding' over the events of the night.
The funeral of a feline may be a strange sight indeed, on a perfectly ordinary night, in a perfectly ordinary street of a perfectly ordinary town—to a perfectly ordinary person. But for those who believe in the extraordinary there's nothing strange about it.	**Add emphasis with repetition.** The phrase 'perfectly ordinary' is repeated four times. This creates emphasis and irony, as a burial organised by cats is anything but perfectly ordinary. A contrast links to the next paragraph to create a smooth transition.
One such person was watching from her back verandah. Before the last few mourners had melted into the shadows she turned to go indoors, the moonlight catching the silver gleams of her tears.	**Use emotive language to evoke an emotional response in the reader.** Here the author describes a human onlooker who has gone unmentioned until now.

NARRATIVE TEXT

Descriptive narrative

WRITING YOUR OWN SAMPLE

Plan your sample on the lines provided.

- **Create an interesting title.** You might consider using a pun on a keyword.
- **Describe the overall scene, giving a general picture of what is happening or has happened.** It is important to build mood as details are presented. In a short description, it may also be appropriate to develop suspense.
- **Use highly descriptive language.** This helps convey precise details about the appearance of important focus objects, people or scenes. Strong description is achieved using a complex sentence structure with multiple clauses.
- **Use sensory descriptions.** Describe visual (sight), auditory (sound), tactile (touch), olfactory (smell) and gustatory (taste) images to help the reader imagine the scene.
- **Use connectives to link sentences and paragraphs together smoothly.** Connective words and phrases like 'next', 'again', 'after a while' or 'presently' can be used to link paragraphs together. You could also use foreshadowing words and phrases to signal that something else is expected to happen, thereby building mild suspense.
- **Use a combination of sensory images to engage as many senses as possible.** Try to engage more senses than just sight and hearing. Include emotional perceptions as you create descriptions.
- **Use verbs to describe the action and adverbs to enhance the descriptions.** Use adverbs to express the ways in which actions are performed.
- **Use authorial intrusion to add variety.** You can address the reader directly, echoing their unspoken thoughts about the description. Use contrast and personification to create interesting imagery.
- **Add emphasis with repetition.** The repeating of words and phrases can create emphasis and irony. Use a contrast to link to the next paragraph to create a smooth transition.
- **Use emotive language to evoke an emotional response in the reader.**

NARRATIVE TEXT

Poetry

READING WORK

Planking

They say it's dead and gone.
We've moved on to
something new.

It had its day in twenty-twelve.
Now far too *yesterday*
somewhat naff.

But I can't let it go.
I see a space
somewhere odd.

An escalator handrail, a ledge
A public wharf or
someplace else.

A beckoning space, makes me try
An awkward climb that
sometimes fails.

I scale this scaffold
Knowing that gravity may triumph
someday soon.

My serene celebration of nonsense
Needs no photo, it's
somehow wrong.

Enticed to assume the familiar position,
I just lie down
and plank.

Paul Faye

- The **title** of the poem describes the topic. Poems may not be named in this literal way. Many have names that require interpretation on multiple levels.
- The **pronoun** 'they' is used to refer to an as-yet unidentified group of people, but we know that this expression usually means 'people generally'.
- A pattern of **capitalisation** of the first two of the three lines in each stanza is established.
- The use of **italics** implies that this word is being spoken by someone.
- A pattern of **repeating** the prefix 'some' is evident by the time we read the second stanza and compare it with the first.
- The **conjunction** 'but' signals that a contrast is to come. In this line we see that although planking has been judged as passé, the poet continues to do it.
- This stanza's **phrasing**, where some places are precisely named, followed by the offhand generalisation 'or someplace else', reveals the poet's determination to plank anywhere he can.
- The verbs 'beckoning' and 'makes' adds **a sense of compulsion** to the poet's behaviour.
- The only negative outcome mentioned in the poem is deliberately **understated**, as if failure to make a climb (which may result in serious injury) is a triviality to the poet.
- **Alliteration** is used to create a repeated 's' sound effect reminiscent of a sharp intake of breath and perhaps a muttered swearword as the planker narrowly avoids a fall.
- This is a **reference** to the common purpose of plankers—to get photos of themselves planking and thereby gain points for bravery and skill.
- The expression 'assume the position' is a common one often applied to scenarios where schoolboys were required to submit to a beating with the cane as a form of punishment. Here the meaning is quite different, with the poet voluntarily assuming the position to be silly.
- The only **reference to the title** and the actual name of the practice appears in the last word of the last line for extra impact.
- The **poet's name** is given.

NARRATIVE TEXT

Poetry

COMPREHENSION WORK

Literal questions

Hint: Read the text carefully to locate specific facts and details.

1 What is this poem's topic?

2 List three places where the poet mentions he has performed this stunt.

3 In the first stanza, what do we find out some people feel about this hobby?

Interpretive questions

Hint: These questions require you to combine facts and details to synthesise the meaning.

4 Which line tells us that the speaker has fallen while trying to plank before?

a a ledge **b** an awkward climb that sometimes fails **c** But I can't let it go

5 Which slang phrase means 'no longer popular today'?

a too yesterday **b** nonsense needs **c** somehow wrong

6 How do you do this stunt?

Hint: Only one answer option is correct. Use the process of elimination to work through the options.

7 Why does the speaker do this stunt?

a to get funny photos of himself **b** as part of his job **c** he just likes doing it

8 Which of these places could be a suitable site for performing this stunt?

a a sofa **b** a grassy lawn **c** a window ledge

9 What are the connotations of the phrase 'a beckoning space'?

a The speaker feels tempted by certain places.

b The speaker needs to make an awkward climb.

c The speaker might fall.

10 Which phrase reveals how the speaker feels about planking?

a something new **b** assume the familiar position **c** my serene celebration of nonsense

Applied questions

Hint: This question requires you to understand a text's implications to infer meaning from the text.

11 What pattern is evident in the last line of each stanza (except for the very last line of the poem)?

12 How old do you think the speaker of this poem is? Explain your reasoning.

NARRATIVE TEXT

SPELLING WORK

List Words

All of the words below appear in the text 'Planking'.

somewhat	beckoning	celebration	familiar	triumph
escalator	awkward	assume	gravity	scale
wharf	serene	nonsense	scaffold	enticed

1 Correct the spelling errors in these sentences. Write the correct form of the misspelt words on the lines.

a It's dangerous to plank on an escelator hand-rail. ____________________

b The window ledge was somewhat akward to reach. ____________________

c I tried to scale the scafold. ____________________

d There were quite a few people down at the warf. ____________________

e We were enticd outside by the sunny weather. ____________________

f There were some familar faces at the gathering. ____________________

g The lake was calm and sereen at sunset. ____________________

2 Solve this puzzle by fitting the list words in correctly.
Hint: Use the existing letter clues to help you.

3 Form eight list words out of these fragments.

sense tri escal ward non umph ent awk
what fold ene iced scaf some ator ser

____________________ ____________________
____________________ ____________________
____________________ ____________________
____________________ ____________________

4 Make phrases containing these abstract nouns.

a awkward ____________________

b serene ____________________

5 Write sentences containing these abstract nouns.

a triumph ____________________

b nonsense ____________________

6 Complete this table by changing the forms of these list words. *Hint: Remember the spelling rules about what we do with the letter e when adding certain suffixes.*

Base word	Add *ed*	Add *ing*	Form an abstract noun
assume	a	b	c
entice	d	e	enticement
celebrate	f	g	h
escalate	i	j	k

NARRATIVE TEXT

Poetry

VOCABULARY WORK

1 Write synonyms for these words from the text 'Planking'. Ensure that you preserve the original meaning as revealed by their context in the text. The words that provide context are shown in parentheses.

a scale (this scaffold) ______________________ **b** (it's had its) day ______________________

c beckoning (space) ______________________ **d** awkward (climb) ______________________

e odd ______________________ **f** they (say) ______________________

g naff ______________________ **h** (beckoning) space ______________________

2 Add your own stanza to the poem, using this scaffold to help you.

I spot a ______________________ (good place for planking)

I ______________________ (verb and adverb in either order)

Someone ______________________. (noun, verb or adjective)

3 How many syllables are there in these words? Circle your answer.
Hint: Think about how they sound when you say them.

a	familiar	1	2	3	4	5
b	serene	1	2	3	4	5
c	scaffold	1	2	3	4	5
d	escalator	1	2	3	4	5
e	triumph	1	2	3	4	5
f	celebration	1	2	3	4	5
g	assume	1	2	3	4	5
h	position	1	2	3	4	5
i	wharf	1	2	3	4	5
j	gravity	1	2	3	4	5

4 Match the prefixes to their endings to form a list of adjectives about planking.

chal	il	biz	de	non	sil
odd	pec	ex	un	dang	risk

a ______manding **b** ______ique **c** ______treme

d ______logical **e** ______arre **f** ______ly

g ______erous **h** ______uliar **i** ______lenging

j ______y **k** ______sensical **l** ______ball

5 Planking is a strange pastime. Complete these idioms about other hobbies and special interests.
Hint: Use the clues in parentheses to help you work them out.

a have a j__________ session (practising music in a band)

b about as exciting as watching p__________ dry (describing a boring activity)

c go and shoot some h__________ (play informally with a basketball)

d keep a p__________ face (maintain a blank expression to hide a good or bad hand of cards)

e burn some r__________ (engage in motorsports with cars or motorcycles)

NARRATIVE TEXT

Poetry

GRAMMAR WORK

Complete this puzzle by writing the correct tense for these verbs into their numbered spaces in the grid.
Hint: 8 across is 'turned (present)' so the answer is a present tense form of the verb 'turned', which is 'turns'.

Across

1 had (present)
3 hears (past)
6 was (present)
8 turned (present)
10 folded (present)
14 choosing (past)
16 will build (past)
17 cared (present)
18 jumped (present)
20 sneezing (past)
22 walked (present)
23 hides (past)
25 storms (past)
26 lazed (present)
27 wrote (present)
29 will meet (past)
32 says (past)
34 raced (present)
36 waves (past)
37 jerked (present)
39 entered (present)
42 bombing (past)
43 kneels (past)
44 did (present)
47 nodded (present)
49 ate (present)
52 was (present)
53 fibbs (past)
54 cried (present)
55 might've (present)
56 imprisons (past)

Down

2 were (present)
4 ended (present)
5 pursued (present)
6 asked (present)
7 gossipped (present)
9 calling (past)
11 went (present)
12 think (past)
13 slept (present)
15 will fail (past)
19 swam (present)
20 snoozed (present)
21 has been (present)
24 quitted (present)
25 see (past)
28 receding (past)
30 growls (past)
31 gives (past)
33 dreams (past)
35 skis (past)
36 worked (present)
38 stood (present)
40 sniffed (present)
41 climbed (present)
45 saw (present)
46 said (present)
48 swatted (present)
50 added (present)
51 scanned (present)

NARRATIVE TEXT

PUNCTUATION WORK

Punctuating poetry

In poetry the regular rules of **punctuation** don't apply. Instead poets use 'creative licence' (artistic freedom), using punctuation marks (or their absence) as creative tools to provide cues about how to say the poem aloud. Some poetic techniques that involve punctuation include the following.

- **Caesura:** Caesura is a mark within the line itself that signals the reader to pause, slowing the pace of the poem. It prevents a poem from having a regular end-rhyme pattern.
- **Lower-case letters:** Capital letters are often ignored, with lower-case letters beginning lines.
- **Enjambment:** This is where one line runs into another with no punctuation mark at the end of a line. The reader continues without pausing because the poet wishes to leave a single idea uninterrupted. It also helps the poem to flow.
- **End stop:** A full stop at the end of a line is known as an end stop when it is used to end a thought or a whole stanza.
- **No punctuation:** Poets frequently use no punctuation at all in an effort to let the words speak for themselves, without imposing interpretive details upon them.

Some poets do use formal punctuation marks in their work, following the traditional rules we apply to regular writing. One such poet is French writer Hilaire Belloc, who wrote *Cautionary Tales for Children* (1907).

1 There are problems with the use of capital letters in the first line of this poem by Hilaire Belloc. Rewrite line 1 with the punctuation errors corrected. *Hint: Look at line 2 to see if line 1 requires a full stop or a comma.*

Line 1 the chief defect of henry king was chewing little bits of string

____

2 List the punctuation marks found in the remaining lines of the poem. Make your list in the order that they appear in the text, but don't write any repeats. Write the name and the symbol of each mark.

Line 2 At last he swallowed some which tied itself in ugly knots inside.
Line 3 Physicians of the utmost fame were called at once; but when they came
Line 4 they answered, as they took their fees, 'There is no cure for this disease.
Line 5 Henry will very soon be dead.' His parents stood about his bed
Line 6 lamenting his untimely death, when Henry, with his latest breath,
Line 7 cried—'Oh, my friends, be warned by me, that breakfast, dinner, lunch and tea
Line 8 are all the human frame requires ...' with that the wretched child expires.

Name	Symbol	Name	Symbol
______	___	______	___
______	___	______	___
______	___	______	___
______	___		

3 Which lines in the first stanza of the poem 'Planking' are enjambed? Write the line number here. __________

4 Which lines of each stanza always begin with lower-case letters: the first, second or third? __________

5 Write the line numbers of the poem's lines that include a caesura. __________

6 How many lines of the poem have an end stop? __________

Poems

Poems are usually designed to be spoken aloud so that the sound effects they produce can be heard. Poetry has specific characteristics that set it apart from prose (or ordinary writing). Poetry is a form of creative expression that requires us to become personally involved in interpreting and responding to it. Learning to identify and comprehend the use of poetic techniques is an important skill. A poet's main aim is to use words economically to explore a theme. Poets hope to move us emotionally and to create extraordinary effects through the use of language.

Scholars tell us that there are three main groups of poetry: narrative, lyrical and dramatic. **Narrative poetry** is story-based, whereas **lyrical poetry** is song-like and emotionally expressive. Lyrical poems are often based on lighthearted subjects and are primarily used to create single impressions. **Dramatic poetry** is often delivered like a speech and is very intense and introspective. The text 'Planking' is a lyrical poem. There are many more lyrical poems in the world than narrative or dramatic.

The **structural features** of poetry may:

- have one or more speakers from whose point of view the poem is delivered
- include elements of story, such as a setting, characters and a plot
- be completely unstructured or have a formal, metered verse structure
- have a clear pattern of rhythm
- be unrhymed or have a clear rhyme scheme
- be musical or chant-like
- have a dramatised crisis or climax
- include a sense of the passage of time
- build to a logical conclusion that reveals the theme
- observe, disregard or partially obey the formal rules of punctuation.

Language features of poetry can include:

- expression in any mode and tense
- introspection (looking inwardly at one's own thoughts and feelings)
- a unifying theme or message
- an emotive tone
- a symbolic or obscure meaning
- similes and metaphors
- alliteration and assonance (repetition of consonant and vowel sounds close together)
- personification
- rhythm
- rhyme
- emotive language
- colloquial language (informal language peculiar to a particular group or place, including slang)
- jargon
- symbolism
- contrast
- repetition (repeating of sounds, words, phrases and ideas)
- onomatopoeia (where a word's spelling reflects the actual sound of the thing being described).

1 What are three elements of story that may be present in a poem?

____

2 What is onomatopoeia?

____

3 What do you think is the theme of the text 'Planking'?

____

4 Revise your knowledge of poetic techniques by completing these definitions. Insert the missing words.

nouns	punctuation	pictured	repeating	speech	names	consonant

a alliteration — repetition of ____________ sounds that are identical or similar in sequences of words positioned closely together

b imagery — a description of something that can be seen and therefore ____________ by the reader

c repetition — the deliberate ____________ of a word, phrase or part of a word to create a pattern

d adjectives — words that describe ____________ more vividly

e pronouns — words that take the place of ____________, such as 'I' or 'you'

f colloquial language — informal language used in everyday ____________, like slang

g informal punctuation — irregular use of ____________ marks to create certain poetic effects

5 Find lines that contain examples of each of these poetic techniques. Complete this table by writing lines from the text 'Planking' in the Example column.

Hint: Use the annotations on the original text to help you.

	Language feature	Example
Imagery	**a** alliteration	• •
	b assonance	•
Structure	**c** repetition	•
Other poetic language features	**d** adjectives	• • •
	e personal pronouns	• •
	f colloquialisms	• •
	g enjambment	• •

NARRATIVE TEXT

Poetry

WRITING SAMPLE

Here are two sample texts showing you how to structure and write different types of poetry.

Beached

Oh! the strength of him,
the power and size of
him.
Majestic in a
cumbersome form,
covered in great grey
sleekness.

Where are his family?
Has he been alone in his
sorrow?
Was his hugeness
wracked with pain?
Was he aware of hurting,
helping hands?

Or, unlike his human
co-inhabitants
on this vast planet,
did he accept the fate of
all creatures
great and small—

Death—undignified and
alone?

Colleen Minett

Driving through Woomera from Coober Pedy

When times are tough
And the going is rough
I will think of my trip
Outback.
Where the land is dry
And the stockmen cry
For the rain that they
sadly lack.

These Aussies brave
Give a cheery wave
To the traveler on the
track.
Scorching sun and sand
Follow travellers overland
and adventure draws
them back.

My eye roams free
Over a grey-brown sea
Of nothingness far and
wide.
Then far up in the blue
Swarms a green-grey hue
Of birds with nowhere
to hide.

Wildflowers will bloom
If the rains come soon
To replenish the parched
and dried.
Great beauty is there
For those who care
And for those who
bravely abide.

- **Use an interesting title that hints at the topic of the poem.** The subject matter of 'Beached' is a beached whale. Or **use a literal title to specify the topic of the poem.** The subject matter of 'Driving through Woomera …' is clearly described in the title.
- **Develop a meaningful structure.** The first stanza of 'Beached' presents the poet's sensory observations of the whale; the second is composed of questions; and the third is a question which the last line ends. The structure of 'Driving through Woomera …' is loosely based on the Australian bush ballad form—it is composed of eight stanzas of even length.
- **Decide on a rhythm.** 'Beached' uses the rhythm of natural language. 'Driving through Woomera …' has a regular and consistent rhythm—it has three beats to each of the first two lines and five beats to the third line of each stanza, which creates a regular rhythm that suggests an ongoing journey.
- **Decide whether you will use a rhyme scheme.** The poet has chosen to use 'free verse' form for 'Beached', with no rhyme scheme or regular rhythm. In ballads, rhyme and rhythm work closely together to produce a musical, sing-song effect, so to describe the rhyme scheme of 'Driving through Woomera…' we need to view it in two halves (of four stanzas each)—its rhyme scheme is AAB CCB DDB EEB.
- **Add details that allow the listener to picture the setting.** Use visual imagery to create emotive effects. In 'Beached' the emotionally evocative image of the whale is created with visual and tactile images ('size', 'great grey sleekness', 'hugeness'). In 'Driving though Woomera …' we read of stockmen, sun, sand, birds, wildflowers, rains and parched, dried earth.
- **Pay close attention to diction.** Words are used as economically as possible. Choice of words is critical in a structured poem.
- **Use alliteration and assonance.** The reference in 'Beached' to 'hurting, helping hands' repeats the 'h' sound that mimics laboured breathing. In 'Driving through Woomera …' the repeated consonants at line 3 of each of the first four stanzas is the hard 'ck' sound. Other examples of alliteration in this poem are seen in the 'scorching sun and sand' and the 'green-grey hue' of birds. Assonant vowels create subtle sound effects that help to unify the sound of the poem.
- **Use an allusion.** Allusions allow you to communicate a lot of meaning using few words. In 'Beached' there is an allusion to the usually positive phrase 'all creatures great and small', an expression that refers to the wonderful diversity of life. In 'Driving through Woomera …' a 'grey-brown sea' invites us to imagine the plains as a vast ocean.
- **Use emotive language.** In 'Beached', 'sorrow' is mentioned at the whale's predicament. The last line expresses a question in the poet's mind about the whale's acceptance of death. In 'Driving through Woomera …', the concept of bravery is a focus—the poet suggests that when facing tough times we should put our troubles into perspective and compare our circumstances with stockmen facing endless drought.
- **Credit the poet.** The poet's name is displayed at the end.

WRITING YOUR OWN SAMPLE

Write your own sample poem in one of the two styles modelled in the sample.

- **Use an interesting title that hints at the topic of the poem.** Or **use a literal title to specify the topic of the poem.**
- **Develop a meaningful structure.** You may choose to write in a pattern of regular stanzas or an unrhymed form with no pattern at all.
- **Decide on a rhythm.** This will be created by the way you organise the poem (into stanzas or without any pattern) and the number of beats you assign to each line, stanza or other unit of structure you choose.
- **Decide whether you will use a rhyme scheme.** You should try to describe the rhyming pattern using the ABAB system. Remember: each time the rhyming sound at the end of a line changes, you add a new letter in alphabetical order.
- **Add details that allow the listener to picture the setting.** Use visual imagery to create emotive effects.
- **Pay close attention to diction.** Choice of words is critical in structured poems. Even in unstructured poetry we must be economical with words.
- **Use alliteration and assonance.** Assonant vowels create subtle sound effects that help unify the sound of the poem.
- **Use an allusion.** Allusions allow you to communicate a lot of meaning using few words.
- **Use emotive language.** Select words that express feelings and evoke emotional responses in your audience. Create an emotive conclusion to end the poem, leaving the audience strongly impacted by your message.
- **Credit the poet.** Place your name at the end.

UNIT 9

PERSUASIVE TEXT

Marketing text

READING WORK

From: Carl Whitman <ceo@easyid.com.au>
Subject: Easy ID
To: Fantasy Land Board <board@fantasyland.com>

Dear Fantasy Land Directors

Thank you for the invitation to submit our proposal to you. I trust you all arrived back in the States safely. We were delighted to spend some time getting to know you at the ID Technology conference in Sydney. We'd like to invite the Fantasy Land Board of Directors to consider using our Easy ID wristbands. You'll find attached to this email a PowerPoint presentation that provides details about the Easy ID system. We trust that you will find it of great assistance in making your decision.

Kind regards,
Carl Whitman, CEO,
Easy ID

PowerPoint—5-slide presentation

SLIDE 1: A simple wristband; a total solution

- the world's leading data management system
- capabilities for promotion, tracking, security, market research and personal ID
- access from a web-based interface

Isn't progress wonderful?

SLIDE 2: Creating the future

- long-life
- colourful
- high-resolution printing
- comfortable to wear
- waterproof

Would you like your business to profit from these features?

SLIDE 3: Simplifying the future

- secure
- simple software
- tamper-proof features
- fully customisable in design

How much simpler could it be?

SLIDE 4: Future opportunities

- web interface
- instant barcode scanning technology
- tracking information

And the entire process takes less than a second to complete. Is that fast enough for you?

SLIDE 5: Welcome to the future

Would you like to see Fantasy Land's branding on an Easy ID Wristband?
We invite you to call us to obtain a free sample, custom-designed for your business.
Why not let Easy ID work for you?

- A polite **opening statement** is used to begin the email.
- A **statement of the sender's goodwill** is included as a mark of respect.
- The **word 'invite' is used**, even though this is actually a request from Easy ID for the recipients to purchase the Easy ID system.
- The **sender's company and brand name** is mentioned early to keep it as the firm focus of the message.
- The directors' **attention is drawn** to the attachment of the email—a PowerPoint presentation outlining the features of the Easy ID system.
- A standard, polite **sign-off statement** is used to end the email.
- The **sender's position** as Chief Executive Officer is added.
- A **one-line statement is used to summarise** and introduce each set of dot points. Here we have a statement of contrast between a difficult problem and a simple solution.
- A bold **claim** about globally acknowledged success is made.
- A **rhetorical question** is used to invite agreement from the reader.
- The **summary statements** that introduce the slides repeatedly use the word 'future' to emphasise the ongoing benefits to be enjoyed by users of the system.
- **Bullet points** are an effective means of summarising key information. By presenting these details in point-form, the burden of reading through a text-heavy page is lightened, increasing the likelihood of the reader noticing all the salient features and benefits.
- The word 'simpler' **repeats the effect** of the phrase 'a simple solution' in the first slide.
- The **repetition** of the word 'future' continues.
- This question specifically **addresses the company by name**, strengthening the call to action in the next line.

PERSUASIVE TEXT

Marketing text

COMPREHENSION WORK

Literal questions

Hint: Read the text carefully to locate specific facts and details.

1 Which word is repeated five times in the PowerPoint slides in the text 'Easy ID'?

a instant **b** future **c** fast

2 What are three characteristics of the wristbands?

a colourful, fully customisable, glow-in-the-dark

b colourful, waterproof, tamper-proof

c comfortable, cheap, environmentally friendly

3 What is the official position of the person presenting the proposal?

a Chief Executive Officer **b** Director **c** Conference President

Interpretive questions

Hint: These questions require you to combine facts and details to synthesise the meaning.

4 Which of these lines presents a contrast?

a a simple wristband; a total solution

b high-resolution printing

c long-life

5 What type of sentence appears last in each slide?

a an interjection **b** an exclamation **c** a question

6 Which company's representatives are in Australia?

____

Hint: Only one answer option is correct. Use the process of elimination to work through the options.

7 What do the directors need to do if they want to obtain a sample wristband made up with their logo on it?

____

8 What does the phrase 'fully customisable in design' mean?

____

9 Why does the process of barcode scanning need to be fast?

____

10 How does the owner of the wristband technology access the information they collect?

____

Applied questions

Hint: These questions require you to understand a text's implications to infer meaning from the text.

11 What is one feature under 'future opportunities' that would enable companies to work out where visitors are in real time?

a tracking information **b** colour-coded **c** customisable

12 What is the reason for the creation of this persuasive text?

____

PERSUASIVE TEXT

Marketing text

SPELLING WORK

List Words

All of the words in the box below appear in the text 'Easy ID'.

invitation	proposal	conference	attached	assistance
presentation	decision	management	capabilities	colourful
resolution	simplifying	technology	obtain	business

1 Look at these list words and circle whether each *c* should be sounded as a 'k' sound or a 'ss' sound.
Hint: Say them aloud to help you decide.

a decision 'k'/ 'ss' **b** capabilities 'k'/ 'ss' **c** colourful 'k'/ 'ss'
d assistance 'k'/ 'ss' **e** conference (first *c*) 'k'/ 'ss' **f** conference (second *c*) 'k'/ 'ss'

2 Which list word has a 'u' that sounds like a short 'i'? ______________________

3 Which of these words from the text 'Easy ID' contains one or more silent letters? Circle them.

delighted wristbands details system technology spend
process personal email designed printing

4 Read these sentences and correct the spelling of two words in each.

a Ristbands carry barcodes that can be scaned. __________ __________
b The directers arived safely back in America. __________ __________
c We'd like to asist you in makeing your decision. __________ __________
d We are confedent that you'll love our propossal. __________ __________
e Here's a simple solushen to your data managment puzzle. __________ __________
f You can acess market research data via a webb interface. __________ __________
g Our product is a colourfull and comfortible product to wear. __________ __________
h We hope you'll considar this oportunity to work with us. __________ __________
i The entire proccess takes just secends to complete. __________ __________
j Ask us for a free sampel printed with a desine of your choice. __________ __________

5 Find three list words with double consonants located next to each other among the list words.

__________ __________ __________

6 Complete these compound words from the text.

a __________bands **b** __________ware **c** __________face

7 Write the missing singular and plural words in the table.

Singular	Plural	Singular	Plural
proposal	**a**	**b**	details
solution	**c**	data	**d**
e	capabilities	business	**f**
opportunity	**g**	**h**	information
i	samples	director	**j**

PERSUASIVE TEXT
Marketing text

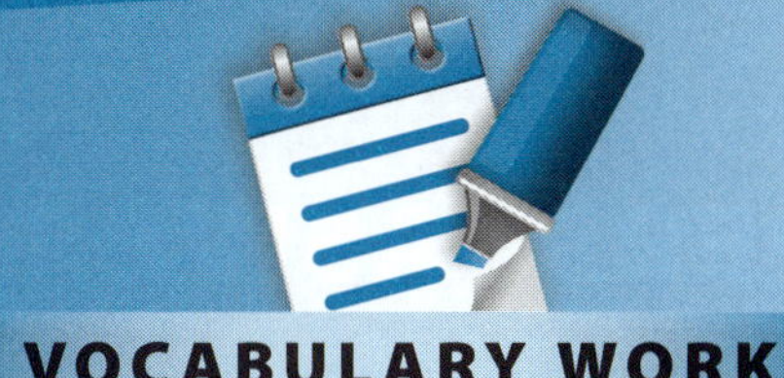

VOCABULARY WORK

1 Find antonyms in the text 'Easy ID' for these list words.

a colourless ____________ **b** detached ____________
c disabilities ____________ **d** mismanagement ____________
e indecision ____________ **f** complicating ____________
g problem ____________ **h** exclusion ____________
i obstruction ____________ **j** lose ____________

2 Change these words into their simplest form base words. *Hint: Think about what the word would look like without a suffix, and remember the 'e' rule.*

a invitation ____________ **b** presentation ____________
c resolution ____________ **d** proposal ____________
e decision ____________ **f** simplifying ____________
g conference ____________ **h** management ____________
i attached ____________ **j** assistance ____________

3 What do these expressions mean? Write definitions in your own words.

a Board of Directors ____________
b data management ____________
c ID ____________
d custom-designed ____________
e high-resolution printing ____________

4 Complete these idioms about the world of business by inserting the missing words.

bottom	personal	ballpark	down	handshake	millionaire	eat
in	losses	show	business	square	world	

a It's none of your ____________.	This matter is private and is not a concern of yours.
b He got a golden ____________.	He received payment to encourage him to retire.
c Let's get ____________ to business.	Let's talk about the main reason for our meeting.
d There's no business like ____________ business.	The entertainment industry is exciting to work in.
e It's nothing ____________, it's just business.	Don't take negative talk and decisions to heart.
f You should cut your ____________.	You should stop doing what is causing you to lose.
g I'm a million bucks short of being a ____________.	I haven't got any money.
h Money makes the ____________ go round.	Everyone on Earth is affected by money.
i I'll bet my ____________ dollar …	I will gamble the last amount of money I have left.
j I'm taking a gamble and I'm all ____________.	I have staked all of my remaining money on this bet.
k The business world is dog ____________ dog.	People in business can be cruel and ruthless.
l Give me a ____________ figure.	I would like a rough estimate of the price.
m We'll have to go back to ____________ one.	We will have to start over from the beginning.

PERSUASIVE TEXT

Marketing text

GRAMMAR WORK

Interrogatives are adverbs that question (or 'interrogate'). They are usually placed at the beginning of a question. Examples are *who, what, how, why, when* and *where.* However, not all questions are phrased using interrogatives. There are many different ways in which questions can be posed, including using the words *are/aren't* and *is/isn't* when seeking a simple *yes* or *no* response.

1 Change all of these questions from the text 'Easy ID' into statements. *Hint: Where you see interrogative adverbs, try removing them and rephrasing the sentence.*

a Isn't progress wonderful? ______________________

b How much simpler could it be? ______________________

c Would you like your business to profit from these features?

____

d And the entire process takes less than a second to complete. Is that fast enough for you?

____

e Why not let Easy ID work for you? ______________________

2 Circle all the prepositions in this passage.

Thank you for the invitation to submit our proposal to you. I trust you all arrived back in the States safely. We were delighted to spend some time getting to know you at the ID Technology conference in Sydney. We'd like to invite the Fantasy Land Board of Directors to consider using our Easy ID wristbands. You'll find attached to this email a PowerPoint presentation that provides details about the Easy ID system. We trust that you will find it of great assistance in making your decision.

3 Find eight adjectives that are used to describe the wristbands in the text 'Easy ID'.

__________ __________ __________ __________

__________ __________ __________ __________

4 Find two adjectives that are used to describe the Easy ID data management system in the text.

__________ __________

5 Find one adjective used to describe the progress of technology in the text. ______________________

6 Circle all the positive adjectives and adverbs in this group.

easy	great	arrived	safely	high	total	comfortable
wonderful	access	simple	consider	fully	attached	secure
instant	free	fast	profit	spend	trust	simplifying

Nominalisation occurs when a verb is used as a noun. For example, the verb *gaming* is an action but it is also the noun that we use to name the activity. We might write *I will be gaming all day today* or *Gaming is a popular hobby.* The first has 'gaming' as a verb; the second as a noun. Here's another example: in the sentence *I will email my boss,* the word 'email' is used as a verb. But in the sentence *I have received an email,* the word 'email' is used as a noun. This means that the word 'email' is a nominalisation.

7 Circle all the nominalised words (words that can be used as verbs or nouns). *Hint: Try putting each word into a sentence to see if it can be used as a noun, then do the same to check whether it can be used as a verb as well. If you can 'do' it but it is also a 'thing', it is a nominalisation.*

tracking	opportunities	progress	email	management
personal	research	printing	second	profit
complete	access	features	sample	business

Apostrophes

We use **apostrophes** for two main functions in writing:

- to make words possessive
- to signal where letters have been omitted when spelling contractions.

Possessive apostrophes show that the noun 'owns' or possesses something; for example, *the pizza's crust* or *the monster's face*. In a contraction formed by joining two words together, we place the apostrophe at the location of any missing letters; for example, *do not* becomes *don't*.

1 Identify the possessive words and phrases out of this selection. Circle *possessive* or *plural* for each of them.

a	States	Possessive	Plural	**b**	Fantasy Land's	Possessive	Plural
c	Directors	Possessive	Plural	**d**	world's	Possessive	Plural
e	wristbands	Possessive	Plural	**f**	features	Possessive	Plural

2 Write out these contracted expressions in full. *Hint: There are two possible answers for f.*

a isn't ________ ________ **b** haven't ________ ________

c might've ________ ________ **d** you'll ________ ________

e can't ________ (one word) **f** I'd ________ ________

3 Now write the missing letters from each of those contractions, as indicated by the apostrophe's position in each one.

a isn't ________ **b** haven't ________ **c** might've ________

d you'll ________ **e** can't ________ **f** I'd ________

4 Write all the hyphenated words found in the text 'Easy ID'.

____

____

5 Find the line number in which each punctuation mark appears and write it on the line provided.

a one semicolon Line number ____ **b** four capital Ws Line number ____

c six question marks Line numbers ______ **d** an abbreviation for 'identification' Line number ___

An **ellipsis** (the plural is ellipses) is a set of three equally spaced full stops (…) to show that something has been left out of a sentence. An ellipsis can also signal an unfinished thought or statement, an interruption, or a pause when someone is speaking.

6 Change this passage by adding an ellipsis in the right place to indicate that something has been left out. *Hint: Use an ellipsis to replace a full stop.*

We could go on forever about the great features of our wristbands. They are secure, tamper-proof, waterproof, high-resolution. Need we go on?

7 Rewrite the dot points from Slide 2 in the text 'Easy ID' in the form of a properly punctuated paragraph of prose (ordinary writing) rather than in the form of a bullet point summary. *Hint: Make the points into a total of three sentences.*

____

____

____

____

PERSUASIVE TEXT

Marketing text

WRITING WORK 1

Persuasive marketing texts

People compose **marketing texts** to persuade other people to buy or accept products, services and ideas. They are usually very well planned and may be the result of a collaborative effort by a team. Marketing texts may be written, spoken or digitally interactive.

The text 'Easy ID' has two parts: an introductory email (or cover letter) and a digital presentation.

Clarity and structure are very important in marketing texts. There should be an attention-grabbing opening statement. This should be followed by a series of points that present the features of the product and how they will benefit the target customer. The presentation must flow logically. It should have an authoritative tone, which can be developed by presenting facts, statistics and other data.

The aim of marketers is to present a positive view of their product or service, avoiding any negative elements. Persuasive language techniques are used to appeal to the target audience's values, emotions and aspirations (dreams). In various media—print, digital or audiovisual—these texts share certain features.

Persuasive marketing texts appear in many forms, so their **structural features** vary greatly from one to another. Some common structural features often used in persuasive marketing texts include:

- an attention-grabbing opening statement
- subheadings
- short blocks of text
- a series of points that present the features of the product
- a logical flow of ideas
- truncated (short, cut-off) sentences
- bullet point lists
- summaries
- graphic features such as text boxes, side bars and pull quotes
- graphs, charts and tables
- a strong call to action, encouraging the target reader to respond.

Language features and techniques that may be used in a persuasive marketing text include:

- repetition
- inclusive language
- vivid imagery
- selective use of first, second and third person
- emotive language that creates a desire to buy or use the item or service being promoted
- analogies (detailed comparisons between things)
- allusions (references to other works, people or events)
- imperatives and challenges
- questions
- rhetorical questions (which don't need or anticipate an answer but are designed to provoke thought)
- specific benefits for the target customer
- an authoritative tone
- facts, statistics and other data
- buzzwords (popular words and phrases designed to appeal to buyers, such as *free*).

1 What are analogies? ______________________________

2 What is the difference between an ordinary question and a rhetorical question?

____

3 What is another word for aspirations? __________

4 Find three rhetorical questions used in the text 'Easy ID'. Write them on the lines below. *Hint: Not all questions are rhetorical.*

____

____

____

5 Write one example of these features and techniques from the email portion of the text 'Easy ID'.

a salutation __________

b emotive language __________

6 What is the call to action in this text? __________

7 Find four buzzwords used in the text and explain why each is appealing to the target reader.

__________ __________

__________ __________

__________ __________

__________ __________

8 What are two specific benefits for the target customer mentioned in Slide 4 of the text 'Easy ID'?

____

____

9 Write a short phrase to describe the subtopic of each of the five slides in the presentation.

Slide 1 __________

Slide 2 __________

Slide 3 __________

Slide 4 __________

Slide 5 __________

10 Repetition is an important tool used for emphasis in persuasive texts of all kinds. What keyword in the text 'Easy ID' is repeated?

____

11 If you had to edit the text 'Easy ID' to contain only four slides, which slide would you delete? Explain your reasoning.

____

____

____

____

PERSUASIVE TEXT

Marketing text

WRITING SAMPLE

Here is a sample text showing you how to structure and write a persuasive marketing text.

Jazz in the Gardens

Join us for an evening of fine foods and smooth grooves set in the city's beautiful Botanic Gardens.

Featuring

- Harpo Dalton and the Goldhorns
- Jaynie Taylor
- Legs Eleven

Listen

Wrap your senses in the silky sax tones of the legendary Harpo Dalton and his band the Goldhorns. Groove along with scat extraordinaire Jaynie Taylor and let your hair down with Legs Eleven, Australia's premier jazz quartet.

Enjoy

Enjoy fruity champagne on arrival and a lavish selection of gourmet treats that will get your tastebuds singing. You'll love our cocktails made exclusively for this prestigious event by celebrity barman Saul Sweetwater.

Indulge

And just when you thought things couldn't get any sweeter, indulge in the delights of a chocolate fountain brought right to your table.

Why not treat yourself to some of life's little pleasures?

Date: April 11: 7:30 pm
Venue: Sydney Botanic Gardens
Gold tickets: $64 Seniors $58
No student concession for Gold tickets
Silver tickets: $54 Seniors $48
Student concession $44

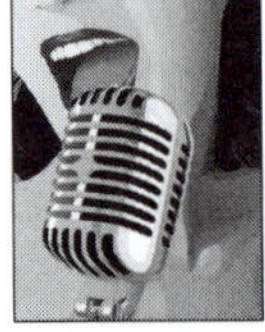

No admission for under-18s.
Book early to avoid disappointment.
Call our hotline: 1800 323 JAZZ for full details or visit info@jazzevents.com.au

- **If possible, use the brand name in the title.** This text is promoting a jazz music event.
- **Make a direct approach to the reader in the opening statement.** In this text we see a direct invitation to the target reader to come to the event. We see strong adjectives including 'fine', 'beautiful' and 'silky'. Rhyme has been used to create impact: the phrase 'fine foods and smooth grooves' is an example of rhyme created with assonant sounds.
- **Use bullet point lists to clearly organise key information.**
- **Use subheadings and short blocks of text to present the main features being promoted.** The ideas are organised into a logical flow. Information is presented that details the specific benefits for the target customer: we see the music, the food and drinks, the treats and the prestige highlighted as the specific benefits to be enjoyed. Vivid imagery engages the physical senses, enabling the target customer to imagine themselves participating in the event. Second person mode creates a sense of inclusion and personal invitation—we read the pronoun 'you' in the descriptions of the benefits to attendees. Emotive language creates a desire to get involved in the event being promoted—words like 'lavish', 'love' and 'prestigious' all appeal to the feelings.
- **Use rhetorical questions.** The question here is 'Why not treat yourself to some of life's little pleasures?'
- **Use highly structured layout to present short lists of data.** In this text we see the date, time, venue and ticket prices presented in this way. Subheadings with colons, bold type and heading hierarchies are used to add clarity and a sense of order. A simple layout promotes clarity and structure.
- **Make a strong call to action.** 'We'll see you there' uses inclusive language, emphasising the personal nature of the invitation, and implying that the target customer, upon buying tickets, becomes part of an exclusive, privileged group.
- **Include an appropriate visual image that complements the item or service being promoted.**
- **Add important information that might detract from the overall impact of the message in a less prominent position.**

Plan your sample on the lines provided.

- **If possible, use the brand name in the title.** At least mention the name of the product or service being promoted.
- **Make a direct approach to the reader in the opening statement.** This encourages them to access the product or service being promoted. Use strong adjectives. Create impact with rhyme.
- **Use bullet point lists to clearly organise key information.**
- **Use subheadings and short blocks of text to present the main features being promoted.** Organise the ideas into a logical flow. Present information that details the specific benefits for the target customer. Employ vivid imagery that engages the physical senses. Use the second person mode to create a sense of inclusion and personal invitation. Use emotive language to create a desire to get involved.
- **Use rhetorical questions.**
- **Use highly structured layout to present short lists of data.** Subheadings with colons, bold type and heading hierarchies can be used to add clarity and a sense of order. Ensure that you use a simple layout to promote clarity and structure.
- **Make a strong call to action** encouraging the target reader to respond to your invitation. Inclusive language can emphasise the personal nature of the invitation.
- **Include an appropriate visual image that complements the item or service being promoted.**
- **Add important information that might detract from the overall impact of the message in a less prominent position.** Perhaps use a smaller typeface.

PERSUASIVE TEXT

Opinion piece

READING WORK

Thanks for nothing

In English, we say 'thank you'. In Hawaiian, it's 'mahalo' … and it never seems to end.

There I was, ready to embark on my USA trip of a lifetime, flying Sydney to New York, with a six-hour stopover in Hawaii. In the departure lounge I was first amused and eventually nauseated by being thanked by Hawaiian Airlines staff 'the island way'. For the traditional Hawaiian 'thank you', take 'aloha', add an 'm' and scramble. They thanked passengers for booking the flight and for actually showing up to catch it. They thanked us for our patronage, our passivity, our parenting skills and our patience, which was fast running out. They '*mahalo*ed' us to the very brink of sanity—as if 'aloha' wasn't already enough.

To be sure, on a hot afternoon when a mountain of a man resplendent in a lime green, palm-tree-themed suit booms Hawaiian greetings at you on a melting tarmac in Honolulu, it sounds welcoming and pleasant. But heard repeatedly in announcements over a fuzzy PA system, it loses the magic somehow. Especially when the message goes like this and especially when you note the inescapable fact that you're still in Sydney.

'Mahalo, ladies and gentlemen. Mahalo for your attention to this announcement. Mahalo for listening carefully. This is the last call for flight HA094 boarding from Gate 35. Mahalo for your cooperation. Mahalo for choosing Hawaiian Airlines. This is the final call for Ms Juanita Margarita Angelina Ballerina Smith. Mahalo. Please make your way to Gate 35 immediately—mahalo—as your flight is leaving. (pause … cough) Mahalo.'

We jetted off—with the tardy Ms Smith safely aboard—at around 6:30 pm. After being relentlessly thanked for our cooperation, for putting our seatbelts on, for eating our dinner, for putting our 'trash' away, for returning our tray tables to the upright position and for listening, I looked out of my window to see Hawaii's islands below us—a cluster of green volcanoes rising steeply out of the blue. They give you the feeling that they just emerged from the sea that morning. Almost as special as the delightful vista was the cheery thought that Elvis had seen them too—and somehow that made up for the humid stench and the mushy airline food.

As we touched down at the scorching Honolulu International terminal, I was reassured to find that no-one had bombed Runway B since 1945, or at least if they had, someone had thoughtfully repaired it. A rainbow welcomed us on arrival—a giant lei in the sky—rewarding us for surviving the long flight. Before I could stop myself, I let a *mahalo* of my own slip out.

Hawaii was hot, which put me in a bad mood that worsened at the sight of the décor in Arrivals. It had a distinctively '80s feel. I didn't see Tom Magnum but I certainly felt his presence. The nostalgia of it all was enough to make you rush out to buy an aloha shirt and grow a moustache. Dazzled by the wicker furniture, the hibiscus-print cushions, the bamboo wallpaper and the inhumane wall murals, I sank damply into a peculiar massage chair offering weary travellers a good jiggle for a modest $5. A lengthy search of the entire terminal building eventually resulted in a surprisingly unfair currency exchange that had me wishing I'd brought a calculator. The massage chair relieved me of my Yankee cash, firstly through the $5 fee and more cunningly by vibrating the coins out of my pocket and into the recesses between the seat cushions that only the most seasoned traveller would dare explore. And I was certainly no seasoned traveller, although I was quite well marinated by the time I planted my feet on mainland USA.

'We hope you enjoyed your flight. Mahalo.'

- This common expression is **ironic**, meaning that the speaker is not thankful at all. It is also a pun, with the meaning being that the people who keep repeating the Hawaiian word for 'thank you' are doing it for no reason.
- This sentence begins a **sequence** detailing the list of things the writer was thanked for, all of which would not ordinarily elicit thanks.
- Italics and quotation marks are used here for **comic effect**. The word has been used as a verb in an unconventional way, by applying the regular verb rule of the past tense.
- This **throwaway line** hints that the author is equally annoyed by the constant habit of saying 'aloha' as well, giving us insight into their attitude as a traveller.
- A strong adjective is used for **comical emphasis** of the silliness of the situation.
- The word 'mahalo' is repeated in a succession of sentences, creating **hyperbole** to prove the author's point and perhaps to provoke an annoyed response in the reader and thus create empathy.
- An unusual verb is used to report that the plane took off. This creates a more **dramatic effect** on the scene being described.
- This is a **reference** to the previously quoted announcement in the terminal building that featured repeated thanks and a message to a late passenger.
- This is an **allusion** to the famous rock'n'roll singer Elvis Presley, who made a number of films in the Hawaiian islands in the 1950s and 60s.
- This is an **understatement** ('reassured' that the runway was still there) and an allusion to the bombing of the Hawaiian naval base at Pearl Harbor in World War II.
- This is an **allusion** to a popular television show in the 1980s called *Magnum PI* about a private investigator who wore aloha shirts and a big moustache. This impression of Hawaii was the dominant one in that period. Ironically, the real Polynesian culture of Hawaii was largely ignored in favour of this kitschy, fabricated television version.
- This is a **humorous euphemism** for a massage, which adds a visual image of the author being shaken (a sight-gag) for amusing effect.
- The writer uses a common **colloquialism** for 'American'.
- The author's major criticism is highlighted once more by making it the last word of the text. The sentence is presented as a flight attendant's announcement to create a **sense of unity** across the text, harking back to the earlier announcements quoted by the author.

Literal questions

Hint: Read the text carefully to locate specific facts and details.

1 What does the word 'mahalo' mean? ____________________

2 What are the 'green volcanoes' mentioned by the writer? ____________________

3 Why did the writer need to conduct a lengthy search of the terminal building in Honolulu?

____

Interpretive questions

Hint: These questions require you to combine facts and details to synthesise the meaning.

4 With what aspect of Hawaii was the writer most impressed?

____

5 To which famous American singer does the writer allude in the fourth paragraph (beginning line 29)?

____

6 What is the purpose of the first sentence of the final paragraph (lines 36–37)?

____

Hint: Only one answer option is correct. Use the process of elimination to work through the options.

7 What is the purpose of the phrase 'on a melting tarmac in Honolulu'?

a to indicate that the climate is hot **b** to reveal the poor condition of the runway

c to describe volcanic lava

8 Which statement is true about the missing passenger who was paged over the public address system?

a she missed her flight **b** she had an unusual name **c** her name was made up to create humour

9 Whose speech is the detail about 'returning our tray tables to the upright position' mimicking?

a Hawaiians **b** the writer's **c** a flight attendant's

10 What is the main purpose of this blog?

a to entertain **b** to provide travel advice

c to assess the services offered by Hawaiian Airlines

Applied questions

Hint: This question requires you to understand a text's implications to infer meaning from the text.

11 To what is the writer alluding in the reference to 'Runway B'?

a a plane crash

b the bombing of Pearl Harbor in World War II

c poor maintenance procedures

12 How could the writer's objection to the use of the word 'mahalo' best be summarised? *Hint: This question requires you to make an informed judgement based on the evidence.*

a The writer thinks that when it is overused it sounds insincere.

b The writer doesn't like thankful people.

c The writer feels that people should only thank him in English.

PERSUASIVE TEXT

Opinion piece

SPELLING WORK

List Words

All of the words in the box below appear in the text 'Thanks for nothing'.

embark	inescapable	listening	terminal	nostalgia
departure	relentlessly	volcanoes	thoughtfully	moustache
announcements	cooperation	vista	worsened	peculiar

1 Circle the correct spelling.

a imbark	embark	embarc		**b** deparchure	departuer	departure
c announcement	anouncement	anouncment		**d** inexcapable	inescapeble	inescapable
e rellentlessly	relentlessly	relentlesly		**f** cooperation	coperashon	cooperashen
g lisening	listening	lissening		**h** volcanoes	volcanos	vollcanos
i vysta	vissta	vista		**j** terminal	terminal	terminel

2 This is a two-step task.

a First circle all the affixes below that appear in the list words.

b Then write the affixes you circled into the boxes below to classify them as either prefixes or suffixes.

iar	*em*	*gia*	*port*	*ity*	*ab*	*ness*	*fully*	*pro*	*auto*	*co*
lessly	*mis*	*able*	*de*	*ments*	*in*	*ice*	*ic*	*sub*	*ing*	*re*

Prefixes		**Suffixes**	

3 Which word in each pair has one or more silent letter?

a island, final **b** delightful, steeply **c** wishing, bombed **d** flight, fuzzy

e myself, listening **f** jiggle, cough **g** thought, currency **h** magic, hour

4 Which word in each pair is spelt phonetically (as it sounds)? Circle your selections.

a patience, green **b** vista, décor **c** attention, jetted **d** mushy, moustache

e dinner, thoughtfully **f** relentlessly, pleasant **g** international, traveller **h** lei, wicker

i enough, mood **j** modest, certainly **k** booking, special **l** position, away

m tarmac, especially **n** planted, Hawaiian **o** embark, search

5 Form twelve compound words out of these parts.

life	air	main	men	paper	some	bow	wall
right	how	run	stop	lines	seat	way	noon
up	after	belts	land	gentle	over	rain	time

____________ ____________ ____________ ____________

____________ ____________ ____________ ____________

____________ ____________ ____________ ____________

PERSUASIVE TEXT

Opinion piece

1 Complete these word families by using the base word to create other related words. The word in capital letters is the base word. You will need to adjust the spelling to form related words, following the usual spelling rules and conventions.

HAWAII **a** ____________ (a person from Hawaii)

DEPART **b** ____________ (left) **c** ____________ (is leaving)

ANNOUNCE **d** ____________ (said) **e** ____________ (speaker)

LISTEN **f** ____________ (hears) **g** ____________ (heard)

VOLCANO **h** ____________ (volcano-like) **i** ____________ (more than one)

COOPERATE **j** ____________ (helpful) **k** ____________ (worked together)

2 Find homophones for these words in the text 'Thanks for nothing'. Write them on the lines provided.

a to ____________ **b** our ____________

c you're ____________ **d** by ____________

3 List all the numbers mentioned in the text. Ignore any repeated instances. *Hint: Some numbers may be shown as numerals, while others may be spelt out in words.*

____________ ____________ ____________ ____________

____________ ____________ ____________

There are many **idioms** that relate to travel—by road, sea, air, rail and many other forms of transport.

4 Fill in the missing words to complete these idioms and their meanings.

minute	red-eye	home	rock	light	traveller
beaten	miss	nothing	itchy	boat	road

a We're all in the same ____________. Everyone else is in the same unpleasant or difficult situation as you.

b to ____________ the boat — to fail to seize on an opportunity by not acting decisively or quickly

c Don't ____________ the boat. — Do nothing to cause trouble in an otherwise stable situation.

d to hit the ____________ — to start out on a journey

e on the ____________ stretch — nearing the end of something, like a work project or a long journey

f Thanks for ____________. — a way of criticising someone for what they did to disadvantage you

g a seasoned ____________ — an experienced tourist who has visited many different countries

h having ____________ feet — desiring to travel to see new places and have new experiences

i He talks a mile a ____________. — He speaks very quickly and is hard to keep up with.

j to go off the ____________ track — to travel via less popular routes to certain destinations

k to travel ____________ — to take very little luggage with you when you travel

l to catch the ____________ — to take a flight departing late at night and travelling until morning

PERSUASIVE TEXT

GRAMMAR WORK

Connectives are words and phrases that have a linking effect in texts. Connective language helps us make transitions from one sentence to the next. They can compare or contrast ideas. They can also show relationships of cause and effect, and indicate sequence.

1 What are three jobs that connectives can do to create transitions in texts?

____________________ ____________________ ____________________

2 Complete the table of connectives by writing each one in the correct column, based on the job it performs in a text.

First	In the same manner	Like	Finally	In contrast	Unlike
Consequently	Similarly	Next	Comparably	As a result	However

Comparing two similar things or ideas	Contrasting two different things or ideas	Demonstrating cause-and-effect relationships	Indicating a specific order or sequence
Just as	Conversely	Since	**a**
b	**c**	For this reason	Second
d	**e**	**f**	**g**
h	Whereas	Accordingly	Then
i	**j**	**k**	**l**

3 Identify the connective words and phrases in these lines. Write the words or phrases on the lines provided. *Hint: They are all connectives that indicate sequence.*

a Line 6 ____________ **b** Lines 23–24 ____________ **c** Line 31 ____________

d Line 34 ____________ **e** Line 42 ____________ **f** Line 47 ____________

4 Use connectives from the choices below to complete these sentences.

like because since although whereas

a ____________ we took off, I haven't left my seat.

b It's strange but ____________ most people like travelling, I detest it.

c Hawaii is a great holiday destination ____________ it is quite expensive to take the whole family.

d Our flight was delayed ____________ of one passenger's late check-in.

e ____________ my travelling companion I too became ill on my last trip overseas.

5 Use connectives from the table in Question 2 to link these pairs of sentences together.

a ____________ let me say, 'Welcome!' ____________ allow me to carry your bags for you!

b A violent thunderstorm rolled in over the airport. ____________ our flight was cancelled.

c I ran out of money while on holiday. ____________ I was unable to do any shopping.

d The islands of Hawaii are very beautiful with many lovely, natural vistas. ____________ they are a popular destination for photographers from all over the world.

e Our helicopter pilot told us some crash stories as we hovered over one of Hawaii's active volcanoes. ____________ I quickly became frightened and couldn't wait until the flight was over.

f Hawaii was very hot. ____________, when I returned home to Hobart, it was freezing cold.

PERSUASIVE TEXT

Opinion piece

PUNCTUATION WORK

1 Find examples of each of the following quotations in the text 'Thanks for nothing' and write them on the lines provided. *Hint: Look for opening and closing punctuation marks.*

a a quoted phrase and a quoted single word in the same line

____________________ ____________________

b a single word quote in italics, where a single word is presented in quotation marks within a sentence

____

c a sentence quote, where a whole sentence is presented in italics at the end of a paragraph

____

2 Write the line numbers where a paragraph quote starts and finishes in the text. *Hint: Look for where a whole paragraph spoken by someone else is quoted in the text.*

Starting line number: ________ Finishing line number: ________

Capital letters signal two main textual features: the beginning of a sentence and the presentation of proper nouns. When you're looking for proper nouns, scan the text for capital letters. Obviously some proper nouns may also be hiding at the beginning of sentences where they would have a capital letter anyway.

3 Find the following proper nouns in the text. Write the answers on the lines provided.

a a man's given name and surname ________________

b a slang term for 'American' ________ **c** a famous singer's first name ________

d NSW's largest city ________ **e** an area of the airport ________

f a woman's name ________________

g an island state ________ **h** an airline ________

i the capital of Hawaii ________ **j** a language ________

k a city in mainland USA ________

4 What do these abbreviations mean? Write definitions in your own words.

a PA system ________________

b HA094 ________________

c '80s ________________

d USA ________________

5 Find these punctuation marks in the text by using the line numbers as hints. To answer, write the word that comes immediately before the punctuation mark or the word that it is within.

a ellipsis (line 2) ________ **b** apostrophe (line 26) ________

c dash (line 23) ________ **d** comma (line 31) ________

e colon (line 23) ________ **f** parentheses (line 22) ________

g apostrophe (line 37) ________ **h** hyphen (line 39) ________

PERSUASIVE TEXT
Opinion piece

WRITING WORK 1

Opinion pieces

An **opinion piece** is a persuasive text that can be written or spoken. It presents the writer or speaker's personal opinion about a topic in the form of an extended response. Opinion pieces are designed to entertain. The composer takes a deliberately extreme or exaggerated position on a simple issue. Humour is often a feature of these texts.

In opinion pieces the impact often depends on the responder's ability to recognise familiar frustrations that arise from everyday scenarios. The composer's tone is very important in persuasive opinion pieces. So are these elements:

- a topic that elicits a strong response
- a number of clear key points that build in intensity from least to most significant
- points presented in paragraphs in a logical progression
- bold statements aimed at provoking a response
- a call for the responder to sympathise and agree with the composer's point of view.

The language style used by a composer is called the **register**. Each register is suited to different situations and audiences. Some registers are highly inappropriate in certain contexts. For example, toilet jokes would not be appropriate in a formal police interview. The choice of language register depends on the composer's purpose, audience and topic.

The five main registers are:

1 **Static register** never changes. It is used in very formal settings like a courtroom.
2 **Formal register** is required in many situations, such as a university lecture.
3 **Consultative register** is less formal. It is used by consultants (including lawyers or doctors).
4 **Casual register** is informal (colloquial). It often includes slang and is used between friends.
5 **Intimate register** is reserved for use by people in close relationships, like two siblings.

Here are some specific **language features and techniques** composers use to create opinion pieces:

- first person narrative mode, to emphasise that this is the composer's personal point of view
- direct addressing of the audience using personal pronouns (for example, *I'm sure you'd agree …*)
- strong adjectives and intensifying adverbs (for example, *hideously ugly*)
- vivid imagery and strong contrasts
- connectives, to create momentum
- emotive language
- truncation (short, cut-off sentences)
- contractions (such as *can't* rather than *cannot*)
- anecdotes (personal stories)
- analogies (detailed comparisons between things)
- allusions (references to other works, people or events)
- imperative tone created with high modality verbs (such as *must* rather than *may*)
- rhetorical questions
- hyperbole (deliberately extreme exaggeration)
- a final punchline.

1 What is another word for level of language usage? ______________________

2 What is the most informal language style? ______________________

3 What is hyperbole? ______________________

4 Which register is most likely to be used in these settings?

a a police report ______________ **b** a family video commentary ______________

c a dental appointment ______________ **d** a wedding ______________

5 Make a list of ten things that the writer of the text 'Thanks for nothing' criticises about his experiences from the time that he enters the airport terminal in Sydney to the time that he finally lands at his destination in New York.

6 Complete the table by identifying the language technique or feature at work in the quotations from the text 'Thanks for nothing'. *Hint: All the answers are listed here. You need to find out which is which!*

alliteration	adjective	metaphor	intensifying adverb	colloquialism for 'American'
visual image	tactile image	repetition	direct speech	allusion (to a TV show)

Quotation from the text	Feature or technique
a Mahalo, ladies and gentlemen. Mahalo for your attention to this announcement. Mahalo for listening carefully.	
b a cluster of green volcanoes rising steeply out of the blue	
c a mountain of a man	
d on a melting tarmac in Honolulu	
e After being relentlessly thanked for our cooperation	
f the delightful vista	
g A rainbow welcomed us on arrival—a giant lei in the sky	
h I didn't see Tom Magnum but I certainly felt his presence.	
i The massage chair relieved me of my Yankee cash	
j 'We hope you enjoyed your flight. Mahalo.'	

PERSUASIVE TEXT

Opinion piece

WRITING SAMPLE

Here is a sample text showing you how to structure and write an opinion piece.

Squid's Seafood Restaurant

✱ **Use a literal title so readers can identify the topic.**

Wondering where your next meal is coming from? Then you can't afford to eat at Squid's. Their prices will certainly leave a bad taste in your mouth—that's guaranteed! And their oysters too. I can assure you Squid's seafood is caught fresh from an open drain near you each and every morning.

✱ **Begin the piece strongly.** This one starts with a question then a bold statement: 'you can't afford to eat at Squid's.' It makes a number of points, working from the minor ones to the most important—the writer starts with the prices and the terrible-tasting oysters. The use of first person mode creates a sense of authentic personal commentary. The conversational style wins readers over to the writer's view.

There's plenty of Australian fare on offer, including Road Kill Roo Burgers and Dolphin Mince soup. You're sure to find eating the Warm Eel Salad with Whale Stomach Gravy a memorable experience, especially when served on the Pike Pikelets (with most sharp bits removed). But here's a positive—all orders come with free chef's hairs, while stocks last!

✱ **Use hyperbole to emphasise your major point or theme.** Here we see imaginative inventions of dishes used to exaggerate the horrors of the food. Irony is employed to create humour—the comment about the chef's hairs implies that the chef is balding. Colloquialisms such as the catchphrase 'while stocks last' add to the humorous effect of the observation about the hairs.

When you dine at Squid's, you can feast your eyes on the view of the hulking Snake Pit floating dock, where if you strain your neck you may even catch a brief glimpse of some clean water. You can inhale diesel fumes straight from the watercraft moored at the Marina. You'll be dazzled by the kaleidoscope of broken glass sparkling away in the sands of the foreshore. And the heady aroma created by boat owners emptying their chemical toilets over the side really complements the taste of the house wine. Watch as seagulls foul the outside tables and frenzied sparrows kill each other over leftover plates of bruschetta. I'm sure you'll agree that these delights are just too good to pass up.

✱ **Use boldly critical statements.** This writer gives the impression that he is airing his views on a pet hate. The idea is that he has a lot to get off his chest about the topic. Strong adjectives and intensifiers add impact to descriptions. Here we read of 'the hulking' floating dock, the 'heady aroma' of chemical toilets and the 'frenzied sparrows'. Switching from short, sharp sentences early in the piece to longer, more complex ones midway through has the effect of illustrating that the writer is getting more emotionally worked up. The writer addresses the audience directly and assumes their agreement, such as in the line 'I'm sure you'll agree.'

But by far the worst thing about this dive is the long waiting times. You could easily make dining at Squid's an all-day experience. If you go in for breakfast, you'll most likely wait until lunchtime for your food to arrive. In fact, some people stay until they're operating off the dinner menu and make a whole day of it.

✱ **Use strong connectives.** They help create a sense of momentum and expectation. The first sentence of the paragraph foreshadows something worse to come. Emotive and descriptive language creates a sarcastic effect—pretending to praise while actually criticising. Here the writer aims to provoke an emotive response in his readers with phrases like 'an all-day experience' and 'make a whole day of it'.

Regular diners at Squid's should be entitled to the following membership bonuses:

- NSW State Ambulance Service Priority Transport
- A free funeral if caused by your dining experience
- McDonald's vouchers.

Who's with me on this?

✱ **Make a final call for your audience's sympathy and agreement with your assessment of the topic.** This writer has constructed a hypothetical list of demands to which diners should be entitled. The list of supposed benefits highlights the imagined risk of illness or death (or at least hunger) associated with dining at Squid's.

By the way Squid's are very happy to accept any credit card. In fact, they still haven't returned mine.

✱ **Finish with a strong final statement.** This one ends with an ironic joke, with the punchline finishing off the piece.

PERSUASIVE TEXT

WRITING YOUR OWN SAMPLE

Plan your sample on the lines provided.

- **Use a literal title so readers can identify the topic.**
- **Begin the piece strongly.** Consider a question followed by a bold statement. From there, add more points to strengthen the argument. Make a number of points, working from the minor ones to the most important. Write in first person mode to create a sense of authentic personal commentary. The personal tone is important if you hope to capture and maintain the interest of your readers. Employ a conversational style to win your readers over to your view.
- **Use hyperbole to emphasise your major point or theme.** Use irony to create humour.
- **Use boldly critical statements.** Try to give the impression that you are airing your views on a pet hate. The idea is that you have a lot to get off your chest about the topic. Use strong adjectives and intensifiers to add impact to descriptions. Switch from short, sharp sentences early in the piece to longer, more complex ones midway through. This has the effect of illustrating that you are getting more emotionally worked up. Directly address the audience and assume their agreement.
- **Use strong connectives.** They help you create a sense of momentum and expectation. Use emotive and descriptive language.
- **Make a final call for your audience's sympathy and agreement with your assessment of the topic.**
- Finish with a strong final statement.

PERSUASIVE TEXT

Film review

READING WORK

Batman is dead (to me)

Only six actors can say they've had the honour of playing the Caped Crusader—oh, make that seven if you must include Ben Affleck. Creator Bob Kane invented the comic-book hero in 1939—Batman, that is, not Ben Affleck.

Although Lewis Wilson was the first actor to play the character, Adam West's incarnation of Batman is the most memorable because of the extraordinarily successful *Batman* television series of 1966–68. The television series was intended to be a lighthearted swipe at the superhero genre. Its ludicrous villains and preposterous death traps set by villains such as the Joker made it great fun to watch. Faithful viewers would tune in—'same bat time, same bat channel'—to see the Dynamic Duo escape certain death with the aid of various items from Batman's famed utility belt.

Later, a series of Hollywood blockbusters returned the Batman character to its original, darker comic-book style. Holy switcheroo, Batman! Bat-fans have been treated to performances by Michael Keaton (*Batman*, 1989 and *Batman Returns*, 1992), Val Kilmer (*Batman Forever*, 1995) and George Clooney (*Batman and Robin*, 1997). The currently reigning and undisputedly superior Bat-actor is Christian Bale, whose performances in *Batman Begins* (2005) and *The Dark Knight* (2008) earned a new generation of fans and millions of dollars in box-office takings.

Now we turn to Ben Affleck's ill-fated turn in the cape in the hideous *Batman v Superman: Dawn of Justice* (2016). The film begins with a cool idea, posing the question of whether Batman's brand of vigilante, vendetta-driven violence is really heroic or just thuggish. But cool soon turns to stone cold. By the end of the ordeal of watching this film, most of the audience have frozen solid.

Batman is presented as a grumpy retired superhero with no logical motive behind anything he does. He explains to Alfred, the butler, that Superman's power to wipe out humanity makes him dangerous. For this reason, and also because he messed up the Batmobile, Batman decides he has to kill him. Unlike every other incarnation of Batman, this one kills people—gleefully. The audience is left unsure whether Batman is a suave saviour or just a belligerent badboy with bats in his belfry.

The perpetual night-time of the setting is depressing, the script is shoddy, the twists implausible and the special effects predictable. I struggled to suspend my disbelief as I watched this pair of souped-up superheroes smash an unconvincing CGI city to smithereens. And to add injury to insult, Hans Zimmer's musical score delivers a truly punishing orchestral assault. As soon as I returned home after seeing this flick, I called Commissioner Gordon to let him know that this time the Caped Crusader really is dead and buried.

- The **title** provides a clue about the reviewer's topic and opinions.
- The fact that the reviewer sees playing Batman as an honour tells us that he admires the character and is a Batman fan.
- The **specific details** pertinent to Batman's origins are given early in the text to establish the context for the review.
- The **connective statement** 'although' signals a contrast to come. The writer contrasts the first actor with the most memorable one.
- We're given the **explanation** that the television series was not meant to be taken seriously and we accept the reviewer's authoritative statement on this.
- One specific villain is mentioned by name, an **allusion** that assumes the reader's prior knowledge of the Batman franchise's characters.
- A common **idiom** that arose from the television series is used to signal to the reader that all Batman fans are united by their knowledge of the world of the character.
- This is a **synonym** for 'successful films'.
- A series of Batman films are presented in **date order**, with no commentary on any except the last two. In this way, the reviewer has set the reader up to receive the evaluation that Christian Bale is the best of the actors to play Batman.
- The **negative language** 'ill-fated' and 'hideous' reveals the reviewer's opinion of the film that starred Ben Affleck.
- An **extended metaphor**, also a play on the word 'cool', is used to describe the audience's reaction to the film that the reviewer dislikes.
- The final two paragraphs are spent panning many aspects of the film—including the plot, the setting, the script and the special effects.
- A **colloquial expression** for a special kind of madness where the victim believes in totally implausible fantasies.
- This **synonym** for 'film' has connotations that the film is being dismissively deemed a trivial, inconsequential one, in contrast to the other films which were called 'Hollywood blockbusters'.
- The reviewer **transitions** into the world of fantasy to make his last definitive statement about the film, implying that Affleck's performance has killed the Batman character forever, at least in his opinion.

PERSUASIVE TEXT

Film review

COMPREHENSION WORK

Literal questions

Hint: Read the text carefully to locate specific facts and details.

1 In what year did Bob Kane create the Batman character?

a 1943 b 1966 c 1939

2 Which two adjectives emphasise the silliness of the television show *Batman*?

______________________ ______________________

3 How many Batman movies have been made since 1988? ______________________

4 Which of the following is correct?

a Adam West was the first actor to play Batman.
b Lewis Wilson was the first actor to play Batman.
c George Clooney was the first actor to play Batman.

Interpretive questions

Hint: These questions require you to combine facts and details to synthesise the meaning.

5 Which of the following is correct?

a The television show version of Batman was the most similar to the original Batman character.
b The films made since the 1980s have portrayed Batman most like the original comic-book character.
c Only the films starring Christian Bale are like the original Batman character.

6 Of which literary technique is the phrase 'vigilante, vendetta-fuelled violence' an example?

____

7 What is the reviewer's opinion of *Batman versus Superman: Dawn of Justice*?

____

8 What criticism does the reviewer make about the setting of the Ben Affleck film in the last paragraph?

____

9 What is the most likely meaning of the abbreviation 'CGI'?

a Computer Graphic Imagery b Commissioner Gordon's Initiative c Convincingly Generated Images

Applied questions

Hint: This question requires you to understand a text's implications to infer meaning from the text.

10 What does the reviewer feel about Hans Zimmer's work in *Batman versus Superman: Dawn of Justice*?

____

11 Why do the words 'same bat time, same bat channel' appear in quotation marks in the text?

a because they need emphasising
b because they are quoting from the television show
c because they are addressing bats

12 Why does the author give this review the title 'Batman is dead (to me)'?

a Because he's disappointed in the latest Batman film and it's diminished his interest in the character.
b Because all the actors who've played Batman are now dead so technically Batman is dead as well.
c Because he never really liked Batman anyway and has now lost interest in the character permanently.

PERSUASIVE TEXT

Film review

SPELLING WORK

List Words

All of the words in the box below appear in the text 'Batman is dead (to me)'.

genre	villains	incarnation	extraordinarily	heroic
memorable	predictable	violence	orchestral	dynamic
successful	preposterous	implausible	disbelief	hideous

1 Find the list words that contain these words.

a carnation ____________ **b** poster ____________

c memo ____________ **d** ordinarily ____________

e predict ____________ **f** imp ____________

g success ____________ **h** hide ____________

i belief ____________ **j** orchestra ____________

k hero ____________ **l** villa ____________

2 Count the number of two-syllable words in the list and write it here: ____________

3 Count the number of three-syllable words in the list and write it here: ____________

4 How many syllables do these words contain?

a implausible ____________ **b** preposterous ____________ **c** extraordinarily ____________

5 This is a three-step puzzle.

a First separate 33 individual words by breaking up these letter chains.
Hint: Fifteen of them are list words.

actgenrehumanitypreposterousideareturned
implausibleblockbustersvillainsBatmanincarnation
superiormemorablecapeextraordinarilycomics
heroicfilmhideousmusicpredictableview
violencechannelsuccessfulbutlerorchestralcity
dynamicfansdisbeliefbrandfun

b Next find the 33 words in the puzzle grid below. Circle each letter as you use it and cross the word off your list. *Hints: The words are hidden in every direction—across, up, down, diagonally and even backwards. Some letters are used by more than one word.*

c Now that you've found all the words, write down the remaining unused letters in order. They will spell out the hidden answer to this question: Who has Batman sworn that he will catch and bring to justice?

Answer: ________________________________

____

C	H	A	N	N	E	L	R	E	L	T	U	B
H	S	N	I	A	L	L	I	V	A	L	L	G
U	I	M	P	L	A	U	S	I	B	L	E	E
M	N	D	R	V	I	E	W	O	T	N	H	X
A	C	H	E	R	O	I	C	L	R	N	E	T
N	A	B	P	O	M	D	C	E	R	U	M	R
I	R	R	O	D	U	I	S	N	A	F	E	A
T	N	A	S	Y	S	S	A	C	T	O	M	O
Y	A	N	T	N	I	B	A	E	C	D	O	R
R	T	D	E	A	C	E	O	O	K	E	R	D
O	I	S	R	M	D	L	M	I	N	N	A	I
I	O	G	O	I	C	I	T	Y	O	R	B	N
R	N	S	U	C	C	E	S	S	F	U	L	A
E	T	H	S	S	A	F	I	L	M	T	E	R
P	R	E	D	I	C	T	A	B	L	E	M	I
U	C	I	O	R	C	H	E	S	T	R	A	L
S	T	C	A	P	E	B	A	T	M	A	N	Y
B	L	O	C	K	B	U	S	T	E	R	S	Y

PERSUASIVE TEXT

Film review

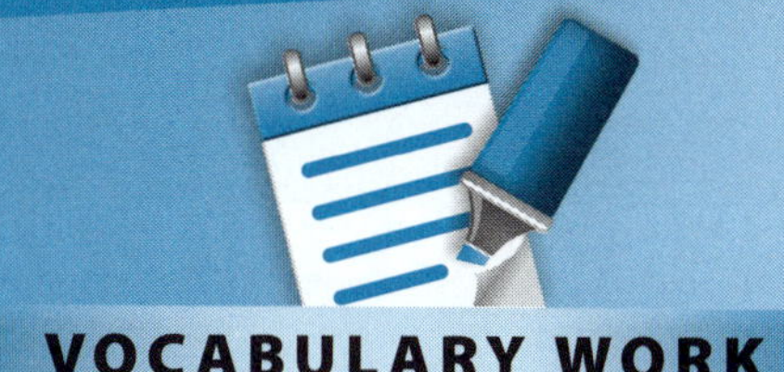

VOCABULARY WORK

1 Look at these terms taken from the text 'Batman is dead (to me)'. Read each one in its context, then when you have worked out their meanings write them next to their definitions.

television series	lighthearted	shoddy	belligerent	certain death
thuggish	ludicrous	motive	ill-fated	box-office takings
superhero	comic-book	perpetual	suave	blockbusters
vigilante	CGI city	smithereens	flick	twists

a ______________________ brutish and mindlessly violent

b ______________________ globally popular films that make massive profits

c ______________________ angry and mean

d ______________________ ridiculous, unrealistic, unbelievable

e ______________________ unauthorised crime fighter who metes out justice as he sees fit

f ______________________ setting created using computer generated imagery

g ______________________ pamphlet with stories made from drawings and text

h ______________________ sequence of programs screened free to air

i ______________________ tiny bits

j ______________________ doomed to failure

k ______________________ sure fatality

l ______________________ film

m ______________________ a fictional character with special powers, often a rescuer

n ______________________ not serious

o ______________________ ongoing, endless

p ______________________ unexpected endings or plot developments

q ______________________ smoothly sophisticated

r ______________________ poor quality

s ______________________ reason for doing something

t ______________________ profits on ticket sales

2 Write the numbers of these Bat-related idioms on the lines provided.

a ____ make someone really annoyed by your behaviour

b ____ unable to see very well (or at all)

c ____ an exclamation about a sudden, unexpected exchange

d ____ someone who has made a silly mistake

e ____ make a telephone call

f ____ hurry to the Batcave by sliding down the Batpoles

g ____ the meeting place and start time will be the same again

h ____ to have something wrong with the way you're thinking

i ____ extremely fast

j ____ didn't react in a surprised way at all

1 'Holy Switcheroo, Batman!'
2 'Same bat time, same bat channel.'
3 'To the Batpoles, Robin!'
4 get on the Batphone
5 didn't bat an eyelid
6 to drive someone batty
7 a dingbat
8 blind as a bat
9 to have bats in the belfry
10 like a bat out of hell

1 Choose the correct verb form in each pair and write it on the line provided. *Hint: You need to make sure the verb matches the specific tense of the sentence.*

a Present tense: Ben Affleck ________________ (played / plays) Batman in the film *Batman versus Superman: Dawn of Justice.*

b Past tense: Adam West ________________ (played / is playing) Batman in the hit TV series of the 1960s.

2 Do the same but without the tense clues this time. *Hint: Use the other words in the sentence as contextual clues to determine the tense.*

a The character of Batman ____________ (is / was) still very popular among fans all over the world today.

b No doubt there ________________ (was / will be) new interpretations of the Batman character to come.

c The Joker ____________________ (will be / was) the villain in *The Dark Knight*, a film released in 2008.

d In 1995 Val Kilmer ____________________ (starring / starred) in *Batman Forever*, a forgettable effort.

e George Clooney's version of Batman ____________________ (was / is) voted underwhelming in the years following its 1997 release.

f Michael Keaton played the character in 1989, redefining how people ____________________ (viewed / views) the character.

g Christian Bale ____________________ (will be / was) remembered as the best Batman for many fans.

3 Organise these alphabetically listed words by writing them in the correct columns.

absolutely	begins	belligerent	called	certainly	channel
character	comic-book	currently	dangerous	dead	delivers
depressingly	dollars	earned	explains	extraordinarily	faithful
fun	generation	gleefully	grumpy	heroic	humanity
idea	implausibly	include	kill	logically	ludicrous
memorable	motive	playing	poorly	power	returned
smash	suave	superior	surely	television	thuggishly
treated	unconvincingly	understated	unsure	viewers	watch

Nouns	Adjectives	Verbs	Adverbs

PERSUASIVE TEXT

Film review

PUNCTUATION WORK

Capital letters

Capital letters are used in two main ways in text. The first letter of a sentence is always capitalised. The first letters of a person's first and last names are capitalised. Proper nouns that name well-known events, places and objects are also worthy of a beginning with a capital letter.

Another use for capital letters is in acronyms and initialisms. An **acronym** is a word that has been created using the first letters of the words that make up a multiple-word name. Acronyms must be pronounceable without adding any other letters, such as vowels. Examples are NATO (North Atlantic Treaty Organisation) and UNICEF (United Nations International Children's Emergency Fund). An **initialism** is very similar. The difference is that an initialism may be pronounced as a series of letters, without actually forming a pronounceable word. Examples include the UK (the United Kingdom) and the FBI (the Federal Bureau of Investigation).

1 Why are the following words and phrases expressed with capital initials? Write your explanations on the lines. *Hint: Use the line numbers to locate the word or phrase and read it in its context in the text 'Batman is dead (to me)'.*

a Batman (line 5) ____________________

b Ben Affleck (line 4) ____________________

c Caped Crusader (line 3) ____________________

d Hollywood (line 15) ____________________

e Now (line 23) ____________________

f CGI (line 39) ____________________

2 What does '1966–68' mean? Write this expression out in words.

____

3 Which line of the text is exclamatory? Line ________

4 Rewrite these statements as questions. *Hint: Sentence starters have been provided to help you.*

a Line 10 Was the television ____________________

b Line 25 But is ____________________

c Line 32 Does Batman ____________________

5 Which words and phrases could be presented in parentheses without altering the meaning or impact of the text? *Hint: The line numbers tell you where to look in the text.*

a Line 9 ____________________ **b** Line 13 ____________________

c Line 32 ____________________

6 Which lines could have exclamation marks added to them to strengthen the impact of the statements? *Hint: There are three.*

____

When we encounter **connectives** in texts, usual practice is to set the connective clause off with a comma. This separates it from the remaining part of the sentence, emphasising a contrast or comparison.

7 In the text 'Batman is dead (to me)' connective statements appear in the lines listed below. Each is followed by a comma. Find all the connective statements and write each one on the line provided.

a Line 7 ____________________ **b** Line 15 ____________________

c Line 27 ____________________ **d** Line 33 ____________________

PERSUASIVE TEXT

Film review

WRITING WORK 1

Reviews

A **review** is an evaluative text written to convey a person's opinion of a particular subject. It may be a film, as in the text 'Batman is dead (to me'), a book, an event, a restaurant, a travel destination or virtually any other subject. When a writer lets readers know their attitude toward their subject through their choice of words, we describe it as **tone**. Most often, readers are led to feel the same way that the author appears to feel about the topic they are presenting. In the Batman review, we notice that the writer's tone is never truly objective (unbiased). Midway through the review, the tone becomes critical of the 2016 film *Batman versus Superman: Dawn of Justice.*

Reviews can be considered informative texts when they are written independently. But certain reviewers are paid to present a positive review of a particular product. These reviews are persuasive texts aimed at making us want to buy or use a product or service. Negative reviews, such as our text, can also be persuasive when the reviewer seeks to influence the reader to adopt the opinion presented in the review. An assessment is made of *Batman versus Superman: Dawn of Justice* and information about the film's contents is presented in a biased way that is aimed at persuading the reader to side with the reviewer.

Some **structural features** of a review include:

- an informative title
- basic information such as names of people and titles of films that the reader may find useful
- paragraphs of information presented in a logical order
- an introductory statement that may include contextual details
- facts, financial figures and statistics about the success of the item
- brief anecdotes
- a clear statement presenting the reviewer's main opinion about the subject
- supporting reasons for the reviewer's opinion
- the personal thoughts and expectations of the reviewer
- comments on the overall style and quality of the subject
- a detailed evaluation of some individual aspects of the subject
- a punchy concluding statement
- a rating system that incorporates visual symbols, such as a five-star rating.

Some common **language features** found in a review include:

- first person mode and second person when addressing the reader directly
- persuasive statements rating the subject under review
- quotes from authoritative people or others linked to the subject
- commands, imperatives and high modality language
- emotive language
- superlatives
- exclamations
- hyperbole (deliberate exaggeration)
- questions and rhetorical questions
- allusions that rely on assumed knowledge
- quotations (when the subject is a film, book or other quotable source)
- informal (colloquial) register and a conversational tone
- strong use of irony
- puns and jokes drawing from the subject as a source
- jargon appropriate to the subject.

1 What is another term for 'objective'? ____________________

2 What is the main purpose of a paid persuasive review? ____________________

____

3 What type of facts are presented using numbers about each Batman film mentioned in the text 'Batman is dead (to me)'?

____

4 What do you feel is the reviewer's attitude toward each of the following? Provide supporting evidence.
Hint: Use quotes from the text as supporting evidence that the reviewer uses to reinforce his opinion.

a the *Batman* television series ______________________________

Supporting evidence: ______________________________

b the film *Batman Begins* ______________________________

Supporting evidence: ______________________________

c the special effects in *Batman versus Superman: Dawn of Justice* ______________________________

Supporting evidence: ______________________________

d the music in *Batman versus Superman: Dawn of Justice* ______________________________

Supporting evidence: ______________________________

5 List ten terms that could be considered jargon related to Batman that the reviewer uses in the text.

______________ ______________
______________ ______________
______________ ______________
______________ ______________
______________ ______________

There is often a strong **link between advertising and reviews**. This is particularly evident on the internet. When you intend to buy a product or use a service, it is likely that you'll google to find a product or service review. Perhaps you want to find out whether a film is worth seeing or an album worth buying. Reviewers on the web are usually paid to write positively about products and services, so you can't always be assured of finding an unbiased opinion. Reviewers should make reasonable and well-informed judgements, avoiding manipulation while still telling what they view as the truth about the subject they are reviewing.

6 From this list of review subjects tick any that you have read, listened to or viewed in a publication, online or on television.

☐ movie	☐ software	☐ album (music)	☐ fashion	☐ toy
☐ restaurant	☐ amusement park	☐ hotel	☐ recipe	☐ mobile phone
☐ cosmetic	☐ car	☐ book	☐ airline	☐ school
☐ medical clinic	☐ car repair shop	☐ pet	☐ online course	☐ concert
☐ motorbike	☐ bicycle	☐ computer system	☐ event venue	☐ scooter
☐ computer game	☐ gaming console	☐ brand of television	☐ furniture	☐ sports shoes
☐ holiday destination	☐ television show	☐ food product	☐ gadget	☐ medication

7 Have you ever been influenced to change your decision to buy or use (or not buy or use) something because of a review you encountered? Circle *yes* or *no*. Yes No

PERSUASIVE TEXT

Film review

WRITING SAMPLE

Here is a sample text showing you how to structure and write a review.

Sample text	Notes
The Phantom: a review by Danny Foong	**Use an informative title that clearly states the topic.**
The Phantom is one of my favourite comic books and I have immense admiration for its creator Lee Falk, so naturally I greeted the news that they were making a multi-million dollar film with great excitement.	**Present an introductory statement that establishes the context.** Basic information such as the title of the film (or the subject under review) and the comic character's creator is included for the reader's reference.
My excitement was rewarded—it's a great film. The plot pits the Phantom (Billy Zane) against the evil Xander Drax (Treat Williams), who hopes to use the power of three magical skulls to control the world. The Phantom teams up with the lovely Diana Palmer (Kristy Swanson), Hero (his horse) and Devil (his pet wolf) to thwart Drax's plans.	**Make a clear statement that provides your overall opinion about the subject.** Here the reviewer clearly states his opinion: 'it's a great film'. The text is structured so that each paragraph presents information in a logical order. The writer has used parentheses to name both the characters and actors in an economical manner.
The plot borrows from two comics, *The Sky Band* and *The Singh Brotherhood* (1936–37), but it incorporates some new twists. Many of the details remained true to the spirit of the original comics. The skull ring's mark, the Jungle Patrol, Dr Axel's Hospital and the vaults of the Phantom's deceased ancestors would delight diehard comic fans.	**Continue building the context for the review by offering solid facts and figures about the subject.** The reviewer explains the similarities and differences between the original comic book stories and the film being reviewed. He adds his personal preferences and observations for the reader's consideration.
However, the few deviations from the comic will no doubt irritate some fans. For example, it's a man who swears an oath upon the skull of his father's murderer to fight injustice rather than a boy. And the skull cave's design is oddly different in the film from the one in the comic. Where is the guard—the Pygmy Bandar—and the curtain of water you have to pass through to get to it? But am I just nitpicking?	**Offer a detailed evaluation of some individual aspects of the topic.** In this text we see the reviewer commenting upon a few minor issues with the film that might irritate some fans and giving supporting reasons for his opinions. But the positive tone is maintained despite these small criticisms. At the end of this paragraph, the reviewer adds a conversational question, 'am I just nitpicking?', to suggest that he views these problems with the film as minor ones and invites the reader to do the same.
Despite these minor detractions, Billy Zane's Phantom is fantastic. He has mastered the quick draw as well as any cowboy and is an expert horseman. Zane's brilliant trademark smile lights up the screen. Also noteworthy was Kristy Swanson's portrayal of Diana Palmer and Catherine Zeta-Jones's performance as Sala.	**Include details about your personal thoughts and expectations as a reviewer.** The statements address the reviewer's own unique insights and emotional reactions to various aspects of the subject under review. Here we see the reviewer using the words 'mastered' and 'expert' to describe the actor's performance. This gives the reader points of reference with which they can agree or disagree.
Director Simon Wincer has unapologetically made this a fan-focused film. Even though Phantom buffs will get the biggest kick out of this movie, anyone who loves action flicks will likely enjoy it.	**Provide specific details such as the name of the director to help reinforce a sense of authority in the comments.** A connective statement ('Even though …') contrasts two types of fans: Phantom buffs and action movie fans.
The Phantom is clean and simple, and doesn't take itself too seriously. The action sequences are terrific and the stunts are absolutely spectacular. Many scenes are set in extremely picturesque locations. The best thing about this film is that it has the feel-good factor of the comic book. True fans must make the effort to get to the cinema and watch it on the big screen.	**Conclude the review with a punchy statement.** This could be a call to action, such as in this text, where the fans are urged to 'make the effort' to see the film on the big screen. The writer reserves the statement about 'the best thing about the film' for his concluding paragraph to ensure that his point is driven home.
My rating: ★★★★☆	**Consider using a rating system that incorporates visual symbols.** Many reviewers use a rating system such as this star-rating one, which adds variety to the text.

PERSUASIVE TEXT

Film review

WRITING YOUR OWN SAMPLE

Plan your sample on the lines provided.

- **Use an informative title that clearly states the topic.**
- **Present an introductory statement that establishes the context.** Include some basic information such as the title of the film (or the subject under review) and other relevant details.
- **Make a clear statement that provides your overall opinion about the subject.** Make sure you state your opinion clearly and concisely. Structure the text so that each paragraph presents information in a logical order. Use punctuation to ensure that your writing doesn't become too wordy.
- **Continue building the context for the review by offering solid facts and figures about the subject.** You may like to address similarities and differences, and discuss your personal preferences and observations for the reader's consideration.
- **Offer a detailed evaluation of some individual aspects of the topic.** This is the point of the review where you might wish to introduce some negative aspects that require comment. Ensure that you give supporting reasons for your opinions.
- **Include details about your personal thoughts and expectations as a reviewer.** Your statements should address your own unique insights and emotional reactions to various aspects of the subject under review. This gives the reader points of reference with which they can agree or disagree.
- **Provide specific details such as the name of the director to help reinforce a sense of authority in the comments.** Use connective statements to make comparisons and contrasts, and to show cause-and-effect relationships.
- **Conclude the review with a punchy statement.** This could be a call to action. Try to reserve a clear statement about 'the best' or 'the worst' thing about the subject under review to ensure that your main opinion is clearly driven home.
- **Consider using a rating system that incorporates visual symbols.** Many reviewers use a star-rating one, which adds variety to the text.

PERSUASIVE TEXT

Online discussion forum

READING WORK

Phantom big cats

Do you believe in the existence of the phantom big cats supposedly hiding out in some parts of Australia?

Add your views to our forum. Log in or sign up to register a new account.

PantherMan: There's some good evidence for the existence of these phantom cats. A couple from Lithgow reported that they've seen catlike scratches up high on tree trunks too tall for ferals or domestics to reach. The same couple have found remains of cattle and sheep that were killed and eaten in a manner consistent with how big cats kill and eat their prey.

Skeptic99: There could be other explanations for the conditions of those animal carcasses. Perhaps they were hunted by dogs or feral pigs, or humans trying to fabricate 'evidence'.

Spooked: Okay—so what about the actual bodies they've found? I saw one photo of what looked like a panther strung up on someone's front verandah. The guy who took the pic said that he cut off the tail and had it examined by experts. They found that it had DNA similar (but not identical) to a feral cat.

Skeptic99: People will do just about anything to get themselves on television or in a news article. And as for photographs, it would be laughably easy to fake such 'evidence' with some simple photo-doctoring software.

PantherMan: Well—the fake photos seem to have fooled some pretty smart authorities. In 2003 the NSW government released a statement to the media that said it was more likely than not that the Blue Mountains big cats were real. And in Victoria a study conducted by researchers at Deakin University concluded that the Australian 'marsupial lion', thought to be extinct, could have survived to modern times in remote rural areas.

Spooked: It definitely is possible that one or two big cats could have bred with our feral cats and produced bigger-than-normal offspring. One story I heard was that there were some American wildcats brought into Australia during the gold-rush years (1850s). But that would mean they've been breeding in secret for over a century without being captured, which is a little hard to believe.

PantherMan: Personally I believe these animals are the offspring of escaped circus animals from the days when circuses travelled all around the country with only minimal security to keep costs down. I mean, how likely would a circus owner be to report to the authorities that they'd accidentally let a big cat slip off into the bush during a tour?

Skeptic99: This whole idea is utterly ridiculous. No-one will ever convince me that these things really exist.

PantherMan
Joined (Dec 4, 2016)
Status: Online
Post count (7)

Skeptic99
Joined (Feb 24, 2015)
Status: Online
Post count (9)

Bosko7
Joined (May 30, 2017)
Status: Offline
Post count (14)

Spooked
Joined (Apr 9, 2015)
Status: Online
Post count (6)

JonSymes
Joined (Feb 3, 2016)
Status: Offline
Post count (2)

RickNZT
Joined (Aug 2, 2015)
Status: Offline
Post count (1)

- The topic is described with a **literal title**. This is known as the 'thread heading'—each new topic is discussed under its own separate thread.
- The forum begins with an **introductory section** containing a question directed at the online reader.
- The user is **encouraged to join the discussion** according to the usual rules of signing in or creating a new account.
- Each participant in the forum is **identified** by a literal or made-up username. The usual rules of punctuation are ignored when creating usernames. They may incorporate numbers and symbols as well as words and letters. Some also add an avatar or photo to personalise the online identity further.
- Each participant is able to post **comments**, often in reply to previous posts.
- The word 'evidence' is shown in **quotation marks** to imply that this evidence is questionable.
- The **informal register** of online forums simulates the conducting of real-life conversation.
- **Non-essential details** are enclosed in parentheses.
- This is a **reference to software products** that are not named by brand but instead according to their function—in this case, altering photos.
- Evidence is provided by one user with a strong **sense of authority** due to the provision of dates and details.
- Online users commonly present personal stories that involved them or that they heard from others. These are called **anecdotes** and may contribute some truths about practical experience but they are notoriously difficult to verify and are therefore disregarded as valid sources of evidence in arguments.
- This **emotive statement** summarises one user's point of view forcefully. The abrupt end signals that this is the last post in the thread but that the discussion may continue in the future.

PERSUASIVE TEXT

Online discussion forum

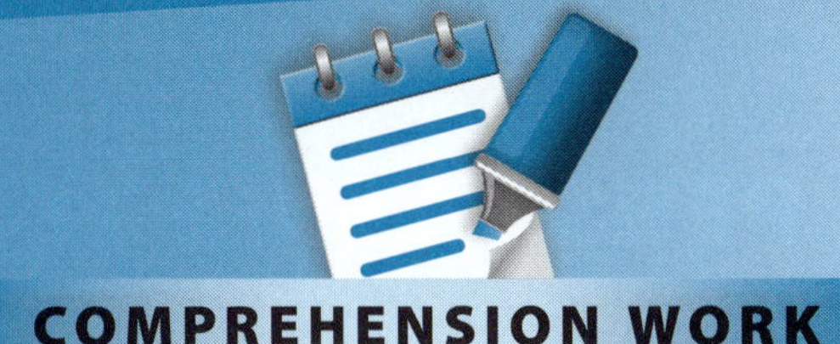

COMPREHENSION WORK

Literal questions

Hint: Read the text carefully to locate specific facts and details.

1 What type of sentence begins the text 'Phantom Big Cats'? ______

2 How many people are participating in this forum? ______

3 To which animal species is 'carcasses' referring in Skeptic99's first comment?

a big cats **b** sheep and cattle **c** feral cats

4 According to Skeptic99, what would be laughably easy to fake? ______

Interpretive questions

Hint: These questions require you to combine facts and details to synthesise the meaning.

5 What evidence prompted DNA testing?

a the dead body of a mysteriously large cat **b** video footage

c cat-like scratches on tree trunks

6 In Spooked's first comment, of which language feature is the word 'pic' an example?

______

7 According to Skeptic99, what motive would people have for faking big cat evidence?

a to get on television or written about in an article **b** to see if people will believe their stories

c to fool university researchers

8 This web forum can best be described as a discussion. Circle *true* or *false*. True False

9 What does the phrase 'pretty smart authorities' mean?

a that the authorities are quite smart **b** that the authorities are quite pretty

c that some authorities are smart, while others are pretty

Applied questions

Hint: This question requires you to understand a text's implications to infer meaning from the text.

10 According to PantherMan if a circus owner had lost a big cat, why would they probably not have made a report?

a They would be too busy to go and look for it.

b They wouldn't care if a few escaped.

c They knew they'd be in serious trouble with authorities.

11 According to the text, the gold-rush years in Australia were in what period?

a the fourth decade of the eighteenth century

b the fifth decade of the nineteenth century

c the fifth decade of the twentieth century

12 What is the main purpose of this text?

______

______

______

PERSUASIVE TEXT

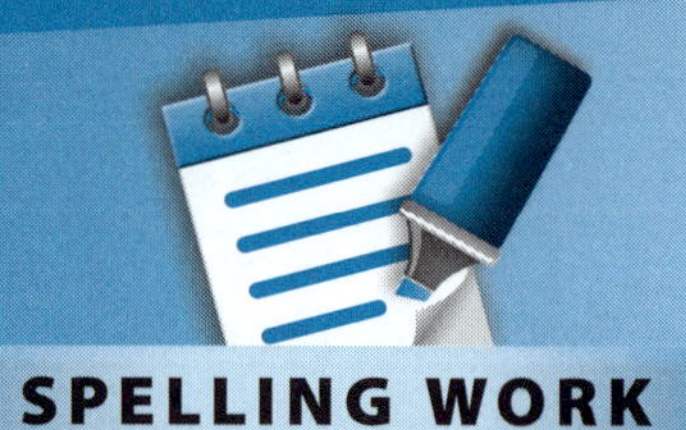

SPELLING WORK

Word List

All the words in the box below appear in the text 'Phantom big cats'.

phantom	explanations	fabricate	government	university
existence	carcasses	television	authorities	offspring
definitely	feral	laughably	marsupial	captured

1 Match these base words with their corresponding list word forms. Write them on the lines provided.

a exist ______ **b** definite ______
c explain ______ **d** fabric ______
e laugh ______ **f** govern ______
g authority ______ **h** capture ______

2 Separate these letter chains into list words. *Hint: They share the letter that links them; that is, the last letter of one is the first letter of the next.*

a phantomarsupialaughably ______ ______ ______
b fabricatexistencexplanations ______ ______ ______
c offspringovernmentelevision ______ ______ ______

3 Form list words that include these vowels and consonants in the same order.

a aua ______ **b** aae ______ **c** mrspl ______
d dfntly ______ **e** ea ______ **f** auoiie ______

4 Write the list words that fit around these affixes (prefixes and suffixes).

a ______ence **b** ______ly **c** ______vision
d ______ably **e** ______ial **f** ______ity

5 Solve these word puzzles by following the instructions.

a F O U N D ______
Change the *o* to an *e*; change the *u* to an *r*; change the *n* to an *a*. Change the last letter to make a word from the text 'Phantom big cats' that means 'wild'.

b C I R C U S ______
Change the *i* to an *a*; delete the next two consonants and replace the letters with *tt*; change the next vowel to an *l* and add an *e* to make a word for a group of cows.

c P A N T H E R ______
Keep the first letter in its place; rearrange the next four letters, then add *om* to make a word for an apparition.

d C A R C A S S E S ______
Delete one *a* and one *s*, add a *t* and an *h* then rearrange to make a word that means 'claws the skin'.

6 Use the prefix at the top of the column to make other words to fill each space. *Hint: Use suffixes like* ed, ing *or* ment *if you get stuck.*

gov	*tele*	*uni*	*laugh*

PERSUASIVE TEXT

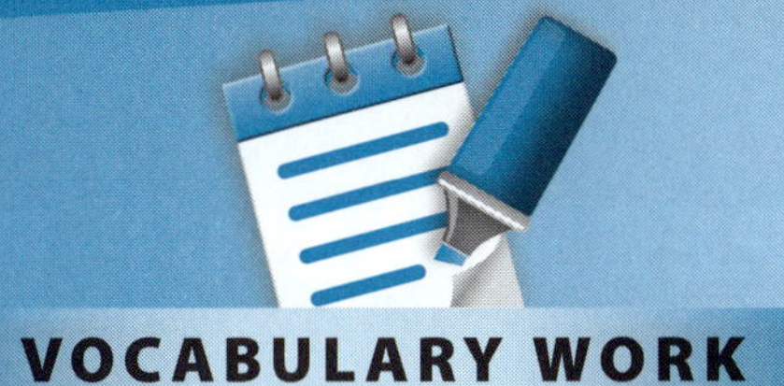

VOCABULARY WORK

1 Circle all the words that relate to cats or feline behaviour.

evidence	past	whiskers	phantom	vanished	cats	cat-like
tail	feral	prey	claws	bred	paw	shadows
scratches	dark	mystery	teeth	photo	panther	lion
spooked	ghost	trail	hunting	local	legends	history
frighten	feathers	sound	roar	target	death	ears

2 Unscramble these jumbled-up names for big cats.

a unilmtoanion (2 words) ______________________

b garaju (1 word) ______________________

c cotbab (1 word) ______________________

d limsulianprao (2 words) ______________________

e nolepasword (2 words) ______________________

f regit (1 word) ______________________

g ugaorc (1 word) ______________________

h ampu (1 word) ______________________

i chateeh (1 word) ______________________

j heatrnp (1 word) ______________________

3 Write each of these words from the text 'Phantom big cats' in the appropriate column, according to whether you consider them to be the language of a skeptic or a believer.

fabricate	fake	actual	extinct	DNA
experts	story	supposedly	study	evidence

Skeptic	Believer

4 First separate these five cat idioms then write them next to their definitions.

you look like something the cat dragged in curiosity killed the cat easy, tiger! she has the tiger by the tail let's not pussyfoot around I'm as weak as a kitten a fat cat when the cat's away the mice will play let the cat out of the bag cat got your tongue?

a ______________________ rich and uncaring toward the poor

b ______________________ Someone is remaining silent.

c ______________________ Being too curious causes trouble.

d ______________________ Workers play up in the boss's absence.

e ______________________ She's in a dangerous situation.

f ______________________ Settle down!

g ______________________ frail

h ______________________ dirty or untidy

i ______________________ reveal a secret

j ______________________ Let's talk straight.

PERSUASIVE TEXT
Online discussion forum

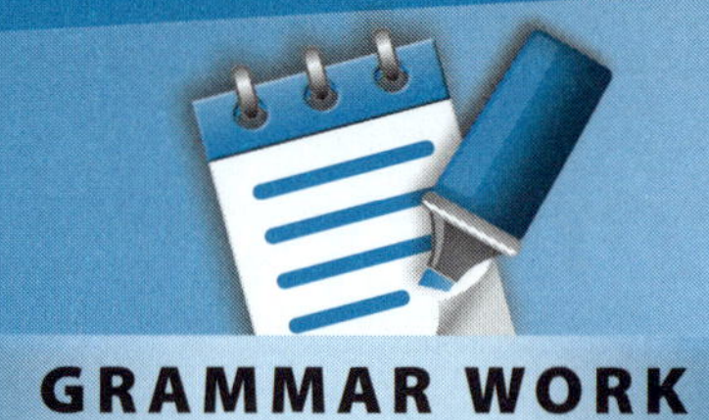

GRAMMAR WORK

Sentence structure

Let's revise the **main features of a simple sentence**. Sentences have a subject and a verb. For example, in the sentence *The panther is an impressive creature* the words *The panther* is the subject and the word *is* is the verb. We can identify the parts of speech in this sentence as follows:

The	*panther*	*is*	*an*	*impressive*	*creature.*
article	noun	verb	article	adjective	noun

1 Identify the parts of speech in these sentences by writing their abbreviated names on the lines underneath; for example, *adj* for *adjective*.

a Evidence suggests big cats exist in Australia.

_____ _____ _____ _____ _____ _____ _____

b A study was conducted by experts at a university.

_____ _____ _____ _____ _____ _____ _____ _____ _____

c The photos of the Lithgow panther were faked.

_____ _____ _____ _____ _____ _____ _____ _____

2 Which of these phrases are written in the present tense? Circle your choices.

Add your views. I shared my views. He logged in. Log in. Please sign up today.

3 Words identifying animal species are common nouns. List all the animal species mentioned in the text 'Phantom big cats'. *Hint: Skim read the text for common nouns and noun phrases.*

______________________ ______________________

______________________ ______________________

______________________ ______________________

______________________ ______________________

______________________ ______________________

4 Circle the abstract noun in each of these pairs of words.

a existence / Victoria **b** thought / researchers **c** phantom / identity **d** possibility / gold

e similarity / photos **f** verandah / security **g** circus / belief **h** bush / secret

5 Find homophones in the text 'Phantom big cats' to match each of these words. Write them in the correct place.

a their ________ **b** knew ________ **c** ewe ________

d bee ________ **e** two ________ **f** pray ________

g won ________ **h** eye ________ **i** tale ________

j sum ________ **k** knot ________ **l** reel ________

m storey ________ **n** herd ________ **o** bean ________

p daze ________ **q** scene ________ **r** bread ________

6 Identify the contractions in these lines of the text 'Phantom big cats'. Write the two words that form the basis for each contraction.

a Line 5 ______________ **b** Line 7 ______________

c Line 16 ______________ **d** Line 46 ______________

PERSUASIVE TEXT

Online discussion forum

PUNCTUATION WORK

The **names** we use as our online identities often lack the formal punctuation style of traditional names. For example, in the text 'Phantom big cats' we see names combined with numbers. Words that aren't part of a person's name (such as adjectives) are included in the online identity tag. Because of the variety of elements used in making online identities, the way we punctuate them has changed from simply using capital initials for proper nouns.

1 List the names of the people involved in the forum.

____

2 Which punctuation mark immediately follows each participant's screen name? ______________

3 What form of punctuation do all the names share in at least one instance? ______________

4 **a** What is it about the text of lines 2 and 3 that sets it apart from the other text? ______________

b What is different about this portion of text's purpose that justifies the use of a different style?

____

c List three common ways of varying the appearance of text to set it apart from the main body text.

__________ __________ __________

5 Why do you think the use of minimal punctuation has become the norm in the online environment?

____

6 Why is the word 'evidence' presented in inverted commas in lines 9 and 14 of the text 'Phantom big cats'?

____

7 Insert the missing punctuation in these sentences by rewriting them on the lines provided.

a theres some good evidence for the existence of these phantom cats

____

b i mean how likely would a circus owner be to report to the authorities that theyd let a big cat slip off into the bush during a tour

____

____

c in two thousand and three the new south wales government released a statement to the media that said it was more likely than not that the blue mountains big cats were real

____

____

____

8 Match these abbreviations and contractions with their full forms by writing the letters on the correct lines.

a deoxyribonucleic acid	______	they've	**b** picture	______	OK
c okay	______	DNA	**d** they have	______	I'd
e university	______	pic	**f** television	______	uni
g photograph	______	TV	**h** I would	______	photo

PERSUASIVE TEXT

Online discussion forum

WRITING WORK 1

Online discussion forums

An **online discussion forum** allows people to converse in the form of written messages about a particular topic. Usually a forum is structured under categories of topics called threads, where people can post their messages in reply to one another. Multiple posts make up each thread. Most forums allow people to read posts without signing in or becoming a member. Threads are displayed from the oldest to the newest.

A member's details—their name and avatar—are usually shown in the left-hand column of the page. Names are varied in format, containing words and numbers. The number of posts a member has made is usually tracked and displayed near their name.

A moderator (or a group of moderators) usually controls what can be posted on the forum, according to rules of behaviour for participants. To ensure that the moderator can keep control, participants must sign up to the forum and become an approved member before they can post anything. Some forums allow users to post as guests so that they can remain anonymous.

Online forums vary in their **style of presentation**. However, most include:

- a page title
- a left-hand column displaying users' names, avatars or photographs
- a post count
- thread headings
- a structure presenting the most recent comments at the top of the page
- a facility for visitors to make comments on the posts
- a comment counter
- counters showing the number of users currently online
- an archive of older posts accessible through links
- a navigation bar.

The **style of language** found in online forums depends upon the topic and the target audience. Generally, though, the style is informal to reflect the idea that the participants are conversing. Some features of language to look out for in online discussion forums are:

- informal expressions
- personal opinions presented forcefully and persuasively
- personalised retorts and challenges to posters with whom people disagree
- personal pronouns
- contractions
- expressions of agreement or disagreement
- presentation of evidence to support the poster's views
- slang, idioms and colloquial expressions that online users understand
- emotive language that describes the poster's feelings and reactions
- jargon specific to the topic
- dates, time stamps and other specific factual details describing or logging usage statistics
- calls to action to encourage others to comment.

1 What name do we give to a page where multiple posts appear on a single topic in a discussion forum?

____

2 What is the job of a moderator? ______________________________

3 What identification elements are shown in the left-hand column of the page of a discussion forum?

____

PERSUASIVE TEXT

Online discussion forum

WRITING WORK 2

The **register** in which discussions are written is usually informal, and may reflect certain aspects of conversational language.

4 Circle the informal words and phrases in this post from the text 'Phantom big cats'. *Hint: There are five.*

Spooked: Okay—so what about the actual bodies they've found? I saw one photo of what looked like a panther strung up on someone's front verandah. The guy who took the pic said that he cut off the tail and had it examined by experts.

5 Now write the formal equivalents of two informal words and phrases you selected.

____________________ ____________________

6 Which is the most emotively charged post in the thread? Use the line numbers to reference your answer.

____

7 List the emotive words or phrases from that post. ____________________

8 How many posts have each of the participants made? Write their names and the post count for each one.

____________ ____________ ____________

9 In your opinion which poster sounds the least convincing? ____________________

Explain your answer. ____________________

____

10 Work out the alliances in the forum.

a Which participants agree with each other's views? ____________________

b Who disagrees with the other two? ____________________

11 With which participant do you agree? ____________________

Explain your reasoning. ____________________

12 Look at the text 'Phantom big cats' and write one example of each of these pieces of evidence on the lines below.

a evidence for the presence of a tall cat-like animal

____

b evidence of an animal that kills and eats livestock

____

____

c a conclusion about some scientifically examined evidence

____

d a story offering a possible explanation for the existence of big cats in the Australian bush

____

____

PERSUASIVE TEXT

Online discussion forum

WRITING SAMPLE

Here is a sample text showing you how to structure an online discussion forum conversation.

Post		Notes
Punctuate or perish?		Give the page a title that encourages participation.
What do you think? Share your views. Please log in first.		Make specific calls to action for users to get involved.
WordPerfect ¶	I have to admit I'm a purist when it comes to language. My text messages may be longer but at least I haven't compromised the language.	**Display users' names and their avatars or photographs.** The format for this information varies widely from one blog to another but should be clear and concise.
GuitarMojo	I agree with WordPerfect on this one—it is scary to think that textspeak could become the norm.	**Include expressions of agreement or disagreement by various users to enliven the debate.** In this one the user affirms their agreement with the previous user's post.
Stimpy13	Like WordPerfect and GuitarMojo, I'm a fan of accurate punctuation, the main casualty of texting.	**Use personal pronouns to make the tone conversational.**
penny101	Shorthand in text messaging saves time space and money. Because of the need to simplify language we should get rid of punctuation altogether.	**Present personal opinions forcefully and persuasively.** The aim here is to recruit the support of other users and people who aren't posting but are reading the forum.
GuitarMojo	But doing away with punctuation would just hinder clear communication, wouldn't it? I mean punctuation marks signal how we read or say something and they do so more concisely than any combination of letters and numbers can.	**Raise opposing arguments, offering evidence.**
Tengreen bottles	I am happy to use SMS language in an SMS, but that's where it should stay. I wouldn't want to see it replace regular language. And don't even get me started on the horrors of trying to use predictive text!	**Use emotive language to describe feelings and reactions persuasively.** Jargon specific to the topic is employed.
penny101	whats wrong with predictive text?	**Informal (or even absent) punctuation is permissible.**
Stimpy13	Look what happens when we remove punctuation. 'The prisoner told the court he was innocent half an hour after he was executed.' Either this prisoner was able to talk after he was dead or there's some punctuation missing. With punctuation it reads like this: 'The prisoner told the court he was innocent. Half an hour after, he was executed.'	**Present evidence that supports your views.** This can be drawn from various external sources. In this example we see the poster using logic to demonstrate the fallibility of written expression when proper punctuation is ignored. This creates a powerful argument that gives weight to the poster's opinion.
GuitarMojo	A good rule of thumb is to use texting for confirmation, not conversation.	**Include witty one-liners, puns or jokes to add variety.** This user relies on rhyming words to make a point.
WordPerfect ¶	Generation Text probably spend more time composing texts than their ancestors did because instead of typing madly away on some dinky hand-held device, they were hard at work in the fields.	**Feature provocative statements that will lead to retorts and challenges.** Here WordPerfect is presenting a thinly disguised criticism of people's overuse of their devices when they should be working.
penny101	WordPerfect—are you implying that people who do a lot of texting have a poor work ethic?	**Present personalised retorts and challenges to posters with whom people disagree so any opposing views are clearly represented.** We're expecting an argument to break out between WordPerfect and penny101.
WordPerfect ¶	No Penny. I'm simply pointing out how much life has changed in the past few generations.	**Use personal pronouns and contractions to create a simple register and informal, conversational tone.**
Tengreen bottles	So what's the texting solution for punctuation devotees? We probably have to concede that a relaxed approach would save typing time and screen space. But should punctuation still be properly applied to written language outside of texting?	**Create statements that summarise the key points being raised in the discussion.** Here the poster takes the middle ground, offering a compromise as the solution.

PERSUASIVE TEXT

Online discussion forum

WRITING YOUR OWN SAMPLE

Plan your sample on the lines provided.

- **Give the page a title that encourages participation.**
- **Make specific calls to action for users to get involved.**
- **Display users' names and their avatars or photographs.** The format for this information varies widely from one blog to another but should be clear and concise.
- **Include expressions of agreement or disagreement by various users to enliven the debate.**
- **Use personal pronouns to make the tone conversational.** Other forms of informal language such as slang, idioms and colloquial expressions are popular with online audiences.
- **Present personal opinions forcefully and persuasively.**
- **Raise opposing arguments, offering evidence.** Draw this evidence from real-life experience, personal anecdotes or your own insights. This can be bolstered by more objective evidence, such as media sources, research study results or trends proven by statistical studies among the population.
- **Use emotive language** to describe feelings and reactions persuasively. Include some jargon specific to the topic but bear in mind the danger of assuming too much knowledge in your readers.
- **Informal (or even absent) punctuation is permissible.**
- **Present evidence that supports your views.** This can be drawn from various external sources. Another way to present evidence is by appealing to logic. The aim is to create a powerful argument that gives weight to the poster's opinion.
- **Include witty one-liners, puns or jokes to add variety.**
- **Feature provocative statements that will lead to retorts and challenges.** This is common fare in the opinion-soaked online environment and is a key reason why people read and engage in discussion forums.
- **Present personalised retorts and challenges to posters with whom people disagree so any opposing views are clearly represented.** These lively exchanges also add interest and excitement to the forum.
- **Use personal pronouns and contractions to create a simple register and informal, conversational tone.**
- **Create statements that summarise the key points being raised in the discussion.** This allows users and non-participating readers to navigate the various arguments that may appear disjointed when they occur over numerous posts. It can also function as a conclusion when a thread is discontinued.

TIPS FOR THE SAMPLE TESTS

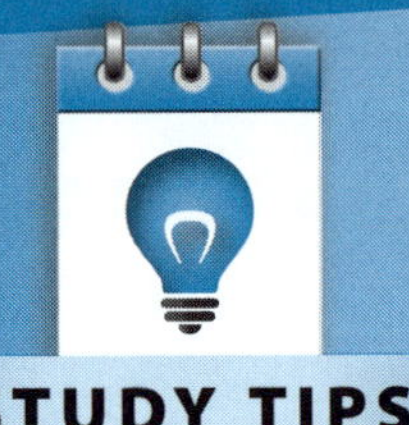

STUDY TIPS

Know what to expect

- Find out from your teacher what knowledge and skills will be assessed in the sample test.
- Find out what format is being used for the sample test.

Revise and rehearse

- Revise the relevant knowledge and skills.
- Write some practice analysis paragraphs about sample texts.

Read carefully

- Read all instructions on the test paper.
- Note the mark allocations. These indicate how much you should write and how much time you should spend on each answer.
- Read the questions before the texts so that when reading the texts you know what to look for.

Make your answers count

- Use handwriting that is clear (not too large, too small or too cursive).
- Use all of the answer spaces provided.
- Be specific in your answers and don't use padding or repetition to make them look longer.

Re-read and check

- Once you have completed a response, re-read it to make sure it actually answers the question. This will only take a few seconds.
- Edit quickly and clearly. If you need to, make corrections using single cross-out lines (not scribbles).

Manage your time

- Write legibly but quickly.
- Ensure you are working through the test efficiently and not spending too much time on each question, or you may not finish the test.
- If you finish early, don't waste the leftover time. Spend that time checking, editing and possibly extending your answers.

Be ready

- Always study English actively. This means using a pen and paper to make notes. It also involves recording grammar rules, language features and definitions of difficult terms.
- If you have prepared thoroughly for the test, you do not need to be nervous. Tests are not designed to trap you, but to give you an opportunity to show how much you know.

Part A Reading and comprehension

Read the following texts and answer the questions that follow on page 125.

Text 1: Informative text—Informative article

Ninjas to the rescue

A trio of muggers were foiled by a troupe of ninjas in Sydney in January 2017.

Three nasty thugs got more than they bargained for when they staged a mugging near Burwood railway station in Sydney. The youths, aged between 16 and 20, had been harassing a German medical student while he was travelling on an inner city train.

When the man refused to hand over his wallet, they followed him from the railway station into a dark alleyway and began beating and kicking him in a cowardly attack. The student, on an eight-week exchange visit to Australia, cried out for help.

And help came in a manner that sometimes happens in the movies, but rarely in real life.

By coincidence, the attack had occurred right outside the Ninja Senshi Ryu training school, where the *ninjitsu** class was being let out for the night.

Imagine the scene—these three delinquents are brutally assaulting an innocent tourist, when out of the shadows emerge five black-clad ninjas, in full traditional gear, running toward them at speed.

The thugs showed by their actions that they did have some measure of common sense—they ran. And they ran fast. Led by *sensei** Kaylan Soto, the ninjas gave chase, giving the attackers the fright of their lives.

The victim came away with minor injuries and had his iPod and phone stolen, but these belongings were recovered shortly afterwards when police arrested two of the three suspects. The third perpetrator is still at large but most likely will be steering clear of dark alleys for some time to come.

****ninjitsu***—a Japanese martial art that emphasises stealth, tactical skill, and specialised knowledge of immobilising enemies through pressure points and lethal weaponry
*****sensei***—a highly skilled ninjitsu instructor

Part A Reading and comprehension

Text 2: Narrative text—Descriptive narrative

An extraordinary undertaking

In a certain garden, still and dark, a strange sight presented itself under the silent witness of the moon. A cluster of seven lithe figures were intently digging at a patch of turf, uprooting it in little clumps.

Their grim purpose was revealed by the strengthening moonlight, which illuminated a sleek, lifeless body stretched out by the widening hole.

A cold breeze shivered through the low brush that formed one border of the garden and the faint scent of wild freesias flavoured the air.

Presently one of the seven signalled for the digging to cease. For a time the mourners stared at the forlorn figure on the grass, their breath creating small puffs of fog that mingled with the night mist.

There was a slight swishing of tails and an audible shaking of forepaws free from the clinging dirt before the little group formed a respectful circle around the gravesite. The scents of earth and grass lingered.

Gathering around the body they tenderly conveyed it to the newly dug cavity. Then, with one accord, they soberly turned their backs on the grave, and in a sudden flurry worked their hind legs to fling the freshly displaced earth over their friend.

Anyone watching this scene may have been struck by the strange sophistication of the ritual. With no human to marshal them and no undertaker to instruct them, the seven animals gave their friend a hero's burial with only the solemn moon presiding. Then one by one they slid away into the deepening night.

The funeral of a feline may be a strange sight indeed, on a perfectly ordinary night, in a perfectly ordinary street of a perfectly ordinary town—to a perfectly ordinary person. But for those who believe in the extraordinary there's nothing strange about it.

One such person was watching from her back verandah. Before the last few mourners had melted into the shadows she turned to go indoors, the moonlight catching the silver gleams of her tears.

Part A Reading and comprehension

Text 3: Persuasive text—Opinion piece

Squid's Seafood Restaurant

Wondering where your next meal is coming from? Then you can't afford to eat at Squid's. Their prices will certainly leave a bad taste in your mouth—that's guaranteed! And their oysters too. I can assure you Squid's seafood is caught fresh from an open drain near you each and every morning.

There's plenty of Australian fare on offer, including Road Kill Roo Burgers and Dolphin Mince soup. You're sure to find eating the Warm Eel Salad with Whale Stomach Gravy, a memorable experience, especially when served on the Pike Pikelets (with most sharp bits removed). But here's a positive—all orders come with free chef's hairs, while stocks last!

When you dine at Squid's, you can feast your eyes on the view of the hulking Snake Pit floating dock, where if you strain your neck you may even catch a brief glimpse of some clean water. You can inhale diesel fumes straight from the watercraft moored at the Marina. You'll be dazzled by the kaleidoscope of broken glass sparkling away in the sands of the foreshore. And the heady aroma created by boat owners emptying their chemical toilets over the side really complements the taste of the house wine. Watch as seagulls foul the outside tables and frenzied sparrows kill each other over leftover plates of bruschetta. I'm sure you'll agree that these delights are just too good to pass up.

But by far the worst thing about this dive is the long waiting times. You could easily make dining at Squid's an all-day experience. If you go in for breakfast, you'll most likely wait until lunchtime for your food to arrive. In fact, some people stay until they're operating off the dinner menu and make a whole day of it.

Regular diners at Squid's should be entitled to the following membership bonuses:

- NSW State Ambulance Service Priority Transport
- A free funeral if caused by your dining experience
- McDonald's vouchers

Who's with me on this?

By the way Squid's are very happy to accept any credit card. In fact, they still haven't returned mine.

SAMPLE TESTS

PAPER 1

Part A Reading and comprehension

Answer the following questions:

Text 1

1 Describe the victim of the mugging. (1 mark)

2 What items did the muggers steal from the victim? (1 mark)

3 Why were the ninjas at the scene of the mugging? (1 mark)

Text 2

4 Which words from the text describe the dead animal? (1 mark)

5 Why do the cats turn their backs on the grave? (1 mark)

6 What is the implied reason that a woman was crying in the shadows at the end of the text? (1 mark)

Text 3

7 What is one source of bad smells at Squid's according to the reviewer? (1 mark)

8 What is the worst thing about Squid's in the reviewer's opinion? (1 mark)

9 What is the writer implying by this line: 'all orders come with free chef's hairs'? (1 mark)

Your Score

/9

Part B Language conventions

Answer the following questions:

Text 1

1 Why are footnotes used in this text? (2 marks)

Text 2

2 Write two examples of olfactory imagery that appeals to the physical sense of smell in the text. (2 marks)

Text 3

3 What does the writer most want to persuade us to do in this text? (2 marks)

Your Score

/6

Part C Comparing texts

Answer the following questions:

Use the number of lines and the allocated marks as a guide to the length of your answer.

1 What differences in the storytelling modes and tenses do you see between Texts 2 and 3? (2 marks)

2 We're given detailed information in both Texts 1 and 2. What is the major difference in the type of information presented in Text 1 compared to Text 2? (2 marks)

3 Which of the three texts do you feel conveys feelings most effectively? Make specific reference to each text. (4 marks)

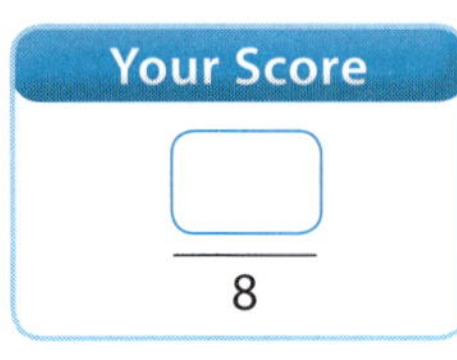

Part D Themes and meaning

Write a paragraph response to the question in the space provided. Use the number of lines and the allocated marks as a guide to the length of your answer.

1 Choose one of the three texts (1, 2 or 3) and write a paragraph summarising its main ideas (themes). These ideas may not be stated directly in the text. (7 marks)

Your Score

7

Part A Reading and comprehension

Read the following texts and answer the questions that follow on page 131.

Text 1: Informative text—Online article

Shipwreck survivor, Hugh Williams

In a strange quirk of history, the survivors of five separate shipwrecks had the name Hugh Williams.

Lucky Hugh!

A man named Hugh Williams survived two separate ferry disasters in the same year. So should this Hugh Williams consider himself lucky or unlucky?

These sinkings occurred in the Menai Strait of Wales and involved the vessels *Tal-y-Foel* and *Abermenai*. Another shipwreck in 1785 saw all aboard drown except another man named Hugh Williams. In 1860 a small ship sank in the same waters. The sole survivor was—unbelievably—a passenger named Hugh Williams. Our tally so far is three men called Hugh Williams who survived a total of four shipwrecks.

Bad Karluk

Historical research turns up yet another shipwreck survivor named Hugh Williams. This fellow was aboard the *Karluk*, an Arctic exploration vessel.

The *Karluk* became trapped in ice, forcing the crew to abandon ship. Most died but among the survivors was our old friend Hugh Williams, a seaman who is fondly remembered for his bravery. Hugh's frostbitten toe had to be removed by a companion to avoid infection. The surgical instrument was a pair of garden shears. And the anesthetic? Ice, of course!

Unlucky for Hugh

But for those parents thinking of naming their son Hugh Williams as a precaution, you may wish to note that not all people with this name survive shipwrecks. The luck of this Hugh Williams ran out.

Michigan's Captain Hugh Williams of Lightship 82 drowned near Buffalo when his vessel went down in the 1913 storm. The captain wrote a final farewell to his wife in indelible ink on a door panel, which was recovered and delivered to his family intact.

The message was brief but poignant: 'Goodbye, Nellie. Ship is breaking up fast. WILLIAMS.'

Part A Reading and comprehension

Text 2 : Narrative text—Journal

First day of freedom

Friday, 30 September 2016

Today is my first day of freedom in nine years. Still can't believe it all happened. But there's no changing history. I'm so grateful that I was able to serve out my sentence in a fairly decent place. It would've been much worse for me if I didn't get moved out of Goulburn. Today, I had the best feed I've had in a looooong time. I couldn't decide between a meatlovers pizza and a cheeseburger and fries, so I had all three! Go son!

Tuesday, 4 October 2016

I'm narrowing down the likely possibilities for my future. First thoughts were landscape gardener or handyman. I've been offered a job behind the bar at my local but I'm reluctant to put myself anywhere near booze at present, because for me booze tends to lead to trouble. So for now I guess I'll stick to yard work until NASA calls me with a better offer.

I'm moving house on the long weekend. Mum and Dad have bought me some basic furniture and dug out some boxes of gear that I'd left in their garage for the past decade! The delivery guy I spoke to said it looks like raining all weekend but I just smiled hearing that. After all those years inside, I couldn't care less if it rained on me and my stuff because at the end of the day I'm free under this big sky and that's all that matters.

Thursday, 6 October 2016

I'm living free and easy in a little fishing town called Lynch's Inlet, near the family farm. I thought I'd try my luck getting work doing small repair jobs and yard work. It's worked out well because I've been able to spend time with my farming folks. It's great being free to earn my own living. I enjoy the freedom that working outside gives me. I work four days a week and spend my free Fridays each week fishing. Who'd have thought that I'd be fixing fences and running after cows instead of fixing bank jobs and running from the cops?

Monday, 28 November 2016

Well, I'm famous! Today the local rag ran a story on my parents' farming enterprise and I had my ugly mug and name on the front page. Fancy having my name appear in print for reasons other than criminal! Things are looking up!

Part A Reading and comprehension

Text 3: Persuasive text—Marketing text

Jazz in the Gardens

Join us for an evening of fine foods and smooth grooves set in the city's beautiful Botanic Gardens.

Featuring

- Harpo Dalton and the Goldhorns
- Jaynie Taylor
- Legs Eleven

Listen

Wrap your senses in the silky sax tones of the legendary Harpo Dalton and his band the Goldhorns. Groove along with scat extraordinaire Jaynie Taylor and let your hair down with Legs Eleven, Australia's premier jazz quartet.

Enjoy

Enjoy fruity champagne on arrival and a lavish selection of gourmet treats that will get your tastebuds singing. You'll love our cocktails made exclusively for this prestigious event by celebrity barman Saul Sweetwater.

Indulge

And just when you thought things couldn't get any sweeter, indulge in the delights of a chocolate fountain brought right to your table.

Why not treat yourself to some of life's little pleasures?

Date: April 11: 7:30 pm

Venue: Sydney Botanic Gardens

Gold tickets: $64
Seniors $58
No student concession for Gold tickets

Silver tickets: $54
Seniors $48
Student concession $44

We'll see you there.

No admission for under-18s.
Book early to avoid disappointment.
Call our hotline: 1800 323 JAZZ for full details or visit info@jazzevents.com.au

SAMPLE TESTS

PAPER 2

Part A Reading and comprehension

Answer the following questions:

Text 1

1 In which country did a man named Hugh Williams survive a shipwreck in the year 1860? (1 mark)

2 What unusual purpose was ice used for by the crew of the *Karluk*? (1 mark)

3 Of which ship was an American man named Hugh Williams the captain? (1 mark)

Text 2

4 In which prison did the writer serve the earlier part of his sentence? (1 mark)

5 Why is there a report about the writer in the local newspaper? (1 mark)

6 Why does the writer turn down an offer of hotel work? (1 mark)

Text 3

7 How much does a Silver ticket for a student cost? (1 mark)

8 How do we know that Jazz in the Gardens is not an event suitable for children? (1 mark)

9 What is meant by the expression 'some of life's little pleasures'? (1 mark)

Your Score

/9

Part B Language conventions

Answer the following questions:

Text 1

1 Identify and explain the meanings of two puns (plays on words) in the text. (2 marks)

Text 2

2 What humorous contrast does the writer create using the words 'fixing' and 'running'? (2 marks)

Text 3

3 Consider the connotations in the name 'Harpo Dalton and the Goldhorns'. What type of act might this be, considering their name? (2 marks)

Your Score

/6

Part C Comparing texts

Answer the following questions. Use the number of lines and the allocated marks as a guide to the length of your answer.

1 What are the specific purposes for which Texts 2 and 3 have been written? (2 marks)

Text 2:

Text 3:

2 What is unique about the structure of Text 2 in comparison to Text 1? (2 marks)

3 Using the content of the text as clues, describe the two different target audiences for Texts 1 and 3. Give specific reasons for your response. (4 marks)

Your Score

/8

Part D Themes and meaning

Write a paragraph response to the question in the space provided. Use the number of lines and the allocated marks as a guide to the length of your answer.

1 Choose one of the three texts (1, 2 or 3) and write a paragraph about its theme. Identify the theme and evaluate how clearly it is presented in the text. (7 marks)

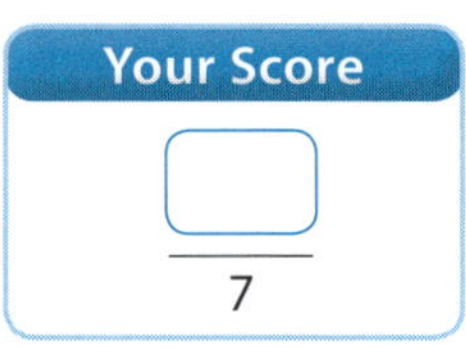

Your Feedback

Part A + Part B + Part C + Part D = /30 = %

ANSWERS

CHECK YOUR ANSWERS

UNIT 1: INFORMATIVE TEXT — BOOK EXTRACT

INFORMATIVE TEXT
Comprehension Work

page 3

1 Meteorologists Storm Field, Sara Blizzard and Dallas Raines.
This is a **literal** question. We read that 'Meteorologists Storm Field, Sara Blizzard and Dallas Raines all report the weather on television' *(lines 8–10)*. Locate this fact in the text.

2 Dr Yankum is a dentist.
This is a **literal** question. We read 'For tooth issues how about making an appointment with one of these dentists? Dr Aichen, Dr Ken Hurt, Dr Puller, Dr Yankum' *(lines 22–23)*. Locate this fact in the text.

3 Early Wynn and Jack Armstrong were pitchers.
This is a **literal** question. We read 'Baseball has its fair share of appropriately named players—pitchers Early Wynn and Jack Armstrong spring to mind' *(lines 36–38)*. Locate this fact in the text.

4 The purpose of this rhetorical question is to prompt readers to think about how famous these two sportsmen are and to emphasise the fact that they are household names across the world.
This is an **interpretive** question. The beginning phrase of the rhetorical question 'Who hasn't heard of …' *(line 34)* is a commonly used expression in rhetorical questioning. The names of the two athletes are very well known so in this way we use our interpretation to arrive at the answer.

5 because cartilage is connective tissue found in the joints in human anatomy that is often injured when doing sports and physical activities
This is an **interpretive** question. Because we are already aware that the text is presenting names that are appropriate for particular professions, we can draw on our knowledge of the term 'cartilage' to arrive at the answer.

6 six
This is an **interpretive** question. We read *(beginning in line 12)* a list of names of people associated with education but the question contains a trap. Only six of the eight people mentioned are actually teachers. By paying close attention to the wording of lines 15–17, we can interpret that the last two people named have school-related jobs but are not teachers.

7 **a** This is an **interpretive** question. To arrive at the answer, we need to consider each option and whether it provides a logical answer to the question. Answer **a** Dr Slaughter is correct because it implies killing and death, not the expected outcome for surgery. We know that Answer **b** Dr Gutman is incorrect because he is a gastroenterologist, not necessarily a surgeon, and his name does not imply anything about surgery. We know that Answer **c** Dr Fillmore is a dentist and his name is relevant to the filling of dental cavities, so it is not correct.

8 **a** This is an **interpretive** question. To arrive at the answer, we need to consider each option and whether it provides a logical answer to the question. Answer **a** is correct because it matches the common expression used to exclaim that we've lost a game. We know that neither Answer **b** nor Answer **c** is correct because neither of those spellings presents a recognisable phrase or word.

9 **b** This is an **interpretive** question. The question says that the name is appropriate for a dentist so we know the answer must refer to an aspect of dentistry. We know that Answer **b** is correct because the name 'plack' sounds like 'plaque', a common aspect of dental care. The first name 'Les' makes it more humorous, as if to mimic a dentist asking patients to brush regularly so they have 'less plaque'. We know that Answer **c** isn't correct because 'Doctor' is actually a term used to refer to dentists. Answer **a** is not correct because we know that there is no such tool.

10 **a** This is an **interpretive** question. We read in line 33 the last part of the section on law. Then we read 'The world of elite sports is replete with aptronyms' *(line 34)*. This is the sentence in which the topic shifts from law to sport. We can work out that Answers **b** and **c** are not correct by checking to see where they appear in the text. If they do not sit between the law and sport sections, they are not correct.

11 **b** This is an **applied** question. We need to consider the logic of each answer option. There is no evidence to suggest that Answer **a** is correct and there's no discussion of their prowess at that sport. We know that Answer **c** isn't correct because the writer explicitly says the opposite in the last line of the text. The process of elimination allows us to arrive at the answer.

12 **c** This is an **applied** question. We need to consider the pronunciation of the name 'Rem Koolhaus' and apply our external knowledge to solve the problem. We can read beyond the lines to realise that the suffix 'haus' sounds like 'house' and that an architect's job involves cool house designs. We know that Answer **a** is incorrect because it falsely asserts that the vowel blend *au* is always pronounced as 'ou'. We know that Answer **b** is incorrect because the name actually does refer to the job of an architect.

ANSWERS

CHECK YOUR ANSWERS

INFORMATIVE TEXT
Spelling Work
page 4

1 **a** specialists **b** confident **c** profession **d** appointment **e** architect **f** elite **g** surgeons **h** represented

2 **a** unusual **b** anatomy **c** defence **d** operation **e** unfortunate **f** champion **g** complaints

3 **a** profession **b** complaints **c** anatomy **d** surgeons **e** architect **f** champion

4 **a** ~~AB~~ELITE/UNUSUAL/REPRESENTED~~ES~~
b ~~DE~~COMPLAINTS/SURGEONS/UNFORTUNATE~~RY~~
c ~~NO~~PROFESSION/ARCHITECT/CHAMPION~~AR~~
d ~~OS~~ANATOMY/CONFIDENT/DEFENCE~~IS~~

5 **a** specialists **b** appointment **c** unfortunate **d** operation

INFORMATIVE TEXT
Vocabulary Work
page 5

1 **a** appropriately **b** protection against loss **c** weather researchers **d** leaders **e** people under medical care **f** skin specialist

2 **a** True **b** False **c** True **d** False

3 **a** issues **b** chose **c** company **d** surgery **e** trust

4 **a** amateurs **b** fortunate **c** usual

5 **a** d **b** b **c** f **d** a **e** c **f** e

INFORMATIVE TEXT
Grammar Work
page 6

1 **a** think **b** hurdling **c** playing **d** expect **e** called **f** need **g** yell **h** visit **i** scratch **j** teaching **k** cycling **l** study **m** reporting **n** become **o** have **p** attracted

2 has

3 lurk, causing, smile

4 report, takes

5 might be called, represented

6 Suggested answers: **a** The teacher asked me a question. **b** The boy didn't want police to question him.

7 **a** report **b** post **c** record **d** issues **e** fear **f** play

8 Suggested answers:
a I watched a news report. The horse was tied to a post. There was no record of the event. We had some issues to discuss. The investigators ran into the building without any fear. We are rehearsing our play.
b I watched the journalist report the news story. You can't post a horse in the mail. The woman didn't record the event in the logbook. This problem issues from two sources. I fear the case will never be solved. Don't play around during rehearsals.

INFORMATIVE TEXT
Punctuation Work
page 7

1 **a** Meteorologists Storm Field, Sara Blizzard, Dallas Raines
b One, Oregon, USA, Cheatham & Steele
c But, Scott Free
d Who, Usain Bolt, Olympic, Tiger Woods
e What, Margaret Court, Australia's

2 **a** I think some of these aptronyms are hilarious!
b Dr Skinner is a very appropriate name for a skin specialist, isn't it?
c Is Usain Bolt a sprinter or a long-distance runner?
d How confident are you that your dental operation will be painless?
e Are you serious—a dentist called Dr EZ Filler worked on your teeth yesterday?
f Get a load of this—my gastroenterologist is called Dr Gutman!
g Can you imagine the embarrassment if Dr Hackman or Dr Kutteroff had to perform an amputation?
h Who'd have thought there'd be a bank called Cheatham and Steele?

3 School teachers seem to fall under the aptronym spell. We know of a metalwork teacher called Mr Steel, a woodwork teacher called Mr Timbers, a biological anatomy teacher Mrs Boddey, English teacher Ms Read, music teacher Mrs Triplett and physical education teacher Ms Cartilage. Other school staff with job-appropriate names are Mr Wheeler, leader of the cycling club, and Pastor Toogood, the school chaplain.

INFORMATIVE TEXT
Writing Work
page 8

1 c

2 a c d

3 The purpose is to inform the reader of an amusing trend that the writer has noticed in language.

ANSWERS

CHECK YOUR ANSWERS

4 **a** the definition of an aptronym
b There is a theory that some people may be attracted to a profession because it reflects their name.
c Three weather reporters have appropriate names, considering their professions.
d Aptronyms have also been discovered among school teachers.
e Medical specialists sometimes have apt names that make patients smile.
f Some medical specialists' names fill the patient with fear.

5 There are two in the text: 'Let's hope you don't find yourself under the care of one of these surgeons … and more positively, Dr Truluck!' *(lines 25–29)* and 'Hey, just for the record, I don't think you suck, Kim. I'm confident you can rise above your name!' *(lines 43–44)*.

6 Two. They are 'An aptronym is a name aptly suited to its owner because of the job they do' and 'The theory is that people who have unusual names are sometimes attracted to the profession they suggest.'

7 Suggested answers:
b school staff
c doctors, dermatologists, gastroenterology and dentists
d surgeons with particularly scary names
e lawyers
f sporting professionals

8 Answers will vary. One suggestion is to reduce the sections on medical practitioners and sports people to contain just a few examples each in order to shorten the text.

9 This is an opinion-based question so answers will vary. Suggested answer: The names of the doctors and dentists seem particularly striking because their names seem certain to undermine the confidence these professionals need to inspire in their patients.

UNIT 2: INFORMATIVE TEXT—INFORMATIVE ARTICLE

INFORMATIVE TEXT
Comprehension Work

page 13

1 Spooky
This is a **literal** question. All you do is look for simple facts in the text. We notice that the text says that 'Spooky the poodle ate a large chocolate Easter bunny' *(line 31)*.

2 boxer shorts and knitted socks
This is a **literal** question. It simply requires you to find a fact in the text. We read that a husky 'loved to eat boxer shorts and knitted socks' *(line 37)*.

3 a pocket knife and nine sewing needles
This is a **literal** question. All you do is look for facts in the text. We can locate the facts about which dogs ate sharp objects by skim reading the text for certain words. We read the terms 'pocketknife' *(line 26)* and 'sewing needles' *(line 28)*. These are sharp objects. While some other objects are mentioned that may have sharp parts, these two objects are the only two mentioned that are classified as 'sharp objects' in their regular, intact form.

4 alliteration
This is an **interpretive** question. It requires you to synthesise the meaning of a common literary technique. You need to read the text carefully and decide which literary technique is present in the quoted line. Alliteration occurs when the same consonant sound is repeated in words sharing close proximity. The repeated consonant sound is the letter *d* in the phrase 'disgraceful doggie'.

5 a veterinarian
This is an **interpretive** question. You need to evaluate the context to make an interpretation of those details. Then you can synthesise the meaning. Sometimes it is helpful to read around the specific detail to get a clearer picture of the wider context. The dog's name, Woof, is given *(line 34)*, and the text says 'When he was finally taken to the vet and given an X-ray, the owner discovered five little duckies inside' *(lines 35–36)*. The words 'and given an X-ray' immediately follow the phrase 'taken to the vet'. When we put these two facts together we can deduce that the vet most likely gave Woof the X-ray.

6 eleven—golden retriever, Jack Russell terrier, Rottweiler, boxer, beagle, Labrador, Chihuahua, poodle, cattle dog, husky, great Dane
This is an **interpretive** question. You need to closely read the text to count the various breeds named. When we list all the breeds, a total of eleven different are mentioned.

7 **b** This is an **interpretive** question. We cannot rely on logic to arrive at the answer because the dogs in the text ate a variety of things unlikely to be mistaken for food. This question requires us to use the process of elimination to find the answer. Answers **a** and **c** cannot be correct because both money and clothing are specifically mentioned in the text as strange things that certain dogs have eaten *(lines 22 and 37)*. This leaves Answer **b** as the only possible answer.

8 **a** This is an **interpretive** question. It requires us to put facts together and use logic to interpret the meaning of the text. We read that a three-year-old great Dane 'began vomiting' *(from line 41)* and then

that 'his owners took him for a scan', and we can conclude that the vomiting was the reason for the scan being sought. We could skim read the text to locate the keywords 'vomiting', 'socks' and 'refusing' to test the suitability of the answer options. We know that Answer **b** can't be correct because it describes the result of the scan rather than the reason for first taking him for a scan. We know that Answer **c** can't be correct because there is no mention of food refusal in the text.

9 **c** This is an **interpretive** question. You need to understand the implications of the title and the writer's tone in the text. We can use our logic and wider experience to reach some conclusions about the writer's attitude from these elements. The focus of the writer seems to be to highlight the strange behaviour of dogs for entertainment purposes. We know that Answer **a** cannot be correct since there is no critical language used that would suggest that the writer dislikes dogs. The second option can also be ruled out because the criticism is only good-humoured. The text would end with suggestions for improvement of the situation if the writer was intending the text to be critical of dogs. This only leaves Answer **c**, which fits as the best answer, considering the lighthearted, amused manner in which the facts are presented.

10 **c** This is an **interpretive** question. It requires you to find a specific phrase in the text and interpret its meaning. We can then use logic to interpret the facts presented to us. We read 'Another weird meal involved a Rottweiler eating a pair of reading glasses, apparently with no ill effects' *(lines 11 and 12)*. We need to apply our vocabulary knowledge to interpret the phrase 'no ill effects': it means that no harm was caused to the dog. We know that Answer **a** cannot be correct, as it states the dog became ill, which is the opposite outcome stated in line 7. We know that Answer **b** cannot be correct, because the dog that ate the glasses did not become ill, which contradicts the point that sickness is caused by dogs eating non-food items. This leaves only Answer **c** as the correct answer.

11 **b** This is an **applied** question. We need to consider the text as a whole and its overall message. The writer registers surprise that some of the dogs were not harmed by what they ate. This indicates that the usual expected outcome would be that the strange objects would harm the dogs. Key words and phrases that help us reach the answer include 'didn't even require surgery' and 'amazingly'. These tell us that the positive outcome wasn't expected. Therefore we can draw the conclusion that the correct answer is Answer **b.** We know that Answer **a** is not correct because the author's amazement that some of the dogs escaped harm tells us this is not the usual outcome. We know that Answer **c** is not correct from our own experience. Most dogs do not eat Christmas lights and for those that do, swallowing glass and metal could not be considered 'harmless'.

12 **b** This is an **applied** question. When we consider all of the facts together and apply reasoning we conclude that the answer must be Answer **b** because of the title *(line 1)*. The answer cannot be Answer **a** because many dogs other than huskies are mentioned in the text. The answer cannot be Answer **c** because our logic and our own experience tells us that the items mentioned in the text were not foods. The answer that fits the facts and the tone of the text is Answer **b**.

INFORMATIVE TEXT

Spelling Work

page 14

1 **a** bizarre **b** lodging **c** weird **d** several **e** cavity **f** disgraceful **g** apparently **h** elastic **i** devoured **j** biscuit

2 amazingly, apparently

3 lodging, swallowing

4 weirder

5 bizarrely, weirdly

6 **a** swallowing **b** numerous **c** diamond **d** amazingly **e** engagement

7 **a** several **b** engagement **c** apparently **d** devoured **e** amazingly **f** numerous

8 **a** one **b** three **c** two **d** two

INFORMATIVE TEXT

Vocabulary Work

page 15

1 **a** Answers will vary. Sample answer: My dog has apparently eaten Grandpa's glasses.
b Answers will vary. Sample answer: A fox terrier tried to eat my engagement ring.
c Answers will vary. Sample answer: Amazingly, the dog that ate four large candles was unharmed.
d Answers will vary. Sample answer: My dog's disgraceful behaviour can be very embarrassing.

2 sticking; getting stuck

3 Suggested answers:
a ordinary, usual **b** ill, unwell, harmed **c** old **d** cheap **e** lost **f** cheap **g** leading **h** up **i** careless **j** partial **k** small, tiny, little **l** thawed, fresh **m** like **n** hated **o** eaten **p** before

ANSWERS

CHECK YOUR ANSWERS

4 a gulp b engaged c lodged d X-rayed

5 a pooch

6 a mutt b mongrel

7 a b b e c f d c
e a f d

INFORMATIVE TEXT
Grammar Work page 16

1 a may b won't c may d can

2 a cannot (or can't) b could not (or couldn't)
c should d will e must not (or mustn't) f will

3 a eagerly b boisterously c silently
d mournfully e judgementally f menacingly
g quickly

4 a rarely b often c regularly d occasionally

5 a wholly b newly c expensively d fully
e daily f lately g bodily h fussily

INFORMATIVE TEXT
Punctuation Work page 17

1 a its b its, its c It's
d it's e it's f its

2 a No apostrophe b No apostrophe c Apostrophe
d Apostrophe e No apostrophe f Apostrophe
g Apostrophe h No apostrophe i Apostrophe

3 a In my neighbourhood, the dogs bark at each other all day long.
b My dog's bark is worse than her bite.
c The husky is a breed of dog that can survive quite well in Siberia.
d My brother received sixteen stitches in his leg after two dogs sank their teeth into it.
e Veterinarians are sometimes compelled to report abusive owners for their neglect of dogs' needs.

INFORMATIVE TEXT
Writing Work page 18

1 It serves as an introduction to the main content of the article.

2 background information

3 direct quotes or quotations

4 the place the event occurred, any unusual details about the crime, clues or evidence left by the criminal, the person(s) who committed the crime, the victim(s) of the crime, the motive for the crime, the date the event occurred, the time the event occurred, the extent of any damage or injuries caused, whether or not the criminal has been caught, lessons to be learned from the incident

5 a True b True c False
d False e True

6 Answers will vary. Sample answers:
a Lost in the Blue Mountains
b Dolphins visit restaurant
c When good Maths teachers go bad
d Breathing fluids?

7 Answers will vary. Suggested answers:
a small children in bushland, the Blue Mountains, a map, search and rescue vehicles/workers
b dolphins swimming, dolphins beached, shallow water, exterior of a seaside restaurant
c a man who looks like a high school maths teacher, a man who looks like a member of an outlaw motorcycle gang, a close-up of a motorcycle, bikie colours on a leather jacket, a tattoo
d a researcher in a science lab, scientific apparatus, a fluid in a flask, a person underwater

8 a pretty unusual b weird meal, pair of reading
c especially bizarre d less fortunate, nine sewing
e some careful surgery f whole frozen
g particularly fussy

UNIT 3: INFORMATIVE TEXT—PROCEDURE

INFORMATIVE TEXT
Comprehension Work page 23

1 c This is a **literal** question. Locate the fact in the text; in this case the name of the café. We read 'At C Ya Latté, we pride ourselves on the precision with which we make our coffee' *(lines 2–3)*. The name is repeated in the same line, telling us clearly the name of the café. We know the answer is not Answer **a** because it is the title of the text. We know the answer is not Answer **b** because it would be an illogical name for a café and because we have already encountered the café's real name twice.

2 three pulls
This is a **literal** question. You need to find a specific detail in the text. We read the procedure for extracting coffee *(from line 10)*, which includes a list of shots and how to obtain them. The answer is in line 14.

3 to empty out the used coffee grounds
This is a **literal** question. You need to use your comprehension to find details in the text. We read the procedure for tapping out the cake of coffee *(lines 25 and 26)*. We read that it 'should come out in one piece' and that the barista should 'discard it immediately'. This tells us that the reason for turning the group handle upside down and tapping it is to dislodge the waste product (the used coffee grounds) from the handle. We also know from the order of the procedure that this would be the clean-up phase.

ANSWERS

4 **a** This is an **interpretive** question. It requires us to interpret the meaning of what we have read. First we need to skim read the section headed 'Steaming the milk—machine method', as it is this activity that the question specifies. We read the instruction to 'begin with half a jug of cold milk' *(line 29)*, which gives us one piece of equipment—the jug. Then we read about using the 'steam wand' *(line 31)*, which is the other piece of equipment involved in steaming the milk.

5 **b** This is an **interpretive** question. You need to scan the text to look for a symbol and read it in context to see what it means *(line 36)*. You also have to consider your own knowledge of temperature measurements and use logic to find the answer. The answer cannot be Answer **a**, as the Celsius scale measures degrees of temperature not points. The answer cannot be Answer **c** as there is no such thing as 'days Celsius'.

6 the product of grinding the coffee beans
This is an **interpretive** question. It requires you to synthesise meaning by putting various facts together to reach a conclusion. We read 'so the grounds are released into the group handle' *(line 8)*. This usage of the word 'grounds' and the verb 'are' tells us that grounds must be a plural word. When we consider that 'ground' is the past tense of 'grind', and that we grind coffee, it becomes clear that 'grounds' must be the products of grinding coffee beans.

7 'Extracting the coffee—machine method' and 'Steaming the milk—machine method'
This is an **interpretive** question. You need to think about the implications of the structure of the text. We can see that the text is organised in two main sections *(lines 6 and 28)* so it is reasonable to conclude that the headings of each section refer to the two key stages in coffee making. We can also refer to our own experience of visiting a café to reach this conclusion.

8 steaming, full of small bubbles and double the size in volume
This is an **interpretive** question. You need to think about the implications of certain parts of the content when they are considered together. We read the word 'steaming' in the heading and the phrase 'break down any large bubbles' *(lines 35–37)*. This tells us that the milk should be steaming, bubbling with small bubbles. We read that the steamed milk should be larger in volume than when it was cold *(line 38)*. All of these facts tell us the answer.

9 **b** This is an **interpretive** question. You need to consider the order in which details are presented in the text. When we read the instruction to 'finish with a swirl or create another pattern' *(line 41)* we can see that the keyword 'finish' reveals this is the final step. The recommendation to pour the milk 'as soon as possible' is not the final recommendation, ruling out Answer **a**. The recommendation about holding the jug at an angle is the second—not the last—recommendation and therefore cannot be correct.

10 **a** This is an **interpretive** question. You have to think about multiple aspects of the text at once. We need to scan the text to work out which of the sets of points has presented them in the same order as they occur in the text. Only Answer **a** does so. Neither Answer **b** nor Answer **c** can be correct as they present the points out of order.

11 incorrect packing of the grounds into the group handle; water pressure too low.
This is an **applied** question. It requires you to make an informed judgement based on evidence from the text. We read that 'If you pack the coffee into the group handle correctly, you can be sure of extracting the perfect shot, which should have a rich reddish brown crema' *(line 20)*. We can infer then that the absence of such a crema must mean that the grounds were packed incorrectly. We also read that 'When making the perfect espresso, it is the pressure that makes the difference' *(line 7)*. This tells us that the pressure is the other likely cause for the failure of the appropriate crema to appear.

12 **a** This is an **applied** question. It requires you to read beyond the lines to consider the purpose of the text rather than just the words. The most logical addition to the procedure text would be a diagram detailing the features of the machine. We know that Answer **b** is not correct because it would serve no purpose for a barista in training to look at a picture of a customer. Answer **c** is also incorrect because although it may be a relevant image to the topic, the image most likely to offer clarity to the text is Answer **a**. Both Answers **b** and **c** are merely decorative, whereas Answer **a** is an illustration that clarifies meaning.

INFORMATIVE TEXT
Spelling Work
page 24

1 **a** angle **b** flavour **c** machine **d** pressure **e** attach **f** maintain

2 **a** attach (attachment)
b maintaining, flavouring, attaching (could also have pressuring, machining, angling, whirlpooling and circling, but these are less commonly known forms)

ANSWERS

CHECK YOUR ANSWERS

3 **a** procedures **b** handles **c** waters **d** wands

4 **a** coarseness **b** extraction **c** preferred **d** consistency

5 whirlpool

6 pressure, preferred, coarseness, attach, espresso

7 extraction

8 machine

9 **a** maintain, day **b** whirlpool, cool **c** released, peace **d** coarseness, board **e** whirlpool, her

INFORMATIVE TEXT
Vocabulary Work
page 25

1 **a** precision **b** procedure **c** set **d** level **e** reddish **f** crema **g** volume **h** swirl

2 **a** around **b** firmly **c** particular **d** press **e** dry **f** inside **g** quickly **h** doubled **i** finish **j** first

3 a barista

4 **a** tea **b** icing **c** cake **d** storm **e** sugar **f** crème **g** cup **h** biscuit **i** cookie **j** piece **k** milk **l** pie

INFORMATIVE TEXT
Grammar Work
page 26

1 **a** coffee **b** machine **c** customer **d** milk **e** staff **f** product **g** aroma **h** café

2 shot, handle, container, coffee, piece

3 attention

4 **a** common **b** common **c** common **d** common **e** abstract **f** abstract **g** abstract **h** common **i** common **j** common **k** abstract **l** common **m** common **n** common **o** common **p** abstract

5 **a** line 10 **b** line 16 **c** line 21 **d** line 24 **e** line 27 **f** line 29 **g** line 34 **h** line 36 **i** line 37 **j** line 40 **k** line 41 **l** line 41–42

INFORMATIVE TEXT
Punctuation Work
page 27

1 **a** clause **b** phrase **c** clause **d** clause **e** phrase **f** clause

2 **a** When the bus pulled up, ten school students ordered six lattes and four cappuccinos between them.
b Although it's not our most popular drink, we've been selling a lot more chai teas lately.
c Despite the hot weather this week, we've been just as busy as ever.
d Since we took on two new baristas last April, we've more than doubled our profits at the café.

3 **a** Two of our regular customers, Theo and Olga, nominated us for a community service award.
b At closing time, one of our baristas tripped and sprained her ankle, giving everyone a nasty shock.
c The barista shook chocolate powder over the frothy drinks then, taking a thin wooden stick in his fingers, he delicately made a swirling pattern on top of each one.

4 **a** To make instant coffee at home you'll need instant coffee powder, hot water, milk and sugar.
b The barista made three coffees, two teas and a hot chocolate.
c We ordered raisin toast, carrot cake, lemon slice, two almond biscuits and a blueberry muffin.

5 equals sign (=)

INFORMATIVE TEXT
Writing Work
page 28

1 Procedure texts teach the reader how to do something using a sequence of logical steps. It may be presented in point form rather than in paragraphs.

2 Answers will be individual. Examples may include 'How to bake a cake' or 'How to fix your washing machine'.

3 Bullet points are used as an effective means of summarising information that needs to be presented in a particular order.

4 **a**

5 subheadings, numbered steps, bullet points

6 explanatory pictures, photos and diagrams

7 **a** pressing **b** Begin with half a jug of cold milk **c** group handle **d** 63–65 °C **e** Extracting the coffee—machine method

8 Answers will vary. Sample answer: The title is suitable for this text because it clearly summarises the content and also suggests its purpose: to help baristas create the perfect cup of coffee.

9 Answers will vary. Sample answer: This text was most likely written by a person in authority over the staff at the café. The text is giving instructions that the writer expects to be followed and the tone is authoritative. The most likely position of the writer

is the owner of the company or the franchisee, the general manager or the head of staff who usually trains baristas.

10 instructions

11
- Select the amount of ground coffee by pressing the appropriate button.
- Press down firmly with the tamp.
- Attach the group handle to the machine and press the button to allow hot water to flow through.
- Turn the handle upside down over the collection container and tap out the cake of coffee.
- Turn your attention to steaming the milk.

UNIT 4: INFORMATIVE TEXT—ONLINE ARTICLE

INFORMATIVE TEXT

Comprehension Work

page 33

1 c This is a **literal** question. Look for a fact. We read that Fleming had 'discovered the antibiotic properties of penicillin, a drug that has saved countless lives' *(lines 9–10)*. The keyword 'life-saving' in the question matches the description of penicillin, the drug that the text says has saved lives. We know that Answer **a** is not correct because the text mentions 'a nasty bacterium', which is not a life-saving drug. We know that Answer **b** is not correct because the text says the petri dish contained 'staphylococcus bacteria', which the life-saving penicillin drug killed.

2 *Olympic* collided with a British warship; *Titanic* struck an iceberg; *Britannic* was torpedoed
This is a **literal** question. It requires you to locate simple facts and details. The detail given in line 33 tells us about the collision, lines 35 and 36 tell us about the iceberg, and line 41 tells of the torpedo attack.

3 once
This is a **literal** question. It requires you to read a detail from the text. At first glance we're tempted to answer 'twice' because we know that Anne encountered the book twice. However, we read that Anne's grandfather had bought the book for her when she was a child *(lines 17 and 18)* so she only bought the book once when she rediscovered it in Paris *(line 20)*.

4 Alexander Fleming (a passenger in a taxi), Neville Ebbin, Willard Manders (the taxi driver), Erskine Ebbin, Anne Parrish, Anne's grandfather and her husband, and Violet Jessop
This is a **literal** question. It requires you to locate multiple details explicitly mentioned in the text. We read about all of these people who are either directly named or indirectly referenced in the text. It's best to list the people in order so that no-one is missed out.

5 1912
This is an **interpretive** question. We have to interpret a fact in the text and use our logic to relate it to other facts we know. We read that 'Violet was assigned to work on the *Olympic's* sister ship, RMS *Titanic*, the following year' *(lines 34–35)*. Earlier we read that Violet was aboard the *Olympic* in 1911 *(line 33)*. Logic tells us that the next year must be 1912.

6 a petri dish
This is an **interpretive** question. It requires you to combine facts and details to synthesise the meaning. The detail given about Fleming's failure to wash up the dish *(lines 4 and 5)* can be combined with the details given in lines 7, 8 and 9 to arrive at the answer. When we read that the staphylococcus bacteria in 'the dish' contained a bacterium that was killed by the mould *(lines 8–9)*, logic tells us that the dish mentioned must be the petri dish mentioned earlier *(lines 6–7)*.

7 c This is an **interpretive** question. We know that the 'unpleasant incident' was the same one mentioned earlier *(line 14)*, the accident that killed Neville Ebbin, because no other unpleasant incident is mentioned until the end of the text, which is clearly a second incident similar to the first. The answer is not Answer **a** because no fight is mentioned, and it is not Answer **b** because Erskine Ebbin died a year after the incident described as 'unpleasant'.

8 c This is an **interpretive** question. It requires you to put various facts and details together and make an interpretation. We know that the setting of this story is Bermuda, a Caribbean island nation, because it says so in line 12. This rules out the hometown being a huge city (Answer **a**) because the Caribbean islands are small and the phrase 'little town' is used in line 12. It also rules out being located in New Zealand (Answer **b**). Both of these answers must be incorrect. We can also use logic to deduce that the coincidence is much more likely to occur when there are few roads and taxis so Answer **c** is the answer that makes the most sense.

9 b This is an **interpretive** question. You can use logic, your own knowledge and the process of elimination to answer it. We read that *Jack Frost and Other Stories* is a children's book *(lines 23–24)* and is at least fifty years old *(line 24)*. Traditionally, children's books published fifty years ago were not accompanied by sound recordings and DVDs so the process of elimination rules out Answers **a** and **c**.

ANSWERS

CHECK YOUR ANSWERS

10 **b** This is an **interpretive** question. To obtain the answer, we need to consider multiple facts drawn from the text. We read that the book had been 'a childhood favourite' *(lines 22–23)* and that for 'sentimental reasons, she bought it' ***(line 26)***. We read later that 'she recalled fond memories of reading those stories as a child' ***(line 28)***, leading us to the conclusion that the correct answer is Answer **b**. We know that Answer **a** is not correct, because although this fact is true, we read that she bought the book before she saw her name written in it *(line 26)*, meaning that this cannot have been her reason for purchasing the book. We know that Answer **c** is not correct because, although we know she is a novelist herself, there is no mention that she wrote the book.

11 **a** This is an **applied** question. We need to use logic to interpret the implications of the text in order to arrive at the answer. The clues about this answer are found in lines 23–24 and 30, where we read that Anne had owned a copy of the book fifty years ago and that the one found in Paris was the very same copy. We know that Answer **b** is not correct because it is the same copy, which is the reason for this story being considered a 'strange coincidence'. The answer cannot be Answer **c** because line 30 tells us that it was Anne's name and old address in America that was written in the book.

12 It is surprising because it involves a number of different elements. The victims were brothers aged a year apart and the accidents occurred a year apart, making the victims the same age when they died. They both used the same moped and rode on the same street. The same taxi driver and passenger were involved, and in both cases the collision led to the death of the rider. This is an **applied** question. It requires you to consider the combined effects of each of these details as well as their implications to arrive at the answer.

INFORMATIVE TEXT
Spelling Work
page 34

1 **a** researchers **b** incidents **c** laboratories **d** novelists

2 bacterium

3 mould and route

4 bought, mould and route

5 laboratory

6 bought

7 **a** mould **b** incident **c** original **d** collided **e** passenger **f** childhood

8 **a** accidentally **b** bought **c** interrupted **d** original

9 **a** e, ea, e **b** ou, e **c** o, i, e **d** a, o, a, o

10 accidentally, bacteria, bought, childhood, collided, incident, interrupted, laboratory, mould, novelist, original, passenger, researcher, route, tattered

INFORMATIVE TEXT
Vocabulary Work
page 35

1 **a** a fungus that grows on organic substances
b crashed into
c way of travelling from one place to another
d torn and falling apart **e** event

2 **a** researcher **b** accidentally **c** interrupted **d** original

3 **a** researcher—knowledge **b** laboratory—chemistry **c** bacteria—disease **d** passenger—travel **e** novelist—literature **f** bought—shopping

4 **a** uninterrupted, unoriginal **b** mouldy **c** researched, routed **d** originally

5 **a** feet **b** stars **c** pot **d** management **e** fate **f** law

INFORMATIVE TEXT
Grammar Work
page 36

1 **a** at, in **b** inside, on **c** beyond

2 **a** off **b** against **c** down **d** over **e** beside **f** into **g** to **h** from **i** in **j** by

3 **a** with **b** by **c** at **d** under

4 in, in, in, of, to, in, of, in, as, along, with, by, with, on (Note: In this text *as* functions as a preposition and has therefore been included in this list)

5 **b** the car's wheels **c** Anne Parrish's luck **d** scientists' discoveries **e** the passengers' deaths

INFORMATIVE TEXT
Punctuation Work
page 37

1 **a** As Fleming repeatedly taught his students, the staphylococcus bacterium is a dangerously infectious bug.
b Is the town of Hamilton in Bermuda?
c Anne Parrish came home from Paris with the very same book she'd owned as a child.
d Imagine the odds of two brothers being killed at the same place by the same driver just a year apart!
e How lucky is Violet Jessop to have survived three accidents at sea?

2 **a** life-saving or germ-killing **b** 17-year-old **c** banged-up **d** bric-a-brac **e** well-used

3 **a** comma **b** apostrophe **c** question mark **d** quotation marks **e** hyphen **f** exclamation mark **g** colon **h** semicolon **i** full stop

4 **a** would have **b** cannot **c** should not **d** they will **e** he had or he would **f** we are **g** have not **h** we will

5 **a** and **b** but **c** because **d** although **e** or **f** while **g** whether **h** except

INFORMATIVE TEXT
Writing Work
page 38

1 non-fiction

2 subheadings, short readable chunks of text, logical order of presentation, connective phrases, visual features

3 An online article. This is because online articles are indexed and organised by their content, using keywords that enable search engines to find only the most relevant articles. In contrast, magazine articles are not usually listed and organised on any kind of database.

4 The writer intends to inform readers about some strange coincidences.

5 **a** appeal, target **b** stories, related **c** large, worldwide **d** indexed, access

6 **a** he'd, she'd
b 'He'd accidentally discovered the antibiotic properties of penicillin.' 'A year later, the same passenger was reminded of this unpleasant incident as he rode in a taxi along that same route with the very same cab driver.' 'There the name of the book's former owner was written—Anne Parrish.'
c Alexander Fleming, The Ebbin brothers, Anne Parrish, Violet Jessop
d 1928, 1974 **e** staphylococcus **f** petri dish
g 209 North Weber Street, Colorado

7 **a** opinion **b** opinion **c** fact **d** opinion **e** fact **f** fact **g** fact **h** fact **i** opinion **j** opinion

UNIT 5: NARRATIVE TEXT—JOURNAL

NARRATIVE TEXT
Comprehension Work
page 43

1 Wednesday, 8 August
This is a **literal** question. Look for a detail in the text. This particular detail is easy to spot as it is written at the beginning of each journal entry.

2 the astronaut's husband or partner
This is a literal question. We need to look at two details from the text. Samuel's name is first mentioned in line 12. You need to notice the message conveyed by the phrase 'him and the kids' *(line 14)*. By looking at these two details together, we can see that Samuel is the person referred to as 'him' in line 13.

3 the Earth as seen from space
This is a **literal** question. It requires you to find a detail in the text. You can do this by skim reading the text for the word 'sphere' and reading it in its context. When we read line 34, we find the word 'sphere'. If we read around that line, starting from line 32 and continuing to line 34, we see that the context in which it is mentioned is a description of the feelings and thoughts of the astronaut when she first went into space.

4 **b** This is an **interpretive** question. It requires you to consider facts and details in combination in order to arrive at a logical conclusion. We read that this mission is the fourth *(line 3)*. When the author mentions her 'last mission' in line 12, she means the mission immediately before this fourth one, which makes it her third mission. We know that the answer cannot be Answer **a** because it has to be her most recent mission before this one, the fourth. The answer cannot be Answer **c** either, because this journal entry is marked 'my fourth and final mission'. In line 12, the phrase 'my last mission' refers to her previous one not this final one.

5 **b** This is an **interpretive** question. It requires us to think about connotations of a term based on the context in which the term appears. The title 'Earthbound' has more than one meaning but to make sense as a title both meanings must refer to something related to space travel or astronauts. The positive meaning of the title is 'bound for Earth' as a destination. The negative meaning is being unable to leave Earth (as an astronaut) again. We know the answer cannot be Answer **a** because this is actually a positive meaning not a negative one. We know that Answer **c** cannot be correct because this contains a misinterpretation of the word 'bound' (meaning 'tied up') and has no relevance to astronauts and space travel.

6 **c** This is an **interpretive** question. It requires you to interpret the meaning of facts and details. The meaning of this detail depends upon an understanding of the colloquialism 'getting your wings clipped'. This means to have your freedom curtailed, such as what happens to chickens when they have their wings clipped to prevent them from flying away. The position of this colloquialism in line 29 of the text also reveals

the meaning, as it is clear from the context that the writer is talking about what will happen after her final mission. We know that Answer **a** is not correct because proceeding with a launch implies freedom not restriction. We know the answer is not Answer **b** because the writer is talking about an experience in space that she will no longer have once she has had her 'wings clipped' and has become 'desk-bound'.

7 c This is an **interpretive** question. It requires you to interpret some details that are revealed in line 15. The context in which the detail is mentioned tells us that the writer was angry at the impact that the NASA employee's comments had upon her family, so we can work out the answer. We know that Answer **a** is incorrect because that employee was mentioned by name as 'Jacko' *(line 9)* and the writer expresses her gratitude that he was able to fix the door, so she is clearly not upset with him. We know that Answer **b** is not correct because this is a reference to the term 'desk sucker' which is a derogatory term for a person who has a desk job at NASA. It cannot literally mean that the person sucks their desk.

8 sad but relieved
This is an **interpretive** question. You need to consider multiple aspects of the text at once. We read the phrase 'profound sadness mixed in with relief' *(line 27)*, which tells us the answer.

9 c This is an **interpretive** question. We need to consider multiple aspects of the text at once. We read that the astronaut hates keeping secrets from her family but that she doesn't want to frighten them so she is forced to do so *(line 13)*. This is clearly the thing she most hates about her job, possibly the only thing, as she makes it clear elsewhere in the text that she loves her job and will really miss her missions. Although she does mention lack of sleep, she doesn't say she hates that drawback and it is only a temporary problem she experiences before a launch, so we can safely say that Answer **a** is not correct. We know that Answer **b** is not correct because the adrenaline surge is something she describes with such intensity *(lines 31–32)* that it is clear that she will miss it.

10 a simile
This is an **interpretive** question. It requires you to interpret and identify a common literary technique. All we need to do is work out which technique is presented in the description. When we read the description we know that descriptive techniques are mainly similes, metaphors, adjectives and contrast. When we work through each one we can see a match between this line of text and the technique of simile.

11 herself
This is an applied question. It requires you to understand the author's likely intended audience, which in turn assumes that you already know about the key features of journals—that writers are writing to themselves. Apply your existing knowledge about journals to solve the question.

12 c This is an **applied** question. We need to consider implications, reading beyond the lines to reach a conclusion. The image of the welcome sign in the last line carries the connotation that the astronaut is choosing to see something positive as she imagines a sign on the satellite. Of course there is no actual sign. The answer cannot be Answer **a** because we are not told this information at all in the article. It can't be Answer **b** either, as there is no other mention of any other NASA employees feeling welcomed by the satellite in space. In addition, a message on a satellite does not constitute any kind of official welcome to the universe.

NARRATIVE TEXT

Spelling Work

page 44

1 mission, satellite, terrify, glittering

2 sphere

3 **a** astronauts, satellite, panorama
b incinerate, mission, glittering
c fatal, failure **d** fourth, launch

4 **a** missions **b** failures **c** launches
d careers **e** spheres **f** satellites

5 **a** astronauts **b** launch **c** satellite
d incinerate **e** glittering **f** adrenaline
g career

6 **a** incinerated **b** terrifying **c** fatality
d launches **e** failed **f** panoramic
g spherical **h** glittered

NARRATIVE TEXT

Vocabulary Work

page 45

1 **a** gamble **b** searing **c** shuttle
d amiss **e** void **f** surreal
g final **h** admit **i** threatening
j restore **k** pressure **l** senses
m survived **n** proceed

2 **a** to do with the stars and space
b wide area **c** round, a sphere

3 **b**

4 **a** Examples: vast, expanding, rapidly
b Examples: brave, training, expertly
c Examples: hot, consuming, fiercely

ANSWERS

d Examples: advanced, orbiting, reliably
e Examples: bold, advancing, resolutely
f Examples: terrible, collided, unexpectedly

5 **a** not thinking clearly; distracted
b strangely distanced from reality
c aliens
d Get ready to start.

NARRATIVE TEXT
Grammar Work page 46

1 **a** my, I, I'm, I, we, I, I'm, I, my, I, I, I, I, we, we, I'll, I, me, I, I, my, my, I'll, I'll, I, my, I, my, me, me
b we, we, we **c** he, him, they, them, him

2 **a** searing **b** fatal **c** final
d profound **e** grounded **f** first
g blue **h** golden **i** black

3 **a** nervous **b** sleepless, sleepy **c** hot
d powerful **e** secretive **f** knowledgeable
g comparative **h** memorable **i** cloudy, cloudless
j golden

4 **a** feeling **b** thinking **c** thank
d told **e** senses **f** hate
g terrify **h** believe **i** inform
j tell **k** sadness **l** relief
m knowing **n** feel **o** understand
p remember **q** dream **r** welcoming

G	A	G	C	S	H	L	H	R	Z
N	I	J	T	M	E	L	E	E	F
I	L	N	R	E	O	N	Q	L	C
L	K	I	F	D	L	W	S	I	X
E	N	S	U	O	Y	L	T	E	U
E	O	P	X	V	R	U	M	F	S
F	W	E	L	C	O	M	I	N	G
S	I	Y	B	W	F	E	H	U	V
U	N	D	E	R	S	T	A	N	D
O	G	P	D	X	E	Y	T	S	S
Q	P	L	N	R	X	B	E	S	E
Z	O	Y	R	T	U	K	E	P	V
T	H	I	N	K	I	N	G	K	E
V	F	S	N	B	D	M	Z	O	I
Y	W	A	M	A	E	R	D	Q	L
D	H	R	S	U	Z	S	V	A	E
T	R	E	M	E	M	B	E	R	B

NARRATIVE TEXT
Punctuation Work page 47

1 **a** I'm feeling just as nervous as I always do before a launch.
b I hate keeping secrets from Samuel and the kids but I don't want to frighten them about the risks.
c I'll tell my family all about my experiences when I get back from this final mission.
d I must admit, I'm looking forward to getting my feet back on the ground.
e Jacko was able to restore power to the pressure door before it was too late.
f I can't believe that someone disclosed the odds of a fatal mission failure to my loved ones.
g Nothing will ever compare to my first experience of going into space.
h Looking back, I remember becoming totally lost in the panorama spread before me.
i The clouds seemed to be brushed onto the background of the sea like oil paint.
j The golden wings of the satellite were glittering in the black void of space.

2 **a** question mark ? **b** full stop .
c exclamation mark ! **d** exclamation mark !
e full stop . **f** question mark ?

3 **a** Yuri Gagarin, John Glenn, Neil Armstrong and Buzz Aldrin are all famous astronauts.
b Many nations use satellites including Australia, Japan, China, Russia and the United States of America.
c The five Space Shuttle orbiters were named *Columbia, Challenger, Discovery, Endeavour* and *Atlantis.*
d The planets in our solar system are Mercury, Venus, Earth, Mars, Jupiter, Saturn, Uranus and Neptune.

NARRATIVE TEXT
Writing Work page 48

1 to record our personal experiences and thoughts

2 conjunctions and connectives

3 an anecdote

4 chronological order

5 Answers will vary but could include: nervous, searing, threatening, incinerate, thank God, hate, terrify, can't believe, fatal, failure, gamble, dangerous, I can't shake the fear, strange, profound sadness, relief, I'll have survived, grounded, get my wings clipped, no one else can understand that feeling, way beyond adrenaline, nothing will ever compare, becoming totally lost, panorama, surreal, like a dream, great, welcoming me to the universe

6 **a** register **b** diary **c** appointment book
d scrapbook **e** chronicle **f** log

7 **a** May Chang **b** Mohendas Gupta
c Marat Samut **d** Cody Jamieson
e Scott Burrell **f** Private Miriam Rosas
g Ringo the Clown **h** Matthew Flinders
i DI Woodbridge **j** Ainsley Ryback

ANSWERS

CHECK YOUR ANSWERS

UNIT 6: NARRATIVE TEXT—BIOGRAPHICAL ARTICLE

NARRATIVE TEXT
Comprehension Work
page 53

1 a hot air balloon
This is a **literal** question. Look for a specific detail in the text. We read that Felix 'travelled to the edge of space in a hot air balloon' *(lines 5–6)*.

2 Taiwan
This is a **literal** question. Locate the specific fact in the text. We read about 'Taiwan's Taipei 101 tower' *(line 15)* so we know that Taipei must be in Taiwan. We can see the pattern of mentioning the country's name first, such as where the text reads 'Malaysia's iconic Petronas Towers' *(line 15)*. We can also rely on our own knowledge that Taipei is the capital city of Taiwan.

3 **b** This is a **literal** question. We need to make a straightforward reading of the text to arrive at the answer. We should look for both numerals and words when trying to locate a numerical figure in a text. The answer is given in line 10 but it is expressed in words rather than numerals. We know that Answer **a** is not correct because this figure (36 000 metres) refers to the height Felix jumped from rather than his speed. We know that Answer **c** cannot be correct because 1000 kilometres per second is a speed that would be impossible for a human being to travel without an aircraft.

4 gravity
This is an **interpretive** question. You need to scan the text to find a specific keyword from the question, in this case 'massive'. We read about 'the massive pull of gravity' *(line 24)*. We can therefore conclude that gravity is the force mentioned in the question.

5 **c** This is an **interpretive** question. It requires you to synthesise meaning by putting various facts together to reach a conclusion. First we need to locate the term 'supersonic' in the text and read it in its context. It appears on line 23.We know that the prefix 'super' means 'above' or 'higher than'. We know that the suffix 'sonic' relates to sound. So we can logically conclude that the term 'supersonic' must mean 'faster than the speed of sound'. The answer cannot be Answer **a** because the context of the term 'supersonic' is about speed rather than height. It cannot be Answer **b** because light speed is not mentioned at all in the text.

6 the helmet's faceplate
This is an **interpretive** question. You can use logic, your own knowledge and the process of elimination to answer it. We need to scan the text for keywords from the questions or synonyms of those keywords. We read 'your helmet's faceplate heats up, stopping you from seeing much' *(lines 7–8)*. In this case the phrase 'stopping you' is used instead of 'preventing you'.

7 It's mostly just spinning.
This is an **interpretive** question. It requires you to find a specific phrase in the text and look at it in its context before using logic to interpret the facts presented to us. First we need to scan the text for the phrase 'video footage' or another similar term ('shot a headcam video') that means the same thing. We read that a headcam video was shot but that it captured mostly just spinning *(line 13)*.

8 **c** This is an **interpretive** question. It requires us to interpret the meaning of what we have read. We need to scan the text for a keyword related to reliability. It could be expressed in another form, such as 'reliable' or 'reliant'. We find the word in line 26, which tells us about the need for a reliable parachute. The answer cannot be Answer **a** because the shooting of video is a non-essential element of the stunt. The answer cannot be Answer **c** as the tower's reliability is something outside Felix and his team's control, so logic tells us this can't be correct. Neither the headcam nor the tower are elements that Felix's team have designed for use in the stunt, leaving only the parachute.

9 **a** This is an **interpretive** question. It requires you to synthesise meaning by putting various facts together to reach a conclusion. Instead of seeking a keyword from the question, this time we need to read for meaning and context. We read that a 'carefully engineered pressure suit and capsule was developed to do the job' *(lines 24–25)*. Looking closer, 'the job' is to enable Felix to withstand supersonic speeds *(lines 23–24)*. When we put these facts together we can arrive at the answer. We know Answer **b** is not correct because a time capsule is not related in any way to supersonic speeds. We know that Answer **c** is not correct because there is no mention at all of the balloon in the section of the text that mentions the suit. Logic tells us that Felix will have jumped out of the balloon by the time the pressure and the pull of gravity come into play in the stunt.

10 **a** This is an **interpretive** question. It requires us to find meaning by looking at the text in a general way for its overall message. When we read the third paragraph we can see that the focus of the explanation of the accomplishment is upon what the team of experts needed to achieve to make the stunt successful. This tells us that the answer is Answer **a**. We know that Answer **b** is not correct because

ANSWERS

CHECK YOUR ANSWERS

we read that 'Felix worked with a team of aerospace experts' *(line 21)*. This tells us that it wasn't a solo accomplishment. We know that Answer **c** is not correct, because Felix went up in the air alone and was not forced to jump out. He went up there with the sole purpose of jumping out to set a new record.

11 humility
This is an **applied** question. We need to consider implications, reading beyond the lines to reach a conclusion. The clue to answering this question is the content presented in direct speech. We read what Felix says about how he thought and felt when he was ready to jump *(lines 18–20)*. The main word that describes a quality of human character is 'humble'.

12 **b** This is an **applied** question. We can view the text as a whole to evaluate the effects of various techniques on the meaning. We note that Felix's main objective at the point of his jump was to come back alive *(line 20)*. This line appears as part of direct speech from Felix in his own words, telling us that Answer **b** is the correct answer. We know that Answer **a** is not correct because the first sentence doesn't mention any emotive word at all. The answer cannot be Answer **c** because, although not being able to breathe *(line 8)* is certainly frightening, it is not a factor mentioned by Felix in the direct speech portion of the text. This tells us that there were factors beyond difficulty breathing that made Felix afraid before he did the jump.

NARRATIVE TEXT
Spelling Work
page 54

1 **a** breathing **b** parachuting **c** plunging **d** hurtling

2 **a** breathed **b** parachuted **c** plunged **d** hurtled

3 **a** atmosphere **b** consciousness **c** plunge **d** metres **e** breathe **f** thousand

4 scientific, adventurer, supersonic, thousand, engineered, parachute, accomplished, atmosphere, consciousness

5 **a** Australian **b** balloon **c** height **d** planet **e** Malaysia **f** oblivion **g** data **h** pressure **i** unlikely **j** staggering **k** helmet **l** aircraft **m** iconic **n** stratosphere **o** withstand **p** efforts

6 The extra letters are:
a s **b** n **c** b **d** n **e** f **f** m

NARRATIVE TEXT
Vocabulary Work
page 55

1 **a** record **b** metres **c** helmet **d** breathe **e** sound **f** aircraft **g** spinning

2 **a** gravity **b** oblivion **c** engineered **d** capsule **e** freefall **f** stratosphere **g** iconic **h** humble **i** crazy **j** limits

3 anytime, faceplate, freefall, withstand, supersonic, anymore

NARRATIVE TEXT
Grammar Work
page 56

1 your, you, you, you're, you, you

2 **a** Felix **b** the team of experts **c** Felix **d** the team of experts

3 **a** Felix was jumping from space.
b Felix will be jumping from space.
c Felix was spinning. **d** Felix is spinning.
e The experts are agreeing on a plan.
f The experts will agree on a plan.
g The record was broken (or has been broken).
h The record will be broken.

4 **a** helmet's faceplate **b** scientific data **c** aerospace **d** stratosphere **e** supersonic **f** pressure suit

5 **a** metres, km/h **b** edge, limits **c** gravity, supersonic

6 Austrian, Earth's, Felix Baumgartner, Malaysia's, Petronas Towers, Taipei, Taiwan

NARRATIVE TEXT
Punctuation Work
page 57

1 **a** capital letter, comma, ellipsis, full stop
b capital letter, slash, full stop, capital letter, comma, full stop
c capital letter, comma, colon, open quotation mark, capital letter, capital letter (I), comma, comma, full stop, capital letter, full stop, close quotation mark
d capital letter, apostrophe, apostrophe, full stop, capital letter, full stop
e capital letter, hyphen, full stop, capital letter, comma, italics (*was*), full stop
f capital letter, comma, comma, capital letter, full stop

2 **a** Felix's helmet
b the team's expertise
c the balloon's ascent

- **d** Taiwan's famous landmark
- **e** the two scientists' expertise
- **f** conquering his fears

3 BASE-jumped, edge-of-atmosphere, record-breaking

4 **a** Well, *was* he wearing a helmet?
b Did Felix report that the feat was a lot harder than he thought it would be?

NARRATIVE TEXT
Writing Work page 58

1 biography and autobiography

2 present

3 photographs, maps, illustrations

4 first or third person

5 indirect speech

6 dates and the names of people, places and events

7 foreshadowing

8 Felix said that when he was standing there on top of the world, he became so humble he did not think about breaking records anymore. He did not think about gaining scientific data. The only thing he wanted was to come back alive.

9 And (you hurtle back), As (a startling bonus), since (you're on the northern side), When (I was standing there), Then (they needed to figure out), After (five years)

10 The feat is a lot harder than he thinks it is. He feels he is about to lose consciousness from the wild spinning that he's enduring during the freefall but he manages to regain control at the critical moments.

11

a Strong	**b** Strong	**c** Strong
d Strong	**e** Neutral	**f** Neutral
g Strong	**h** Neutral	**i** Neutral
j Strong	**k** Strong	**l** Neutral

UNIT 7: NARRATIVE TEXT— DESCRIPTIVE NARRATIVE

NARRATIVE TEXT
Comprehension Work page 63

1 **a** This is a **literal** question. Locate the fact in the text. We read that 'After overheating on his long walk he found the rain a welcome relief, so the boy didn't move straight away' ***(lines 9–10)***. The word 'overheating' tells us that Peter was hot from his long walk. We know the answer cannot be Answer **b** because we read that Peter was 'Shaking drips from his head' ***(line 12)***. The answer cannot be Answer **c** because the text does not say that Peter enjoyed getting soaked and his later decision to take shelter tells us logically that this is not the right answer.

2 the rain shower
This is a **literal** question. Look at the literal meaning of the words around the keyword. The sentence in question appears right after the description of the rain becoming heavier ***(lines 17–18)***. The word 'it' refers to whatever noun or verb came immediately before it in the text. This tells us that the word 'it' refers to the rain shower.

3 **c** This is a **literal** question. Locate a specific detail given in the text. We read that Peter 'noticed that a man seated on a bench in the park hadn't bothered to move either' ***(lines 11–12)***. This tells us the answer specifically. The answer cannot be Answer **a** because the suit is first mentioned after Peter had already noticed the man because he hadn't moved out of the rain ***(line 20)***. We know that Answer **b** is not correct because we learn that Peter couldn't see his face ***(line 25)***.

4 **a** This is an **interpretive** question. It requires you to interpret the meaning of a common phrase. You need to read the text carefully and decide what its logical meaning must be. The answer cannot be Answer **b** because the idea of sheltering is not at all the same as settling. Answer **c** is not correct because the expression 'sitting there' indicates that Peter was still, not adjusting his sitting position.

5 **a** This is an **interpretive** question. You need to read the text closely and evaluate the context to make an interpretation of the keyword 'swung'. Then you can synthesise the meaning. Sometimes it is helpful to read around the specific detail to get a clearer picture of the wider context. We read that Peter 'grasped hold of a lower branch, swung himself up and sat down' ***(lines 13–14)***. The implication of the word 'swung' is that it happened in a single, easy motion, which tells us that Peter had no difficulty climbing the tree. We cannot tell from the text whether Peter was a gymnast so Answer **b** cannot be the answer. The text does not specify that the climb took Peter a long time so we know that Answer **c** isn't correct.

6 broad and waxy
This is an **interpretive** question. It requires us to put stated facts together and use logic to interpret the meaning of the text. The leaves are described as being 'broad' and 'waxy' ***(line 15)***. We know from real life that broad leaves would provide more shelter than narrow ones and that wax helps water to run off surfaces, so we can conclude that these two qualities of the leaves are the factors that improved the shelter from the rain.

ANSWERS

CHECK YOUR ANSWERS

7 as a drizzle
This is an **interpretive** question. We need to consider the connotations of certain words. We find that the rain is threatening to become 'more than a drizzle' *(line 16)*. This implies that until that point in the shower, the rain was just a drizzle.

8 **b** This is an **interpretive** question. We need to apply our interpretation to determine the meaning of the text. We read a direct statement that 'Peter could hear the rain becoming heavier' *(line 17)*. When we consider the position of this statement in the text, we can see that this is the time that Peter first knew the rain was becoming heavier. The answer cannot be Answer **a** because we find out at the end of the description that the man in the suit was a statue, so he couldn't have got up. We know that Answer **c** is incorrect because the statement about people running for cover occurs in line 35 right near the end of the text, well after the time that Peter hears the rain becoming heavier.

9 distinguished and refined
This is an **interpretive** question. It requires you to notice the details about how the man's appearance is described, then apply your knowledge to decide which of these words are adjectives. We read about the man's bearing (the way he held himself) *(line 30)* and the two adjectives 'distinguished and refined' are used to describe him.

10 **a** This is an **interpretive** question. It requires you to interpret the meaning of the terms 'narrative' and 'the third person'. When we remember that this is a descriptive story, we realise that it is classified as a narrative. This rules out the other two answer options. We know that Answer **b** is not correct because it is neither an informative text nor delivered in the second person. We know that Answer **c** is not correct because it is not persuasive and not delivered in the first person.

11 He was in disbelief that the man was still sitting in the rain.
This is an **applied** question. It requires you to consider the text's overall point—to deceive the reader into thinking, as Peter did, that the 'man' is a real person. When we read lines 39–40 in its context we can see that Peter shakes his head in disbelief. The question is designed to trick you into thinking that it is referring to the first time Peter shakes his head, which occurs in line 12 when he tries to get raindrops off his head.

12 'He hadn't moved an inch.'
This is an **applied** question. We need to consider the connotations of the text, reading beyond the lines. The subtle hint conveyed in the expression in lines 28–29 suggests the reason why the man was behaving differently from everyone else was because he wasn't a man and he couldn't move.

NARRATIVE TEXT
Spelling Work
page 64

1 **a** impressions **b** statues **c** angles **d** gentlemen

2 **a** benches **b** faces **c** bushes **d** buzzes **e** inches **f** branches **g** boxes **h** hisses

3 gentleman, nobility, sheltered, drenching

4 **a** gentleman—suffix **b** impression—suffix **c** vigorously—suffix **d** nobility—suffix **e** intrigued—prefix **f** upright—prefix **g** sculpted—prefix **h** torrential—suffix **i** scurried—suffix **j** disappeared—prefix

5 **b** reach, reaches, reaching **c** form, forms, forming **d** rain, rains, raining **e** notice, notices, noticing **f** decide, decides, deciding **g** lean, leans, leaning

NARRATIVE TEXT
Vocabulary Work
page 65

1 **a** after **b** had **c** bad **d** upper **e** imperfectly **f** appeared **g** different **h** possible **i** visible **j** closed **k** lighter **l** further **m** couldn't **n** awake **o** up **p** belief

2 we scurried away; I sculpted a statue; he leapt under the shelter

3 **a** weather **b** hair **c** man **d** caught **e** eyes **f** seat **g** nature **h** human

4 **a** clouds **b** hair **c** rain **d** suit **e** shirt collar **f** iron statue **g** sky

5 **a** torrent **b** vigour **c** shelter **d** impress **e** intrigue **f** noble **g** sculpt **h** appear **i** scurry **j** drench

6 **a** cats **b** day **c** bone **d** week **e** fair **f** silver **g** lightning **h** pours **i** night **j** sprung **k** drowned **l** sun **m** showers **n** dawn **o** bolt **p** storm

NARRATIVE TEXT
Grammar Work
page 66

1 **a** long **b** welcome **c** good, sturdy **d** lower **e** broad, waxy

2 **a** smartly **b** freely

3 **a** steadily increasing **b** perfectly tailored

4 Answers will be individual.

ANSWERS

CHECK YOUR ANSWERS

5 Answers will be individual.

6 a grey, iron b quickly, sudden c unexpectedly

NARRATIVE TEXT

Punctuation Work

page 67

1 a the tree's branches b the people's movements
c the bush's leaves d the boss's car

2 a the boys' mistake b the park's trees
c the trees' trunks d the seasons' changes

3 the man's head, Peter's head

4 a didn't b hadn't c could've
d doesn't e he'll f they'd

5 The man was still sitting there! He must have been soaked to the skin!

6 No

7 Line 29: There was something about the man's bearing that intrigued Peter—distinguished and refined, yet content to sit in the drizzling rain with not a care for the damage to his lovely suit.

8 a After his long walk, the rain was a welcome relief. The boy didn't move straight away.
b Shaking drips from his head, Peter looked around. He spotted a good, sturdy tree to climb.
c The hair disappeared into a grey shirt collar, the colour identical to the suit. It permitted no glimpse of his neck.

9 As Peter stayed under the tree, trapped by the grey sheet of rain, it suddenly dawned on him that the man he was looking at was an iron statue.

NARRATIVE TEXT

Writing Work

page 68

1 Descriptive narratives may be part of an overall narrative or may exist as a single, standalone text. They may be non-fiction, unlike novels, which are classified as fiction.

2 They link sentences together.

3 similes and metaphors

4 The voice does not intrude into the text. It describes the scene from an observer's point of view.

5 These are sample answers only. Any phrase or sentence that presents a visual, auditory or tactile stimulus is acceptable.
a dark, grey clouds; the grass under his feet was scorched and shrivelling into tinder-dry clumps; heat haze; it started to rain; a man seated on a bench in the park; shaking drips from his head; a good, sturdy tree; a lower branch; broad, waxy leaves; the grey sky; smartly dressed; a perfectly tailored suit, charcoal grey; curly hair; cut close; sculpted; the hair disappeared into a grey shirt collar; the colour identical to the suit; steel-grey hair; the steadily increasing rain; his head was still upright; the man's bearing; distinguished and refined; the drizzling rain; his lovely suit; Peter climbed down; a torrential downpour; people everywhere scurried for cover; running to their cars; water flowed freely onto Peter's head and shoulders; drenching him through; he shook it off vigorously; he leapt back under the tree; he peered through the leaves and the rain; shaking his wet head; the man was still sitting there!; the grey sheet of rain; the man he was looking at was an iron statue
b it started to rain; Peter could hear the rain becoming heavier; the steadily increasing rain; the drizzling rain; the heavens opened in a torrential downpour; water flowed freely
c hot and sticky; humid summer weather; the grass under his feet was scorched and shrivelling; baking the town; heat; it started to rain; shaking drips from his head; he grasped hold of a lower branch; swung himself up; broad, waxy leaves; leaned a little closer against the trunk; steadily increasing rain; the drizzling rain; the heavens opened in a torrential downpour; water flowed freely; coursed down his back; drenching him through; he shook it off vigorously; shaking his wet head; soaked to the skin

6 Answers will vary. A sample answer is: Peter sat crouched like a little brown bear trying to stay dry.

7 a park in a town

8 a the present b Cars are mentioned.

9 adverbs

10 a dark b grey c humid
d summer e tinder-dry f long
g good h sturdy i lower
j broad k waxy l grey
m curly n steel-grey o drizzling
p lovely q torrential r wet
s iron

UNIT 8: NARRATIVE TEXT—POETRY

NARRATIVE TEXT

Comprehension Work

page 73

1 Planking, a craze where people would find weird places to lie down and have a photograph of themselves taken. Often these places were high up, hard to reach and dangerous.
This is a **literal** question. You simply need to read the title.

2 escalator handrail, a ledge, public wharf and a scaffold
This is a **literal** question. Look at the literal meaning of the words in the text.

ANSWERS

3 That it's 'dead and gone', old, 'too yesterday' and 'somewhat naff'.
This is a **literal** question. Look at the literal meaning of the words in the text. These expressions all mean that most people don't plank anymore and don't think it is new or exciting at all.

4 **b** This is an **interpretive** question. It requires you to interpret the meaning of certain words and phrases. You need to read the text carefully and decide what its logical meaning must be. We read the words 'awkward climb' and 'sometimes fails' *(lines 15 and 16)*, telling us that not all of the speaker's climbs are successful. When we apply logic to this, we can see that this must mean he sometimes falls while attempting to plank. We know that Answer **a** cannot be correct, as it says nothing about failure. We know the answer cannot be Answer **c** because this refers to the speaker's habit of planking, not 'letting go' of a structure.

5 **a** This is an **interpretive** question. We need to look beyond the literal meaning of the phrase to find its meaning in slang terms. Slang is a special way of speaking where words and phrases come in and out of usage as fashions change and social changes occur. When something is said to be 'yesterday' it means that it was popular in the past but is no longer fresh and new. We know that Answer **b** is not correct because this is not a phrase but simply two words appearing in succession. Both belong to other phrases ('my serene celebration of nonsense' and 'needs no photo'). The phrase offers us nothing about the popularity of planking. We know that Answer **c** is not the answer as this expresses the idea that the speaker doesn't follow the tradition of actually having photos taken of himself planking, but it says nothing about the popularity of the hobby.

6 According to the poem you climb up somewhere and lie down flat.
This is an **interpretive** question. We need to consider the connotations of certain words and put some details together to reach the answer. We read 'I see a space somewhere odd' *(lines 9 and 10)*, 'A beckoning space, makes me try An awkward climb' *(lines 14 and 15)* and 'Enticed to assume the familiar position, I just lie down and plank' *(lines 23–25)*. These lines tell us in sequence how planking is done.

7 **c** This is an **interpretive** question. You need to closely read the text and evaluate the context to make an interpretation of words and phrases that give us clues about his motivation. Then you can synthesise the meaning. We read 'But I can't let it go' *(line 8)* and 'A beckoning space, makes me try' *(line 14)*, and finally 'My serene celebration of nonsense' *(line 20)*. The words 'I can't let it go' tell us he wants to keep doing it. The word 'beckoning' tells us it attracts him. The words 'serene celebration' tell us that he finds planking a peaceful 'celebration', a positive expression that suggests that he just likes doing it. We can also use the process of elimination to find the answer. We know that the answer cannot be Answer **a** because it 'Needs no photo, it's somehow wrong' *(lines 21 and 22)*. We know that Answer **b** cannot be correct as there is no mention of his job and the places he chooses have no relationship to one another as a workplace.

8 **c** This is an **interpretive** question. It requires you to notice the details about the sites that are mentioned, then apply your logic to decide which of the alternatives offered in the question is most like those in the poem. Answers **a** and **b** are both unsuitable answers as a sofa and a grassy lawn are not small, high-up spaces. It would not be unusual to see a person lying flat on a sofa or a lawn. Therefore the answer must be Answer **c**.

9 **a** This is an **interpretive** question. We need to consider the connotations of the phrase 'a beckoning space' and read around that phrase to determine what it means from the context. When we read the whole stanza we see that the speaker is urged or tempted to try a climb that sometimes fails, and the following stanza notes that he is defying gravity and taking a risk. Both of these clues tell us that the connotations of 'a beckoning space' are that he is 'tempted' against his better judgement to try to get to the space and plank there. Although Answer **b** is not correct, it is partially true. An awkward climb follows the temptation so the order is wrong. We know that Answer **c** is not correct because the risk of falling does not imply anything about 'beckoning'.

10 **c** This is an **interpretive** question. It requires you to interpret the meaning of the three lines mentioned in the answer options. We need to look for words that describe feelings or thoughts. This principle rules out the Answers **a** and **b**. Neither Answer **a** nor Answer **b** suggest anything about the speaker's feelings. In fact, the context tells us that Answer **b** is a reference to how others feel about planking, not how the speaker feels. He uses the word 'enticed', meaning that planking attracts and tempts him in a positive way, so Answer **c** must be the answer.

11 The last line of each stanza is composed of two words (except for the very last line of the poem). The first word has two syllables, beginning with the prefix 'some', and the second word has just a single syllable.
This is an **applied** question. It requires you to consider the text's overall structure and look for a pattern. When we look for patterns, we can count syllables and words, and look for rhythms and rhyme.

ANSWERS

CHECK YOUR ANSWERS

12 The speaker is probably in his early twenties.
This is an **applied** question. We need to consider the connotations of the text, reading beyond the lines and applying our outside knowledge to interpret the text's meaning. The clue 'It had its day in twenty-twelve' tells us the year that planking was popular (and perhaps for a few years after 2012). We can apply our logic and outside knowledge of the main social group that keep up with new trends to conclude that the planking enthusiasts were most likely teenagers. This means that if the speaker was a teenager (of around 15–18 years old) in 2012, we can work out his approximate age today by adding the years since 2012 to what he was when the craze was popular.

NARRATIVE TEXT
Spelling Work
page 74

1 **a** escalator **b** awkward **c** scaffold **d** wharf **e** enticed **f** familiar **g** serene

2

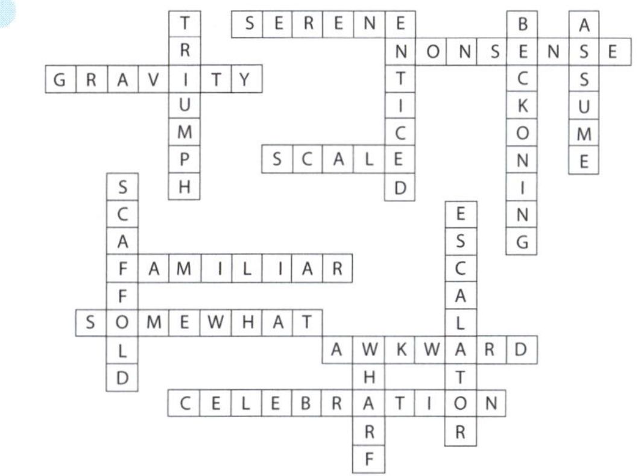

3 nonsense, somewhat, triumph, scaffold, escalator, enticed, serene, awkward

4 Answers will be individual. Sample answers: **a** an awkward moment **b** a serene afternoon

5 Answers will be individual. Sample answers: **a** Our team will triumph on the field tonight. **b** What is this nonsense about you quitting your job?

6 **a** assumed **b** assuming **c** assumption **d** enticed **e** enticing **f** celebrated **g** celebrating **h** celebration **i** escalated **j** escalating **k** escalation

NARRATIVE TEXT
Vocabulary Work
page 75

1 **a** climb **b** time, era **c** calling, enticing, tempting **d** difficult, challenging **e** weird, strange **f** people **g** unfashionable, daggy **h** place, spot

2 Answers will be individual. Refer students back to the poem for samples.

3 **a** 4 **b** 2 **c** 2 **d** 4 **e** 2 **f** 4 **g** 2 **h** 3 **i** 1 **j** 3

4 **a** demanding **b** unique **c** extreme **d** illogical **e** bizarre **f** silly **g** dangerous **h** peculiar **i** challenging **j** risky **k** nonsensical **l** oddball

5 **a** jam **b** paint **c** hoops **d** poker **e** rubber

NARRATIVE TEXT
Grammar Work
page 76

NARRATIVE TEXT
Punctuation Work
page 77

1 The chief defect of Henry King was chewing little bits of string.

2 capital letter, full stop, semicolon, comma, quotation marks, dash, ellipsis

3 lines 2 and 3

4 the third

5 lines 10, 13 and 20

6 eleven

NARRATIVE TEXT
Writing Work
page 78

1 a setting, characters and a plot

2 a word where the spelling reflects the actual sound of the thing being described

ANSWERS

CHECK YOUR ANSWERS

3 The poet seems to be saying that planking is an example of a pursuit that is illogical. He hints at a lesson—we won't always understand why some people enjoy doing odd things but we shouldn't let it bother us.

4 **a** consonant **b** pictured **c** repeating **d** nouns **e** names **f** speech **g** punctuation

5 **a** 'twenty-twelve', 'space somewhere', 'scale this scaffold', 'someday soon', 'serene celebration', 'nonsense needs no'
b 'had its day', 'twenty-twelve', 'no photo'
c the prefix 'some' in every third line of the stanzas
d dead, new, naff, odd, public, beckoning, awkward (used as an adverb), wrong, familiar
e I, me, my
f 'dead and gone', 'had its day', 'far too yesterday', 'naff', 'I can't let it go'
g the second and third lines in each stanza

UNIT 9: PERSUASIVE TEXT—MARKETING TEXT

PERSUASIVE TEXT

Comprehension Work

page 83

1 **b** This is a **literal** question. Find details from the text. When we skim read the text we can see that the word 'future' is repeated numerous times throughout and is present in each slide's subheading.

2 **b** This is a **literal** question. Locate facts and details in the text. We read in slides 2 and 3 the list of the wristbands' features, which includes these specific characteristics. Neither Answer **a** nor **c** is correct because the attributes do not match the details in the slides.

3 **a** This is a **literal** question. You need to recognise synonyms that are used for particular details and search for slightly different words from those in the question. We read that Carl Whitman's position is 'CEO' *(line 13)*, which stands for 'Chief Executive Officer'. The answer cannot be either Answer **b** or **c** because the word 'Director' or the title 'Conference President' would've been part of Carl Whitman's email sign-off.

4 **a** This is an **interpretive** question. You need to look at language-related matters, such as meanings conveyed by certain words, phrases or symbols. The line in the question contains a semicolon, a punctuation mark often used to create a contrast between the two portions of the sentence. The words 'simple' and 'total' are not exactly opposites but when placed together they create a contrast, as we wouldn't normally expect gaining a 'total solution' to be a 'simple' process. The answer cannot be Answer **b** because there is no contrasting language presented. The answer is not Answer **c** because the phrase 'long-life' presents no contrast either.

5 **c** This is an **interpretive** question. You need to consider multiple aspects of the text at once and look at language-related matters, such as meanings conveyed by certain words, phrases or symbols. The statements that form the subheadings are all questions, as evidenced by the presence of question marks and the phrasing. The answer cannot be Answer **a** as an interjection is usually a single word, such as *Hey!* The answer cannot be Answer **b** as there are no exclamation marks present and the phrasing doesn't fit that definition.

6 Easy ID
This is an **interpretive** question. You have to synthesise meaning by putting various facts together to reach a conclusion. We read that Easy ID is the company on whose behalf Carl Whitman has sent the email *(lines 8, 10 and 14)*. We also read that the Fantasy Land directors are back in the States (America) *(line 6)*, so we know that they can't be in Australia. This leads us to synthesise the interpretation that Easy ID is based in Australia and that the Fantasy Land directors paid them a visit from the USA.

7 call them to obtain a free sample
This is an **interpretive** question. It requires you to interpret the meaning of facts and details. The meaning of some parts of the text may not be obvious from just a straightforward reading. When we put certain facts and details together we can arrive at a logical answer. We read the call to action in the invitation to 'call us to obtain a free sample, custom-designed for your business' *(line 43)*. When we apply our logic to interpret this statement, we can see that any item custom-designed for a particular business would carry that business's branding and logo.

8 It means that the wristbands can carry any design, logo, colours, brands and other visual features the customer may want.
This is an **interpretive** question. We need to think about the connotations of words—meanings that extend beyond the words on the page. We read in slide 3 that Easy ID are 'simplifying the future', which implies that customised designs are simple for the customer to obtain because Easy ID take care of customising the product.

9 because of the large number of people who need to be scanned and tracked upon entry to Fantasy Land
This is an **interpretive** question. It requires you to interpret the meaning of facts and details. The meaning of some parts of the text may not be obvious from just a straightforward reading. We read that the target customer is 'Fantasy Land', which we can infer is some type of amusement park or entertainment venue. We can also infer that they would deal with a high volume of customers, who all need to be processed through a ticketing and tracking system. So logic (and our own real-world experience) tells us that to keep their operation running smoothly, the process of scanning would need to be fast. We also read the question 'Is that fast enough for you?' *(lines 39–40)*, which implies that speed of processing is an important feature of the product.

10 via a web interface
This is an **interpretive** question. It requires you to make small but important distinctions between ideas. We read the phrase 'web interface' *(line 36)*, which is grouped together with the scanning and tracking elements of the data management process. This tells us that the web interface is the means through which the owner of the technology accesses the information they collect.

11 **a** This is an **applied** question. We need to apply assumed knowledge, information or understanding that the writer assumes you possess already. Our experience of identification technology, even through paper-based tickets, tells us that scannable products enable the issuing company to track the movement of customers through their doors.

12 to sell the Fantasy Land directors the Easy ID wristband technology
This is an **applied** question. It requires us to make an informed judgement or evaluation based on evidence from the text. It also requires us to read beyond the lines to understand implications. We can see by the persuasive techniques of repetition, emotive language, contrast, the highlighting of features and benefits of the product, and the call to action that this text has been created to persuade the target customer to buy the product.

PERSUASIVE TEXT
Spelling Work
page 84

1 **a** 'ss' **b** 'k' **c** 'k' **d** 'ss' **e** 'k' **f** 'ss'

2 business

3 delighted, wristbands, technology, designed

4 **a** wristbands, scanned **b** directors, arrived **c** assist, making **d** confident, proposal **e** solution, management **f** access, web **g** colourful, comfortable **h** consider, opportunity **i** process, seconds **j** sample, design

5 **a** attached **b** assistance **c** business

6 **a** wristbands **b** software **c** interface

7 **a** proposals **b** detail **c** solutions **d** data **e** capability **f** businesses **g** opportunities **h** information **i** sample **j** directors

PERSUASIVE TEXT
Vocabulary Work
page 85

1 **a** colourful **b** attached **c** capabilities **d** management **e** decision **f** simplifying **g** solution **h** invitation **i** assistance **j** obtain

2 **a** invite **b** present **c** resolve **d** propose **e** decide **f** simplify **g** confer **h** manage **i** attach **j** assist

3 **a** the people in charge of a company
b a system for working with business information
c identification
d created specifically for a customer's unique needs
e very clear and detailed appearance of printed text and images

4 **a** business **b** handshake **c** down **d** show **e** personal **f** losses **g** millionaire **h** world **i** bottom **j** in **k** eat **l** ballpark **m** square

PERSUASIVE TEXT
Grammar Work
page 86

1 **a** Progress is wonderful!
b It couldn't be any simpler.
c We're sure you would like your business to profit from these features.
d And the entire process takes less than a second to complete. That will be fast enough for you.
e Let Easy ID work for you.

2 Thank you **for** the invitation **to** submit our proposal **to** you. I trust you all arrived **back in** the States safely. We were delighted **to** spend some time getting **to** know you **at** the ID Technology conference **in** Sydney. We'd like **to** invite the Fantasy Land Board **of** Directors **to** consider using

our Easy ID wristbands. You'll find attached **to** this email a PowerPoint presentation that provides details **about** the Easy ID system. We trust that you will find it **of** great assistance **in** making your decision.

3 comfortable, high-resolution, waterproof, colourful, long-life, tamper-proof, secure, fully customisable

4 leading, fast, simple, instant

5 wonderful

6 easy, great, safely, high, total, comfortable, wonderful, simple, fully, secure, instant, free, fast, profit, trust, simplifying

7 tracking, progress, email, research, printing, profit, access, features, sample, management

PERSUASIVE TEXT

Punctuation Work

page 87

1 **a** Plural **b** Possessive **c** Plural **d** Possessive **e** Plural **f** Plural

2 **a** is not **b** have not **c** might have **d** you will **e** cannot **f** I would or I had

3 **a** o **b** o **c** ha **d** wi **e** no **f** woul or ha

4 web-based, long-life, high-resolution, tamper-proof, custom-designed

5 **a** Line 16
b Lines 1, 6, 7, 10, 13, 28, 41, 42, 43 and 44
c Lines 21, 28, 34, 40, 42 and 44
d Any of the following: Lines 2, 7, 8, 10,19, 42 and 44

6 after the word 'resolution'

7 Answers will vary. A sample answer: Our wristbands have a long life and are colourful due to high-resolution printing. They are comfortable to wear and waterproof. Would you like your business to profit from these features?

PERSUASIVE TEXT

Writing Work

page 88

1 detailed comparisons between things

2 A question is posed in order to obtain an answer. A rhetorical question doesn't need or anticipate an answer but is designed to provoke thought.

3 dreams

4 Isn't progress wonderful? How much simpler could it be? Is that fast enough for you? Why not let Easy ID work for you?

5 **a** Dear Fantasy Land Directors,
b trust, delighted, like, invite, assistance, easy, kind, regards

6 We invite you to call us to obtain a free sample, custom-designed for your business. Why not let Easy ID work for you?

7 technology: Appeals to the target customer's sense of progress and the belief that high-tech resources provide an advantage in business.
easy: Simplifies the technology to make it sound accessible and user-friendly.
solution: Promises to solve problems for the target customer.
progress: Implies advancement and being ahead of the competition.
leading: Asserts the idea that the seller is the first to market with the product.
instant: Implies speed and ready access.
future: Implies that the customer will benefit for some time to come from a decision made today.
free: Suggests that the customer is getting something for nothing and has nothing to lose.
custom-designed: Implies the value of uniqueness.

8 web interface, instant barcode scanning technology, tracking information, high-speed data processing

9 Slide 1: a total data management system
Slide 2: quality wristbands
Slide 3: security features
Slide 4: technological capabilities
Slide 5: contact Easy ID for a sample

10 the word 'future'. Students may also answer with variants of the words 'simple' and 'easy'.

11 Answers will be individual. The slides to keep are the first and the fifth. Any of the other three could be removed without sacrificing the key message.

UNIT 10: PERSUASIVE TEXT— OPINION PIECE

PERSUASIVE TEXT

Comprehension Work

page 93

1 'Mahalo' means 'thank you'.
This is a **literal** question. We read in the subtitle 'In English we say "thank you". In Hawaiian, it's "mahalo"'. Locate this fact in the text.

2 the Hawaiian islands
This is a **literal** question. Just before the reference to the green volanoes, we read that the writer saw 'Hawaii's islands below us—a cluster of green volcanoes' *(lines 26–27)*. The description after the dash describes the Hawaiian islands. Locate this fact in the text.

ANSWERS

CHECK YOUR ANSWERS

3 to find a place where he could exchange his Australian currency for American coins to put in the massage chair
This is a **literal** question. We read earlier in the text that the writer found a massage chair but had no American coins to operate it *(lines 41–46)*. The next sentence tells us how the 'lengthy search of the terminal building' ended. The question requires us to make the connection between these two details. A third fact to notice is the 'surprisingly unfair currency exchange' *(lines 42–43)*, which tells us that the writer was converting money from Australian to US dollars.

4 the attractive view of the Hawaiian islands from the air
This is an **interpretive** question. We don't read anything positive about Hawaii until the writer describes the view from his window. The writer notes that a thought that occurs to him is 'almost as special as the delightful vista' *(lines 28–29)*. When we interpret this, it becomes clear that the view is the most special thing and, because there are no other aspects described in this way throughout the article, the view was the most impressive aspect of Hawaii for the writer.

5 Elvis Presley
This is an **interpretive** question. It requires you to interpret an allusion (reference to a well-known fact outside of the text). The allusion is in the third paragraph *(line 29)* and refers to Elvis Presley, a world-famous American singer. Most people associate the name 'Elvis' with Elvis Presley, who famously visited Hawaii and made a Hollywood film there. By interpreting the allusion, we can arrive at the answer.

6 to describe the setting and criticise it at the same time
This is an **interpretive** question. To find the answer, we need to work out the writer's purpose by looking closely at his choice of words. We read about the décor of the terminal building and we can see that the writer is being ironic when he says he was 'dazzled by the wicker furniture, the hibiscus-print cushions, the bamboo wallpaper' *(lines 39–40)* because these are odd things to consider dazzling. He remarks, as if surprised, that there was wallpaper and calls the murals 'inhumane' *(line 40)*. When we interpret all of these phrases, it becomes clear that the purpose is to describe the setting and at the same time to criticise its appearance.

7 **a** This is an **interpretive** question. We read throughout the text words and phrases that describe the heat—'on a hot afternoon', 'the humid stench' and 'Hawaii was hot' *(lines 13, 30 and 36)*—so we simply need to interpret the phrase 'melting tarmac' as a reference to the effects of the hot climate. We know that Answer **b** is not correct because Hawaii's international airport is a major tourist hub and would not logically have a melted runway. We know that Answer **c** is not correct because it is clear that the writer is just imaginatively linking the idea of Hawaii's volcanoes with a hot tarmac.

8 **c** This is an **interpretive** question. It requires you to locate a specific fact in the text—a passenger's name—and then use your interpretive skills. You need to think about the reason the writer put this fact in the text. Readers don't really need to know the late passenger's name, so the reason must be to create a particular effect. Because of the large number of rhyming syllables in the name, we can assume that it was made up to create humour. Answer **a** is not correct because we read that Ms Smith was 'safely aboard' when they jetted off. We know that Answer **b** is wrong because her name includes the name of a cartoon mouse, 'Angelina Ballerina', which is unlikely to be someone's real name.

9 **c** This is an **interpretive** question. It requires you to interpret an allusion to a common expression used by flight attendants preparing a cabin for landing. The answer cannot be Answer **a** because all of the other details given are about the activities of the flight attendants while on the plane—before landing in Hawaii. Even if some of the flight attendants were Hawaiian there is a better answer, so we can rule out Answer **a** using the process of elimination. We know the answer is not Answer **b** because we read that the passengers were being thanked for cooperating with the routines supervised by flight attendants.

10 **a** This is an **interpretive** question. It requires you to interpret the text by identifying its most important features. The writer doesn't seem to be recommending a visit to Hawaii so the answer is not Answer **b**. There is no final judgement made about the airline so the answer is not Answer **c**. The presence of descriptive details, humour and irony tells us that the main purpose of this text is to entertain.

11 **b** This is an **applied** question. It requires you to understand a text's implications to infer meaning from the text. There is no mention of a plane crash, and logically we would expect the runway to have been repaired had there been such a crash, so the answer is not Answer **a**. International airports have strict guidelines about maintenance procedures and it doesn't make sense that the writer would expect there to be problems with maintenance, so the answer is not likely to be Answer **c**. The date '1945' provides the best hint that the writer is making an allusion to a famous historical event—the bombing of Pearl Harbor in World War II.

12 **a** This is an **applied** question. It requires you to make an informed judgement based on the evidence. You can apply the process of elimination to find the correct answer here. The answer is not Answer **b** because it would be highly unlikely that any person really hates being thanked. Answer **c** is also unlikely to be the answer because nowhere in the text does he express the view that people should only use English to say 'thank you'. In fact, he lets a 'mahalo' slip out when he finds himself grateful to have reached Hawaii. The best answer is Answer **a**, since the first part of the article seems to focus on the overuse of the word 'mahalo'. The title is a play on the words of a common phrase—'thanks for nothing'—an ironic statement that people say when something bad happens. The use of quotation marks around the word 'thanks' in the title allows us to see another interpretation: people who say 'thanks' for no reason. Over-thanking people does seem insincere, so we can safely decide that the correct answer is Answer **a**.

PERSUASIVE TEXT Spelling Work

page 94

1 **a** embark **b** departure **c** announcement **d** inescapable **e** relentlessly **f** cooperation **g** listening **h** volcanoes **i** vista **j** terminal

2 **a** *iar, em, gia, fully, co, lessly, able, de, ments, in, ing, re*
b Prefixes: *em, co, de, in, re*
Suffixes: *iar, gia, fully, lessly, able, ments, ing*

3 **a** island **b** delightful **c** bombed **d** flight **e** listening **f** cough **g** thought **h** hour

4 **a** green **b** vista **c** jetted **d** mushy **e** dinner **f** relentlessly **g** traveler **h** wicker **i** mood **j** modest **k** booking **l** away **m** tarmac **n** planted **o** embark

5 lifetime, seatbelts, airlines, runway, mainland, afternoon, gentlemen, upright, wallpaper, somehow, rainbow, stopover

PERSUASIVE TEXT Vocabulary Work

page 95

1 **a** Hawaiian **b** departed **c** departing **d** announced **e** announcer **f** listens **g** listened **h** volcanic **i** volcanoes **j** cooperative **k** cooperated

2 **a** too **b** hour **c** your **d** buy

3 six-hour, flight HA094, Gate 35, 6:30 pm, 1945, '80s, $5

4 **a** boat **b** rock **c** miss **d** road **e** home **f** nothing **g** traveler **h** itchy **i** minute **j** beaten **k** light **l** red-eye

PERSUASIVE TEXT Grammar Work

page 96

1 comparing and contrasting, showing cause and effect, indicating sequence

2 **a** First **b** Like **c** Unlike **d** Similarly **e** However **f** Consequently **g** Next **h** In the same manner **i** Comparably **j** In contrast **k** As a result **l** Finally

3 **a** first or eventually **b** After being **c** As we **d** Before I could **e** eventually **f** by the time

4 **a** Since **b** whereas **c** although **d** because **e** Like

5 **a** First then Second or Next
b Consequently, As a result, Therefore, For this reason or Accordingly
c Consequently, As a result, Therefore, For this reason or Accordingly
d Consequently, Therefore, For this reason or Accordingly
e Consequently, As a result, Therefore, For this reason or Accordingly
f Conversely, In contrast, Whereas or However

PERSUASIVE TEXT Punctuation Work

page 97

1 **a** 'thank you' and 'mahalo' **b** '*mahalo*ed' **c** 'We hope you enjoyed your flight. Mahalo.'

2 Starting line number: 18 Finishing line number: 22

3 **a** Tom Magnum **b** Yankee **c** Elvis **d** Sydney **e** Arrivals **f** Ms Juanita Margarita Angelina Ballerina Smith **g** Hawaii **h** Hawaiian Airlines **i** Honolulu **j** Hawaiian **k** New York

4 **a** public address system
b Hawaiian Airlines flight number ninety-four
c the 1980s **d** United States of America

5 **a** 'mahalo' **b** Hawaii's **c** off **d** terminal **e** 6:30 pm **f** pause **g** '80s **h** hibiscus

ANSWERS

CHECK YOUR ANSWERS

PERSUASIVE TEXT
Writing Work page 98

1 register
2 intimate
3 deliberate extreme exaggeration
4 **a** static or formal **b** casual or intimate **c** consultative **d** formal or casual
5 being thanked by Hawaiian Airlines staff over and over; the hot afternoon upon landing in Hawaii; repeated announcements over a fuzzy PA system; being welcomed to Hawaii while still in Sydney; the humid stench on the plane; the mushy airline food; the décor in Arrivals; the wicker furniture; the hibiscus-print cushions; the bamboo wallpaper; the inhumane wall murals; a surprisingly unfair currency exchange
6 **a** repetition **b** visual image **c** alliteration **d** tactile image **e** intensifying adverb **f** adjective **g** metaphor **h** allusion (to a TV show) **i** colloquialism for 'American' **j** direct speech

UNIT 11: PERSUASIVE TEXT—FILM REVIEW

PERSUASIVE TEXT
Comprehension Work page 103

1 **c** This is a **literal** question. Locate the fact in the text. We read that 'Bob Kane invented the comic-book hero in 1939' *(lines 4–5)*. We know that Answer **a** is not correct because 1943 is not mentioned anywhere in the text. We know that Answer **b** is not correct because this is the starting date for the television series based on the character which had to have been invented much earlier.

2 'ludicrous' and 'preposterous'
This is a **literal** question. Locate specific words in the text. We read that the television series had 'ludicrous villains' and 'preposterous death traps' *(line 11)*. These adjectives both emphasise silliness.

3 seven: *Batman* (1989), *Batman Returns* (1992), *Batman Forever* (1995), *Batman and Robin* (1997), *Batman Begins* (2005), *The Dark Knight* (2008) and *Batman v Superman: Dawn of Justice* (2016)
This is a **literal** question. You need to locate specific facts and details from the text and put them all together so they can be counted. You can easily locate all the films by scanning the text for italicised titles. To solve the issue of dates, look at the numbers shown in parentheses next to each title. Each one that is dated after the year 1980 can be considered 'since the 1980s' and should be included in the count.

4 **b** This is a **literal** question Find the information in the text. We read that 'Lewis Wilson was the first actor to play the character' *(line 7)*. This tells us the answer. We know that Answer **a** is not correct because we read that 'Adam West's incarnation of Batman is the most memorable because of the extraordinarily successful *Batman* television series' *(line 9)*. This tells us that Adam West's performance was memorable but not the earliest. We know that Answer **c** is not correct because George Clooney is mentioned as the star of a film released in 1997, long after the first movies, so he cannot have been the first actor to play Batman.

5 **b** This is an **interpretive** question. You need to synthesise meaning by putting various facts together to reach a conclusion. We read that the films made since the 1980s 'returned the Batman character to its original, darker comic-book style' *(lines 15–16)*. This tells us that the answer must be Answer **b**. We read that the television series was a 'lighthearted swipe' at the genre *(line 10)*, which indicates that it was not faithful to the original creator's vision. Therefore the answer cannot be Answer **a**. We know that Answer **c** is not correct because the Christian Bale films only began in 2005. If it were only his films that were like the original character, this would contradict the reviewer's statement in lines 15–16.

6 alliteration
This is an **interpretive** question. Look at language-related matters such as meanings conveyed by certain words, phrases or symbols. In this case it is a literary technique. We know that alliteration is the repetition of consonant sounds in close proximity. We read the expression 'vigilante, vendetta-driven violence' *(lines 25–26)*, which has four 'v' sounds, a clear example of alliteration.

7 He has a very negative opinion of the film.
This is an **interpretive** question. Think about the connotations of words—meanings that extend beyond the words on the page. We read expressions like 'ill-fated turn in the cape', 'thuggish', 'grumpy' and 'depressing', which leave us in no doubt about the reviewer's feelings. Further, in lines 27–28 the reviewer overtly states his view of the film's impact on the audience. He does so again in lines 34 and 35, and his final statement (and the title of the review) tells us clearly that he doesn't like the film at all.

8 It is always night-time.
This is an **interpretive** question. Look at language-related matters such as meanings conveyed by certain words, phrases or symbols. We read that 'the

ANSWERS

perpetual night-time of the setting is depressing' *(line 36)*. This tells us the specific emotive response of the reviewer to the setting.

9 **a** This is an **applied** question. We need to apply assumed knowledge—information or understanding that the writer assumes you possess already. Because the letters 'CGI' fit with the phrase 'Computer Graphic Imagery' we know that Answer **a** is the correct answer. Although the letters also match the other phrases, they can be proved incorrect because Answer **b** is silly, mentioning a character in the film, and Answer **c** is not a very technical-sounding term. We also need to consider whether either of those definitions makes sense in light of the fact that film industry professionals use the term to refer to all kinds of films, not just Batman films. The context gives away the real answer.

10 He found it a punishing assault on his senses and he thinks that the music was a disaster.
This is an **interpretive** question. Think about the connotations of words—meanings that extend beyond the words on the page and make small but important distinctions between ideas. First we need to interpret the question and what Hans Zimmer's work is. The mention of 'Hans Zimmer's musical score' tells us that he was responsible for creating and directing the music in the film. The words 'injury', 'punishing' and 'assault' reveal the reviewer's feelings about the music.

11 **b** This is an **applied** question. Use logic to find the answer. When we apply our logic, we can see that Answer **c** is not correct because this text is a film review addressing movie-goers not bats. We can see that Answer **a** is a more reasonable answer but the phrase 'same bat time, same bat channel' is an odd one to use unless it is a direct quote. In addition, it is not actually emphasising anything but simply mirroring what was said on the television show. Therefore the most logical answer is Answer **b**. The 1966–68 television show often ended with this line spoken by the narrator, asking viewers to tune in next time.

12 **a** This is an **applied** question. Consider multiple aspects of the text at once. When we consider the fact that more than half of the text is spent criticising the film, the answer is clear. We also need to think about why this particular title has been chosen for the text and how the title links up with the last line—a joke that the reviewer intends to announce Batman's death to the fictional character, Commissioner Gordon, who in the television show and films has wrongly thought Batman was dead on a few occasions. We know that Answer **b** is not the answer because logic tells us that the ages of these actors who played Batman in the 1990s and beyond cannot make them old men today. We also know from our extra-textual experience that actors like George Clooney, Christian Bale and Ben Affleck are very much alive. The answer cannot logically be Answer **c** as this reviewer has clearly liked Batman for many years, so at least the first part of that statement is incorrect.

PERSUASIVE TEXT
Spelling Work

page 104

1 **a** incarnation **b** preposterous **c** memorable **d** extraordinarily **e** predictable **f** implausible **g** successful **h** hideous **i** disbelief **j** orchestral **k** heroic **l** villains

2 three: genre, villains, violence

3 six: successful, orchestral, disbelief, heroic, dynamic, hideous

4 **a** 4 **b** 4 **c** 6

5 **a** act, genre, humanity, preposterous, idea, returned, implausible, blockbusters, villains, Batman, incarnation, superior, memorable, cape, extraordinarily, comics, heroic, film, hideous, music, predictable, view, violence, channel, successful, butler, orchestral, city, dynamic, fans, disbelief, brand, fun

b

C	H	A	N	N	E	L	R	E	L	T	U	B
H	S	N	I	A	L	L	I	V	A	L	L	G
U	I	M	P	L	A	U	S	I	B	L	E	E
M	N	D	R	V	I	E	W	O	T	N	H	X
A	C	H	E	R	O	I	C	L	R	N	E	T
N	A	B	P	O	M	D	C	E	R	U	M	R
I	R	R	O	D	U	I	S	N	A	F	E	A
T	N	A	S	Y	S	S	A	C	T	O	M	O
Y	A	N	T	N	I	B	A	E	C	D	O	R
R	T	D	E	A	C	E	O	O	K	E	R	D
O	I	S	R	M	D	L	M	I	N	N	A	I
I	O	G	O	I	C	I	T	Y	O	R	B	N
R	N	S	U	C	C	E	S	S	F	U	L	A
E	T	H	S	S	A	F	I	L	M	T	E	R
P	R	E	D	I	C	T	A	B	L	E	M	I
U	C	I	O	R	C	H	E	S	T	R	A	L
S	T	C	A	P	E	B	A	T	M	A	N	Y
B	L	O	C	K	B	U	S	T	E	R	S	Y

c all the crooks in Gotham City

PERSUASIVE TEXT
Vocabulary Work

page 105

1 **a** thuggish **b** blockbusters **c** belligerent **d** ludicrous **e** vigilante **f** CGI city **g** comic-book **h** television series **i** smithereens **j** ill-fated **k** certain death **l** flick **m** superhero **n** lighthearted **o** perpetual **p** twists **q** suave **r** shoddy **s** motive **t** box-office takings

2 **a** 6 **b** 8 **c** 1 **d** 7 **e** 4 **f** 3 **g** 2 **h** 9 **i** 10 **j** 5

ANSWERS

CHECK YOUR ANSWERS

PERSUASIVE TEXT
Grammar Work
page 106

1 **a** plays **b** played

2 **a** is **b** will be **c** was **d** starred
e was **f** viewed **g** will be

3 Nouns: television, humanity, channel, character, comic-book, motive, fun, power, viewers, generation, dollars, idea
Adjectives: memorable, understated, dangerous, faithful, ludicrous, suave, superior, heroic, grumpy, belligerent, unsure, dead
Verbs: begins, smash, kill, called, delivers, include, playing, explains, watch, returned, treated, earned
Adverbs: extraordinarily, currently, gleefully, implausibly, poorly, depressingly, unconvincingly, logically, thuggishly, certainly, surely, absolutely

PERSUASIVE TEXT
Punctuation Work
page 107

1 **a** because it is the name of a fictional character and is therefore a proper noun
b because it is an actor's name and therefore is a proper noun that requires initial capitals
c because it is a well-known nickname for Batman and is a proper noun
d because it is a district of Los Angeles, USA and is a proper noun
e because it is the first word of a sentence which should be capitalised
f because it is an initialism, which is always expressed in capital letters

2 It means the years 1966, 1967 and 1968.

3 Line 16: Holy Switcheroo, Batman!

4 **a** Was the television series intended to be a lighthearted swipe at the superhero genre?
b But is Batman's brand of vigilante, vendetta-driven violence really heroic or just thuggish?
c Does Batman decide he has to kill him?

5 **a** (of 1966–68)
b ('same bat time, same bat channel')
c (and also because he messed up the Batmobile)

6 Line 28 (after 'frozen solid'), Line 35 ('with bats in his belfry'), Line 43 ('really is dead and buried')

7 **a** Although Lewis Wilson was the first actor to play the character,
b Later,
c By the end of the ordeal of watching this film,
d Unlike every other incarnation of Batman,

PERSUASIVE TEXT
Writing Work
page 108

1 unbiased

2 to persuade the reader to buy a particular product or use a particular service

3 the release dates of each film

4 **a** He likes the series and enjoyed its irony.
Supporting evidence: 'the extraordinarily successful *Batman* television series', 'great fun to watch'
b He liked the film, particularly Christian Bale's performance as Batman.
Supporting evidence: 'The currently reigning and undisputedly superior Bat-actor is Christian Bale, whose performances in *Batman Begins* (2005) and *The Dark Knight* (2008) earned a new generation of fans and millions of dollars in box office takings.'
c He didn't like the film at all and thought the special effects were poorly executed.
Supporting evidence: 'Ben Affleck's ill-fated turn in the cape in the hideous *Batman v Superman: Dawn of Justice*.' 'But cool soon turns to stone cold. By the end of the ordeal of watching this film, most of the audience have frozen solid.' 'a grumpy retired superhero with no logical motive'. 'Unlike every other incarnation of Batman, this one kills people—gleefully.' 'depressing', 'shoddy', 'implausible', 'predictable', 'I struggled to suspend my disbelief', 'unconvincing', 'this time the Caped Crusader really is dead and buried.'
d He hated the music.
Supporting evidence: 'And to add injury to insult, Hans Zimmer's musical score delivers a truly punishing orchestral assault.'

5 the Caped Crusader, the Joker, 'same bat time, same bat channel', the Dynamic Duo, utility belt, Holy switcheroo, Batman!, Batman, Robin, Bat-fans, Bat-actor, Alfred, the butler, the Batmobile, Commissioner Gordon

6 Answers will be individual. The answer can be Yes or No.

UNIT 12: PERSUASIVE TEXT—ONLINE DISCUSSION FORUM

PERSUASIVE TEXT
Comprehension Work
page 113

1 a question
This is a **literal** question. Read the first sentence and decide whether it is a statement, an exclamation or a question. The punctuation mark at the end tells you it is a question.

2 three
This is a **literal** question. Locate some facts and details from the text. We can see the names of each participant written immediately before their post, so if we skim read down the left-hand side of the page we can see that there are three user names: PantherMan, Skeptic99 and Spooked.

3 **b** This is a **literal** question. Locate some facts and details from the text. We read the phrase 'those animal carcasses' *(line 13)*. The determiner 'those' tells us that the carcasses are 'the remains of cattle and sheep' mentioned earlier *(line 6)*. We know that the answer cannot be either Answer **a** or Answer **c** because big cats and feral cats are predators not the victims of predators. We also know that the answer cannot be Answer **c** because the scratches on tall trees is evidence that feral cats are not involved, being too short.

4 photographs of big cats in the area
This is a **literal** question. Locate specific words in the text. We read the phrase 'laughably easy to fake' *(line 24)* so we need to read around this phrase to establish the context. We read the phrase 'and as for photographs' *(line 23)*, which is a dependent clause that points toward the very next statement that they would be easy to fake. We can therefore conclude that the photographs are the subject of the sentence.

5 **a** This is an **interpretive** question. We need to read the key phrase in its context to work out the meaning. In Spooked's first comment, we read about the photo taken of a creature that was captured and killed. This is the 'dead body of a mysteriously large cat'. The remaining lines of Spooked's post reports that DNA testing was performed on the remains. The answer cannot be Answer **b** because you cannot perform DNA tests on footage. The answer cannot be Answer **c** for the same reason. Only Answer **a** offers actual physical evidence that can be subjected to testing.

6 an abbreviation (of the word 'picture')
This is an **interpretive** question. You need to look at language-related matters such as meanings conveyed by certain words, phrases or symbols. In this case we need to work out which language feature involves shortening a word. We know that this technique is abbreviation. When we read \ that a man took a photo of a panther-like animal *(line 17)* and then we read the word 'pic' *(line 19)*, we can see that these words refer to the same thing. This tells us that 'pic' must be an abbreviation of the word 'picture'. Our knowledge outside the text also affirms that this is a common abbreviation used online.

7 **a** This is an **interpretive** question. We need to synthesise meaning by putting various facts together to reach a conclusion. We read that Skeptic99 believes people may be motivated to fake evidence to get on television or to be the focus of an article published in the media *(lines 22 and 23)*. Skeptic99 also says that the stories are 'ridiculous' *(line 48)*, which tells us that she doesn't feel people would necessarily fake very believable stories. This rules out Answer **b**. We know that Answer **c** is probably not correct because DNA evidence exists that university researchers consider compelling and DNA evidence cannot be easily faked by hoaxers. The most logical answer, as stated in the words of the poster, is Answer **a**.

8 true
This is an **interpretive** question. We need to consider multiple aspects of the text at once. The title, the layout features with the user names presented before each post, the content of the post, the disagreement and agreement on certain matters among the participants and the flow of ideas all reveal that this web forum is a discussion. The invitation at the beginning is to 'add your views to our forum', which is essentially signalling that it is a discussion. Our extra-textual knowledge also tells us that online forums like this are usually discussion-based.

9 **a** This is an **interpretive** question. We need to interpret the meaning of facts and details. We read that PantherMan calls the authorities 'pretty smart' *(lines 26–27)* and he is using this phrase as part of his argument that the photos are unlikely to have been able to fool government and university researchers. Because the tone of the rest of the post is informal and colloquial we can conclude that the word 'pretty' is being used as a synonym for 'fairly', so the poster is writing about brainpower not beauty. We know that Answer **b** is not correct because their physical appearance is irrelevant and we wouldn't call researchers 'pretty'. This also rules out Answer **c** because there are no distinct groups made among the authorities. We can see that the words 'pretty' and 'smart' are being used in a different sense from that suggested by Answer **c**.

10 **c** This is an **applied** question. We need to consider facts and details in specific combinations to arrive at a logical conclusion. The answer is clearly Answer **c** because the process of elimination can be applied to rule out the other two. It is also the most logical. Logic tells us that no one would use busyness as an excuse not to look for an escaped big cat! This rules out Answer **a**. Logically Answer **b** can't be correct either, as big cats are valuable animals and the owners would most

certainly care about an escape. Even if they didn't value the animal itself they'd still be concerned that it could cause harm or damage which would create expense and trouble for the owner, so this answer can't be correct.

11 **b** This is an **applied** question. We need to interpret facts using additional knowledge from outside the text. This question is testing your understanding of the way we refer to past centuries. It can be confusing to some students to realise that we always point forwards in time from a date in the past. So a date in the 1800s is part of the nineteenth century. Since the year 2000 we've been living in the twenty-first century, which will end in 2100. The decade is easily determined by the number 50, which refers to the decade of 1950 to 1959. We know that Answer **a** is not correct because that would give us a date of 1940, contradicting the date given in line 38 of the text for the decade of the gold rushes. We know that Answer **c** is not correct because the twentieth century would be 1950, not 1850, again a mismatch for the date given in the text.

12 to discuss the evidence for and against the existence of big cats in Australia
This is an **applied** question. We need to apply thinking skills to develop insights and personal opinions, reading beyond the lines to understand implications. By considering the title, the invitation in the first few lines of the text, the participants' comments and the flow of those comments, we can deduce that the purpose of the text is to host an open discussion about the evidence for and against the premise that big cats exist in parts of Australia.

PERSUASIVE TEXT
Spelling Work
page 114

1 **a** existence **b** definitely **c** explanations **d** fabricate **e** laughably **f** government **g** authorities **h** captured

2 **a** phantom, marsupial, laughably
b fabricate, existence, explanations
c offspring, government, television

3 **a** laughably **b** carcasses **c** marsupial **d** definitely **e** feral **f** authorities

4 **a** existence **b** definitely **c** television **d** laughably **e** marsupial **f** university

5 **a** feral **b** cattle **c** phantom **d** scratches

6 Answers will vary. Samples include:
gov: govern, governs, governed, governing, government, governor
tele: telecast, telephone, telephoned, telephonist, telephony, teleport, telegraph, televise, television
unify, unifies, unifying
uni: universe, universal, universes, universally, university, unicycle, unilateral, unite, unites, uniting, united,
laugh: laughs, laughter, laughed, laughing, laughable

PERSUASIVE TEXT
Vocabulary Work
page 115

1 whiskers, cats, cat-like, tail, feral, prey, claws, bred, paw, scratches, teeth, panther, lion, hunting, roar, ears

2 **a** mountain lion **b** jaguar **c** bobcat **d** marsupial lion **e** snow leopard **f** tiger **g** cougar **h** puma **i** cheetah **j** panther

3 Skeptic: fabricate, fake, supposedly, story, extinct
Believer: DNA, experts, study, actual, evidence

4 **a** a fat cat **b** Cat got your tongue?
c Curiosity killed the cat.
d When the cat's away the mice will play.
e She has the tiger by the tail. **f** Easy, tiger!
g I'm as weak as a kitten.
h You look like something the cat dragged in.
i let the cat out of the bag **j** Let's talk straight.

PERSUASIVE TEXT
Grammar Work
page 116

1 **a** noun, verb, adjective, noun, verb, preposition, noun
b article, noun, auxiliary verb, verb, preposition, noun, preposition, article, noun
c article, noun, preposition, article, proper noun, noun, auxiliary verb, verb

2 Add your views. Log in. Please sign up today.

3 cats, big cats, panther, cattle, sheep, dogs, feral pigs, feral cat, marsupial lion, American wildcats

4 **a** existence **b** thought **c** identity **d** possibility **e** similarity **f** security **g** belief **h** secret

5 **a** there **b** new **c** you **d** be **e** to **f** prey **g** one **h** i **i** tail **j** some **k** not **l** real **m** story **n** heard **o** been **p** days **q** seen **r** bred

6 **a** there is **b** they have **c** they have **d** they had

ANSWERS

CHECK YOUR ANSWERS

PERSUASIVE TEXT
Punctuation Work
page 117

1. PantherMan, Skeptic99, Spooked
2. a colon
3. a capital letter
4. **a** italics
   b It provides an introduction to the forum.
   c italics, bold, all capitals, underlining, different type size, wider or narrower kerning, different typefaces
5. Because screens are getting smaller we need faster, briefer and less complicated ways to compose messages. Adding punctuation marks requires secondary screen and keyboard pages.
6. because the writer is using the term sarcastically, as if to imply that it is not real evidence at all
7. **a** There's some good evidence for the existence of these phantom cats.
   b I mean, how likely would a circus owner be to report to the authorities that they'd let a big cat slip off into the bush during a tour?
   c In 2003 the NSW government released a statement to the media that said it was more likely than not that the Blue Mountains big cats were real. (Answers could also have the full form of 'New South Wales').
8. **a** DNA **b** pic **c** OK **d** they've
   e uni **f** TV **g** photo **h** I'd

PERSUASIVE TEXT
Writing Work
page 118

1. thread
2. to control what people post on the forum
3. the member's name and avatar
4. Okay, they've, strung up, the guy, pic
5. Okay (an expression of agreement), they have, hung up with rope, the man, picture
6. Lines 48–49, Skeptic99's last post
7. utterly ridiculous, No-one will ever convince me
8. PantherMan 3; Skeptic99 3; Spooked 2
9. Answers will vary. The most reasonable answer is that Skeptic99 is the least convincing because they simply offer speculations and alternative theories about the evidence that researchers have actually studied.
10. **a** PantherMan and Spooked **b** Skeptic99
11. Answers will be individual. Explanations of reasons should relate to evidence presented by each poster.
12. **a** There are cat-like scratches up high on tree trunks too tall for ferals or domestics to reach.
    b The same couple have found remains of cattle and sheep that were killed and eaten in a manner consistent with how big cats kill and eat their prey.
    c They found that it had DNA similar (but not identical) to a feral cat.
    d the Australian 'marsupial lion'

SAMPLE TEST 1

SAMPLE TESTS
Part A Reading and Comprehension
page 126

1. The victim was a German medical student who was on an eight-week exchange visit to Australia.
2. his iPod and phone
3. They happened to be on the scene because their *ninjitsu* class was being held in a building in that alleyway.
4. 'a sleek, lifeless body stretched out by the widening hole.'
5. so that they can use their hind legs to fling the dirt and fill in the grave
6. The implication is that she knows the dead cat or perhaps one of the other cats and is sad because it has passed away. She may also be moved by the extraordinary sight of a group of cats hosting a funeral.
7. an open drain, the food itself, the diesel fumes from the watercraft and the heady aroma of the chemical toilets
8. the long waiting time
9. that the kitchen and the chef's practices are unhygienic and customers are likely to find hairs in their food

SAMPLE TESTS
Part B Language Conventions
page 127

1. They are used to provide definitions for Japanese words that are about the art of *ninjitsu*.
2. 'the faint scent of wild freesias' and 'The scents of earth and grass'
3. Stay away from Squid's restaurant.

SAMPLE TESTS
Part C Comparing texts
page 127

1. Text 2 is written in first person, past tense mode. Text 3 is written in second person, present tense mode.

2 Sample answer: The information in Text 1 is non-fiction, whereas the information given in Text 2 is fictitious.

3 Sample answer: The narrative text 'An extraordinary undertaking' conveys feelings most effectively because the writer utilises emotive language and sensory imagery. This text also has the most emotionally charged topic of the three texts: death and a funeral.

SAMPLE TESTS

Part D Themes and meaning page 128

1 Sample answer: The writer of Text 1 presents us with an illustration of the old adage that 'crime doesn't pay'. The writer implies that sometimes people are lucky enough to experience natural justice. In this case the proximity of the *ninjitsu* training centre to the scene of the crime was fortuitous for the mugging victim. In addition to rescuing him from further harm, it also had the effect of teaching the muggers a frightening lesson that they deserved because of their crime.

The writer of Text 2 is presenting a mysterious scene in which a cat has died and is being buried in some kind of ceremony by its friends. The theme suggested by the text is the idea that death affects all living creatures and is a universally sad and unpleasant experience. In addition, the writer seems to suggest that how the living deal with death is important.

The writer of Text 3 is presenting a very negative review of a restaurant. The theme is the many bad features of the dining experience offered at Squid's. The point of this text is to warn prospective diners of the restaurant's poor quality, value and service.

SAMPLE TEST 2

SAMPLE TESTS

Part A Reading and Comprehension page 132

1 Wales

2 Ice was used as an anesthetic in an operation to remove a frostbitten toe.

3 Lightship 82

4 Goulburn

5 The newspaper ran a story on his parents' farming enterprise and he was named and photographed as part of the business.

6 because he wants to avoid alcohol as he says 'for me booze tends to lead to trouble'

7 $44

8 We know that children aren't invited because of the statement 'No admission for under 18s' and also because of the advertised alcohol to be served to guests.

9 good music, good food, chocolate, alcohol, pleasant surroundings and entertainment

SAMPLE TESTS

Part B Language conventions page 133

1 There are three main puns. The first subheading 'Lucky Hugh!' is a pun on the phrase 'Lucky you!' It means that the men named Hugh were lucky to have survived these shipwrecks. The second pun is 'Bad Karluk', a play on the phrase 'bad luck' because it is indeed bad luck to be involved in a shipwreck. The name of the ship in this story is the *Karluk*. A third pun can be seen in the subheading 'Unlucky for Hugh' which calls to mind the expression 'lucky for you' or 'unlucky for you'. This section is so named because the Hugh Williams in this wreck did not survive the disaster. All three puns include the word 'luck'.

2 He contrasts his old life of crime—running from the police after robbing banks—with running around after cows when they've broken through fences. 'Who'd have thought that I'd be fixing fences and running after cows instead of fixing bank jobs and running from the cops?'

3 This sounds like a jazz band's name, with the lead musician and/or singer being Harpo Dalton. It's likely that the name 'Goldhorns' is a reference to the brass instruments in the band so it could be a full jazz band with a brass section. It could also be that the lead musician is a sax player, considering the description of 'the silky sax tones of the legendary Harpo Dalton'.

SAMPLE TESTS

Part C Comparing texts page 133

1 Text 2 is a series of journal entries written only for the writer's personal reference. It has been written as a record of his feelings and experiences after his release from prison.

Text 3 is a marketing text written specifically to persuade a target audience to purchase tickets to a jazz music event.

2 Text 2 is structured in sections that are individual journal entries. They are organised in date order. The structure is typical of a journal or diary and has not been designed to achieve any particular effect on the reader because the writer himself is the

only target audience. The structure of Text 1 is also arranged in sections but these are based on three related but distinctly different topics. The structure of this text is designed to maximise the reader's interest by using short blocks of text and a series of related subheadings.

3 Text 1 is targeting young adult and adult readers who are interested in trivia and history. The target readers would most likely have strong literacy skills because of the style of language, the puns and allusions in the text. Text 3 is targeting young adults and mature adults who like jazz music. The majority of young people tend to like other genres of music more than jazz. However, the student concession tickets tell us that the organisers are trying to appeal to a wide audience. The target audience would likely have enough money to spend on champagne and food, features of the event that have been used to attract their interest.

SAMPLE TESTS

Part D Themes and meaning page 134

1 Sample answers:
The theme of Text 1 is the amazing nature of coincidences. Recounting stories about the coincidental survival of different people with the same name is a very effective means of presenting this theme. The mysterious nature of coincidence and the role that fate and chance play in everyday life are the key ideas conveyed very strongly by the stories of these men named 'Hugh Williams'. The use of the subheadings also reinforce the theme.

The theme of Text 2 is summarised by the title. The text is all about second chances. The writer has the opportunity to view life from a new perspective after having been imprisoned for many years. The nine-year sentence he served is not the focus of the text. Rather, the massive contrast between his life in prison and his new-found freedom is used to present the theme very effectively. Because the text is written in his own words the impact of the theme is strengthened.

The theme of Text 3 is the value of indulgence in life's pleasures. Like most marketing texts this one aims to attract people to the product, service or event being offered by appealing to their physical senses and emotions. The text presents imagery that appeals to the sense of hearing and taste in particular, which enables the writer to deliver the theme powerfully and persuade the target audience to buy tickets to the event.

NOTES

NOTES